P9-DOB-641

WORK IN PROGRESS

A Guide to Writing and Revising

SECOND EDITION

— Beck —

14-09

WORK IN PROGRESS

A Guide to
Writing and Revising

SECOND EDITION

Lisa Ede

OREGON STATE UNIVERSITY

St. Martin's Press   New York

To my students
and
(of course)
to Gregory

Senior editor: Mark Gallaher
Development editor: Edward Mitchell-Hutchinson
Managing editor: Patricia Mansfield-Phelan
Project editor: Cheryl Friedman
Production supervisor: Alan Fischer
Text design: Nina D'Amario/Levavi & Levavi
Graphics: G&H Soho
Cover design: Diane Andrews
Cover photo: Jim Finlayson

Library of Congress Catalog Card Number: 90-71630

Copyright © 1992 by St. Martin's Press, Inc.
All rights reserved. No part of this publication may be reproduced,
stored in a retrieval system, or transmitted by any form or
by any means, electronic, mechanical, photocopying, recording,
or otherwise, except as may be expressly permitted by the applicable
copyright statutes or in writing by the Publisher.

Manufactured in the United States of America.
65432
fedcb

For information, write:
St. Martin's Press, Inc.
175 Fifth Avenue
New York, NY 10010

ISBN: 0-312-04831-9

Acknowledgments

Chris Anderson, "Reruns Redux," from *Northwest Magazine*, December 18, 1988. Reprinted by permission of the author.

Lynne V. Cheney, "Students of Success," from *Newsweek*, September 1, 1986, © 1986, Newsweek, Inc. All rights reserved. Reprinted by permission.

From *The Little Rhetoric and Handbook*, 2/e by Edward Corbett. Copyright © 1982, 1977 by Scott, Foresman and Company. Reprinted by permission. Adapted from "Discovery through Questioning: A Plan for Teaching Rhetorical Invention," by Richard Larson. *College English*, November 1968. Copyright 1968 by the National Council of Teachers of English. Reprinted with permission of the publisher and the author.

Acknowledgments and copyrights are continued at the back of the book on pages 262–263, which constitute an extension of the copyright page.

To Instructors

With the first edition of *Work in Progress*, I wanted to write a theoretically sophisticated but commonsensical and relatively brief textbook, one that would enrich but not dominate the life of the classroom, one that would support but not impose a collaborative approach to the teaching of writing. Traditional textbooks have too often placed students and teachers in opposition: the teacher acts as the provider of knowledge, the students as passive absorbers of this wisdom. *Work in Progress* would, I hoped, foster the development of a genuine collaborative community, one grounded in mutual respect and a shared commitment to inquiry. Learning and teaching are, after all, both works in progress.

Work in Progress has, fortunately, been successful enough to warrant a second edition; thus, it continues as a work in progress for me. In working on this second edition, I have attempted to build upon the strengths of the first edition and to respond to the needs and suggestions of instructors and students who have used the text. The central goals of this second edition of *Work in Progress* are unchanged; these goals are reflected in a number of features that characterized the first edition, including

- full discussion of the concept of the rhetorical situation
- explicit support for and reinforcement of collaborative learning and writing activities
- extensive attention to the process of reading, and to reading and writing as dynamic, interdependent activities
- full discussion of the demands of academic writing
- a strong emphasis on the importance of social context and of textual conventions of writing
- a variety of student and professional examples, including numerous comments by students about their writing practices
- activities interspersed throughout the text, as well as at the end of each chapter, which encourage students to apply the concepts and strategies discussed in the text

Perhaps the most significant change in this second edition is the introduction of a new chapter, "Writers Reading." This chapter develops and strengthens the discussion of the rhetorical situation by helping students understand that the forms of writing are not arbitrary. Writers and readers are involved in a conversation that requires them to be aware not only of their own intentions but also of language and its conventions.

The discussion of reading in Chapter 9 has been revised to emphasize, and provide concrete strategies for, the practice of "strong" reading. Those familiar with the text will also discover that in this edition connections between Parts I and III are more clearly and consistently made evident. Also included in this edition of *Work in Progress* are additional readings, including "short short" stories by Jamaica Kincaid and Mary Robison. Finally, with this edition I continue my effort to convey complex theoretical ideas in a manner that is neither intimidating nor irrelevant to students.

Work in Progress is divided into three major parts. Part I, "Writing: An Introduction," comprises four chapters:

- Chapter 1   Writers Writing
- Chapter 2   Understanding the Writing Process
- Chapter 3   Understanding the Rhetorical Situation
- Chapter 4   Writers Reading

These four chapters establish the conceptual and pedagogical framework for the text. Together, they enable students to develop a sophisticated yet commonsensical understanding of writing as a means of communication, the writing process, and the rhetorical situation. The discussion and activities in these chapters also encourage students to begin to think of themselves as writers participating in a community of writers.

Part II of *Work in Progress*, "Practical Strategies for Writing," includes the following four chapters:

- Chapter 5   Strategies for Successful Invention
- Chapter 6   Strategies for Successful Planning and Drafting
- Chapter 7   Strategies for Successful Revision: Managing the Revision Process
- Chapter 8   Strategies for Successful Revision: Revising for Style and Structure

As the title of Part II suggests, these four chapters introduce students to a variety of practical strategies they can use as they plan, draft, and revise. Rather than emphasizing a single, prescribed series of steps or strategies that students must follow, *Work in Progress* encourages students to develop a repertoire of strategies they can use (working alone and with others), depending upon their purpose and situation.

Part III of *Work in Progress*, "Connections: Writing, Reading, and Reasoning," consists of three chapters:

- Chapter 9   Understanding the Reading Process
- Chapter 10   Understanding Academic Audiences and Assignments
- Chapter 11   Understanding Academic Analysis and Argument

This final part of *Work in Progress* initiates students into the reading and writing they will do as members of the academic community. Students learn approaches to analyzing texts that will help them read more critically and write more effectively. The text offers suggestions for analyzing disciplinary conventions and for understanding what is expected for assignments. In these and other ways, *Work in Progress* shows students ways to approach the writing of academic analysis and argument.

Work in Progress is an innovative textbook, but it is also a practical textbook. It provides a conceptual framework and activities that stimulate effective classroom instruction, yet it also offers teachers considerable autonomy and flexibility. Some teachers will particularly appreciate *Work in Progress*'s emphasis on reading and on academic writing, for instance, while others may draw more heavily on its numerous collaborative, workshop-oriented activities. The *Instructor's Manual to Accompany Work in Progress* provides further elaboration of ways in which the text can be used.

Before I wrote *Work in Progress*, acknowledgments sometimes struck me as formulaic or conventional. Now I recognize that they are neither; rather, acknowledgments are simply inadequate to the task at hand. Coming at the end of the preface—and hence twice marginalized—acknowledgments can never adequately convey the complex web of interrelationships that make a book like this possible. I hope that those whose support and assistance I acknowledge here not only note my debt of gratitude but also recognize the sustaining role that they have played, and continue to play, in my life.

I would like to begin by thanking my colleagues at the Center for Writing and Learning at Oregon State University. I could accomplish little in my teaching, research, and administration without the assistance, encouragement, and friendship of Barbara Hogg, Jon Olson, Laurel Ramsey, and Lex Runciman. They, as well as our writing assistants, have taught me what it means to collaborate in a supportive, productive fashion. Others in the English department, my second academic home, supported me during the years when I wrote, and then revised, this text. I would like particularly to thank the English department's remarkably efficient and humane administrative staff—Anterra, Teri Custis, Diane Slywczuk, and Jennie Waite-Phillips, who not only typed, printed, and photocopied countless copies of drafts of this book but also encouraged and teased me, depending on my needs at the time.

I have dedicated this book to my students, and I hope that it in some way reflects what *they* have taught me over the years. I also owe a great debt of gratitude to another friend and teacher, Suzanne Clark, who allowed me to persuade her to interrupt her own important works in progress to collaborate with me on the *Instructor's Manual*. Colleagues and students play an important role in nurturing any project, but so do those who form the intangible but indispensable community of scholars that is one's most intimate disciplinary home. Here, it is harder to determine whom to acknowledge; my debt to those composition theorists who have led the way or "grown up" with me is so great that I hesitate to list the names of specific individuals here for fear of omitting someone deserving of credit. I must, however, acknowledge my friend and frequent coauthor Andrea Lunsford, who writes with me even when I write alone. And I would also like to thank the many dedicated teachers of composition I have worked and talked with over the years. By their example, comments, suggestions, and questions, they have taught me a great deal about the teaching of writing.

A number of writing instructors took time from their teaching to read and comment upon drafts of this edition. Their comments and suggestions have enriched and improved this book. These reviewers include Chris Anderson of Oregon State University; Andrea Berger of Ohio University; Wendy Bishop of Florida State University; Deborah Bosley of the University of North Carolina at Charlotte; Sharon Crowley of Northern Arizona University; Marvin Diogenes of the University of Arizona; Theresa Enos of the University of Arizona; Robert Inkster of Saint Cloud State University; Mary McMullen-Light of the University of Kansas; Linda Palmer of California State University at Sacramento; and Jane Smith of Winthrop College.

I wish to thank the dedicated staff at St. Martin's Press, particularly Edward Mitchell-Hutchinson, whose supportive but tough questions have challenged me to clarify and extend my ideas, and Cheryl Friedman, whose patient attention to detail proved invaluable.

Finally, I want to (but cannot adequately) acknowledge the support of my husband, Gregory Pfarr, who by his example has shown me what it means to be both dedicated to your work and in love with life. I'm trying, Gregory.

LISA EDE

To Students

If you are like many of my students, you're feeling a little nervous about how you'll do in the composition class you're just beginning. You may feel unsure of your abilities. (Most writers do.) You may wonder if your previous writing classes adequately prepared you for college work. Or, if you've been out of school a while, you may feel a bit rusty. You may be thinking that you wouldn't mind a little advice about how to succeed in this important class. When it comes to advising other students about how to succeed, either in a specific course or in college, students truly are the experts. During the last several years I have asked students at the end of our writing class to answer a single question: "Now that you've almost completed this class, what advice would you give to a student just beginning a composition course like this one?" I've shared their responses with students at the start of subsequent writing classes, and I'd like to share them with you now. Here, then, is what my students would like to tell you about how you can get the most out of, and do the best in, your writing class.

Perhaps the most often repeated advice involves *time*. The following suggestions are typical of those made by many students.

> Start the composing process early. Really think about what you're writing. If you start early, with a strong topic, and really think about what you're writing, you'll be in much better shape.
>
> *BOB DWONCH*

> Don't procrastinate—getting an early start will give you more time to revise and improve your essays. Using your time wisely will also allow you more time to think about what you have written and be more critical of your own writing.
>
> *GARY ETCHEMENDY*

> Give yourself time to write, revise, get a response, and then revise again. Choose a topic that you know enough to write about.
>
> *PAUL AUSTIN*

Students also emphasize the importance of *attitude* and of benefiting from your instructor's advice and experience.

> Take your writing seriously. Most writing that I've seen other students compose is done only because it's required. That's a mistake, as I see it.
>
> *STEVE GREAGOR*

Don't take the class lightly. It is a lot of work, but you can learn a lot if you let yourself.

MARSHA CARPER

Take a hard look at the comments your teacher makes on your paper and try to understand what they mean. Keep in contact with your teacher and get an understanding of what he/she sees as weaknesses or strengths in your writing. Ask your teacher for help if you feel you need it.

SKIP ZWAHLEN

After spending a term working intensely on their writing, students also recommend cultivating a *writing process* that encourages creativity and the development of ideas while providing ample time for revision.

Take charge of your writing. If you're stuck with the introduction, go on to something else. The main thing is to get started so that ideas can start flowing.

CECELIA PANG

Recognize that your main job in writing a first draft is to write something that you can *revise* into a better draft. Try to keep your process moving, so you can gain momentum. And if possible leave time between writing and revising to give you perspective.

DODIE FORREST

Use a word processor, if you can. It makes writing a lot easier, especially when you're doing many revisions.

BEN FLESKES

And, finally, students advise writing in a *style* that feels comfortable and enables you to express your ideas effectively.

Be openminded about style. I think that it's important to try to develop your own way of writing. Use what you learned in other writing classes, but build on it.

LISA DeARMOND

Don't worry about trying to write in a fancy style. Just be true to your ideas, and try to write clearly.

AMY HARRISON

My own experience teaching composition indicates that all these suggestions make good sense. I hope you will think about what these students say and take their advice. After all, they have become experts by writing regularly, and so will you.

LISA EDE

CONTENTS

PART ONE

WRITING:
AN
INTRODUCTION

CHAPTER 1

WRITERS WRITING

Why do people write? Let's take a look at some representative writing situations.

A psychiatric social worker takes notes, jottings that make sense only to him, as he meets for the first time with a client. Later, after reviewing the client's history with colleagues at a staff meeting, he will use these notes to write a summary recommending appropriate therapy for the client.

A consulting engineer meets with her working group; they decide to submit a proposal for a major construction project. Knowing they have just a month to meet the deadline, she assigns duties to group members. Some will begin research on technical issues, others will consult with resource people within the firm, and still others will begin writing nontechnical sections of the draft. Her role will be to organize the group effort and edit the final proposal.

A college student in mathematics education decides to keep a journal during his student teaching practicum. He uses the journal to reflect on his students' problems, to record observations about the school where he is teaching, to analyze the effective-

3

ness of his lesson plans, and to cope with the inevitable highs and lows of his first experience in the classroom. At the end of the term, for an advanced seminar in his major, he draws upon the journal to write an essay on the relationship between theory and practice in mathematics education. "It's a good thing I kept that journal," he tells a friend. "It helped me get beyond clichés about teaching to what I really know works in the classroom."

A *newly hired* manager of a department store *meets with her supervisors to discuss her store's goals for the next three months. Wondering how she is actually going to meet these goals, she goes back to her office, asks her secretary to hold all calls, and brainstorms at the computer for two hours. When she is done, she has the outline of a plan to present to her staff for discussion. Afterwards, she will incorporate the group's ideas in a memorandum to her supervisors.*

A *team of* government safety inspectors *visits a meat-processing plant for its annual inspection. After three days of interviews and observations, they compile an annotated list of problems that have appeared since their last visit.*

A student in an introduction to literature class *learns that she must write an analysis of Mrs. Ramsey, a character in Virginia Woolf's* To the Lighthouse. *After working on ideas for her essay, the student almost gives up in frustration: she still can't decide what to write. Suddenly, she decides to write down all the questions she has about Mrs. Ramsey and think about how different characters in the novel would answer them. Her strategy works! She writes furiously, then rewards herself with coffee and cookies.*

After visiting her grandchildren, a retired teacher *realizes that they know very little about what her own parents and grandparents were like. So she spends several days writing about them. When her grandchildren are older, she will make copies of her recollections for each of them.*

As you can see, people write for a variety of reasons. Many people write because they are required to. Term papers, business letters, reports, proposals, articles in magazines—most are written by a person, or a group of persons, who has been asked to take on the responsibility for the project. Sometimes this writing simply reports the results of analysis or observations, as in the safety inspector's list. But often the writing functions in more complex ways, providing the means by which individuals solve problems, make difficult decisions, or better understand complex situations.

People also write to fulfill important personal needs. The grandmother describing her parents and grandparents, bringing them to life for her grandchildren, writes because she wants to record her family's history. The student teacher uses his journal to help understand, and survive, his difficult but rewarding first experience in the classroom. People write to solve problems or interact with others in the world, but the write to look inward as well.

Exploration

What do you typically write, and why? Make a list of the kinds of writing you regularly do. (Be sure to include *all* kinds of writing, even shopping lists and class notes.) What kinds of writing do you do most often and what kinds least often? What generally are your reasons for writing? Which of your writing experiences typically are productive and satisfying? Unproductive and unsatisfying? Write one or two paragraphs exploring why some writing experiences are productive and satisfying while others are not.

UNDERSTANDING HOW WRITING WORKS

At first glance, the writers described above might seem to have little in common. But if you look more closely, you can see a number of similarities—similarities that can tell you something about how writing works.

1. All these people are writing under some sort of pressure, either external (from a job or school) or internal. They *need* to write.
2. The writing that they do *matters* to these people; it helps determine how successful they are in school or on the job or how they feel about themselves.
3. These writers are not working in isolation; they are writing in a specific context or situation. As writers, they are influenced by such factors as these:
   - their reason for writing
   - the issues they want to explore or points they want to make
   - the readers for whom they are writing
   - textual conventions, like report or business letter formats, that help define the form their writing takes

- their feelings about the writing they need or want to do
- the amount of practice they have had with a particular kind of writing
- external factors, such as deadlines and the availability of information

4. No matter what they write, from the moment they begin to think about their writing, these individuals are faced with a complex series of *choices*. To make practical decisions about their writing, these writers ask themselves questions such as the following as they write and revise:

   - What do I hope to accomplish? Are my goals for the writing realistic, and do they respond to the needs, interests, and expectations of my readers?
   - How can I most effectively organize and develop my ideas?
   - How much supporting detail, and of what types, do I need to provide?
   - Do I know enough about my subject? Do I need to do additional reading and research?
   - What tone or style should I adopt, given my subject, purpose, and audience?

   These writers may not ask these questions in the same way and at the same time in their writing process, but they all understand the importance of considering these and other issues.

5. These individuals recognize the significant role that writing plays in their personal and professional lives. Writing doesn't necessarily come easily to them, but they are willing to spend the time and energy necessary to write well. Writing, they know, is important *work in progress*.

Exploration

The previous exploration asked you to consider the role that writing plays in your life and the kinds of writing experiences that you find productive and unproductive. Now recall a particularly successful writing experience when you were able to achieve the goals you had set for yourself. (Don't limit yourself to academic writing, by the way.) What factors enabled you to complete this writing successfully? Write a paragraph or more describing this experience and analyzing the reasons you were successful.

_____ MAKING CHOICES: DEVELOPING _____
RHETORICAL SENSITIVITY

How do writers make choices as they compose? Successful writers, like those described at the beginning of this chapter, draw upon *all* their resources when they write. They use their knowledge of writing gained through reading, and they also analyze their own situation as writers. They think about their purpose—the meaning they wish to communicate, their reasons for writing—and their readers. They explore their own ideas, challenging themselves to express their ideas as clearly and carefully as possible. They play with words and phrases, sentences and paragraphs, to make their writing stylistically effective. In all of these activities, successful writers are demonstrating their *rhetorical sensitivity*—even though they might not use this phrase to describe their thinking and writing.

You may not be familiar with this phrase, either. It derives from the word *rhetoric*, which means the art or discipline of effective communication. Rhetoric is one of the oldest fields of intellectual study in Western culture; it was first formulated by such Greek and Roman rhetoricians as Isocrates (436–338 B.C.), Aristotle (384–322 B.C.), Cicero (106–43 B.C.), and Quintilian (A.D. 35–96). Originally developed to meet the needs of speakers, rhetoric eventually was applied to written texts as well.

Recognizing the key elements of rhetoric

Rhetoric involves the following key elements:

1. *one or more writers* who have (or must discover) something to convey
2. *one or more readers* with whom the writer (or writers) would like to communicate
3. a written discourse or *text*—an essay, poem, set of directions, letter, report, or other writing—that makes this communication possible

The relationship among these elements is dynamic. As Chapter 9, "Understanding the Reading Process," emphasizes, communication between writer and reader is not a one-way operation, like a radio tower transmitting messages to be passively decoded. Writers select and arrange language to express their meanings, but readers are equally active. Readers don't simply decipher or decode the words on the page; they draw upon their own experiences and expectations as they read. As a student, for instance, you naturally read your economics textbook differently than you read a popular novel. You also know that the more experience you have reading certain kinds of writing—science fiction novels or the sports or financial pages of the newspaper, for example—the more you get out of them.

Seeing the elements of rhetoric in context

Writing and reading do not occur in a vacuum. Like all people, writers exist in a particular time and place; they are influenced by the environment in which they live and by the institutions within which they work. Neither students nor businesspersons, to cite two examples, are free to write whatever they wish. Their participation in larger institutions limits their freedom, just as it also provides opportunities for communication with others. A student writing an essay about a controversial issue and a middle-level manager writing an annual sales report are both taking advantage of institutionally sanctioned opportunities to communicate their own ideas. But if the student and the manager wish to have their ideas taken seriously, if they wish to be effective with their intended audience, they know that they must write in a form acceptable to their readers.

How do forms or genres become acceptable to readers? Like languages, such forms as the business letter and scientific report develop over time. And like languages—which evolve in response to the needs of particular people in particular times and places—forms also respond to the needs of readers and writers. The scientific report and the business letter, for instance, evolved along with and in response to the rise of modern science and of Western capitalism.

Different forms of writing thus have histories, just as languages and countries do. As a college student, you regularly write essays, but you may be unaware of the history of this form, which the Frenchman Michel de Montaigne (1533–1592) helped establish. If you studied the history of the essay, you would learn how the personal narrative essay and the professional or scholarly essay developed and the reasons why they differ in subtle but important ways. Though personal narrative and professional or scholarly essays all have introductions, for example, the form and purpose of these introductions vary because the situation of these writers and readers varies. In Chapter 4, "Writers Reading," you will see how one writer, psychologist John Flavell, adapted the introductions to three essays on the same topic when writing for three different journals, *Psychology Today*, *American Psychologist*, and *Cognitive Psychology*.

It is interesting to learn how forms like the essay developed, but you don't need to take a class on the history of the essay to write an effective essay. By reading a variety of essays and by using the rhetorical sensitivity you have already developed through your experiences as a reader and writer, you can learn a great deal about the conventions of essay-writing. The discussion of the rhetorical situation in Chapters 3 and 4, and of reading in Chapter 9, will help you increase your rhetorical sensitivity to written communication.

Application

An example may help you see how you can use the rhetorical sensitivity you have already developed to increase your understanding of various forms of writing. Let's suppose you want to write a letter to apply for a summer job. You may not know the appropriate format for such a letter, and you undoubtedly do not know the history of how this particular form of written communication developed. Yet by drawing upon your commonsense rhetorical sensitivity, you can understand why those in business encourage writers to follow a particular format when writing a letter of application.

In the *St. Martin's Handbook*, Andrea Lunsford and Robert Connors give students the following advice about how to write a successful letter of application.

> A letter of application is the first "version" of you that a prospective employer will see. As your personal ambassador, it should be absolutely flawless—in format, spelling, grammar, punctuation, mechanics, and usage.
>
> You may want to begin by reviewing your résumé, deciding which areas to emphasize and what information to add. Although each letter will take a somewhat different form, most letters of application consist of three main sections.
>
> *Introduction*. State your reason for writing, and name the exact job for which you are applying. Tell the reader how you learned about the job.
>
> *Body*. Describe, as specifically as possible, either your educational or work experience, whichever is more relevant.
>
> *Conclusion*. Emphasize your interest in the position and your willingness to learn. Request an interview at the employer's convenience. Say when you will follow up with a telephone call if you plan to do so.

Why do Lunsford and Connors begin by observing that "a letter of application is the first 'version' of you that a prospective employer will see"? What are some of the consequences of this situation for those applying for positions?

How does Lunsford's and Connors's advice reflect their awareness of the situation of those *reading* job application letters—employers who are probably reading many letters of application for a single position? Why, for instance, does it make sense for job applicants to begin by listing the exact job for which they are applying and the way they learned about the job?

Write a few paragraphs describing what you have learned about the format of letters of application by reflecting on the situation of both job applicants and the employers reading these letters.

Understanding rhetoric—a writer's perspective

What difference does it make to you as a writer that reading and writing occur in a context and that readers and writers both draw upon and adhere to certain forms and conventions? It means that as a writer you are both limited and free. You can not ignore the situation within which you are writing or the forms and conventions your readers expect you to follow. But unless you are writing a legal contract or filling out a renter's agreement, you also have considerable flexibility and opportunities for self-expression.

An example from my experience in writing *Work in Progress* may help clarify this point. When I started, I knew that I needed to follow certain conventions. Some of these conventions—such as the requirement that a textbook have headings, subheadings, and activities at the end of each chapter—are very general; others are more specific to composition textbooks. I didn't feel burdened or limited by these conventions; in fact, they reassured me, for they provided a framework I could use to develop my ideas. When you write, you must work within conventions appropriate to your situation, purpose, and subject, but these conventions generally are enabling, not limiting.

Demonstrating rhetorical sensitivity

You should now have a clearer idea what I mean when I say that effective writers demonstrate rhetorical sensitivity. Writers who demonstrate rhetorical sensitivity consider all the elements of rhetoric when they compose. They think about their own purposes and intentions—the meanings they want to convey to readers. They reflect on the image of themselves, the writer's *persona*, that they want to create in their writing. They consider the needs, interests, and expectations of their readers. And they draw upon the knowledge they have gained about language through speaking, listening, reading, and writing. No one would attempt to write a science fiction novel, for instance, without reading many such novels carefully beforehand. Reading examples of the kinds of writing they wish to do is one of the most important ways that writers, whether professional novelists or college students, develop rhetorical sensitivity.

All writers, including you, have some degree of rhetorical sensitivity. Because you learned language as a child and have used language constantly in your daily life ever since, you have already developed sensitivity to oral language. When you converse with others, you automatically adjust your language to the situation. You naturally speak differently when you chat with friends than when you talk with your minister, employer, or teacher, for instance.

If you are like many students, you may be more confident of your ability to communicate effectively through oral language than through written discourse. How can you increase your rhetorical sensitivity as a writer? You can do so by reading broadly, writing often, and discussing your writing with others. Helping you to achieve this rhetorical sensitivity is also, of course, a major goal of this textbook and of your composition course.

_____ USING COMMONSENSE ANALYSIS _____
TO UNDERSTAND WRITING "RULES"

Writing is hard but rewarding work. Sometimes people think that they can make that hard work just a little easier by establishing rigid rules. You may have been warned, for instance, never to use the pronoun *I* in your writing. This rule may have confused you; you may not have understood what's so terrible about having a few *I*'s sprinkled throughout your essay.

If you think commonsensically about how language works, drawing upon the rhetorical sensitivity you have developed as a reader and writer, you can begin to understand how rules like this got established. More importantly, you can decide when this and other rules make sense—and when they are overly rigid or unnecessarily limiting.

Let's look at the rule I've just mentioned: *Never use* I *in your writing*. At least one of your past teachers may have told you this—

but why? Have you ever had a conversation with a person who spent the entire time talking about himself or herself? "I did this." "I did that." "I was sick, but now I'm better." It's not fun to talk with self-centered, self-absorbed people, and most of us are careful to avoid constantly referring to ourselves when talking with others. The same is true of writing—perhaps even more so since readers can't butt in and force writers to pay attention to them. That's one good commonsense reason to avoid sprinkling your writing with too many *I*'s. Also, most academic writing—the kind that most concerned your teacher—focuses on facts or on your analysis of them, not on yourself. If you are writing an essay exam analyzing the causes of the civil rights movement in the South, your instructor is interested in your ability to define and explain these causes, not in your personal opinion of the civil rights movement. So that's another reason to avoid peppering your essay with lots of *I*'s.

There's a kernel of commonsense wisdom, then, in some teachers' prohibition against using *I*. The problem is that there are times when *I* is exactly the *right* pronoun to use—when you're describing a personal experience, for example, or when you want to show that an observation truly is your own opinion. Rather than adhering rigidly to rules like this one that may or may not make sense in a specific situation, you can use your rhetorical sensitivity to make decisions as you write and revise.

Application

Think of several writing "rules," such as the one just discussed, that you've never understood or fully accepted. List as many of these rules as possible. Then choose one of the rules you listed and write a brief explanation of why you question it.

Group Activity

Bring your response to the previous Application to class. Working with a group of classmates, discuss your lists, and select one writing rule that you agree may be questionable or too rigidly applied. To report your conclusions to the class, choose one person to record the group's answers to the following questions about that rule:

1. Why do the members of your group think that this writing rule may be questionable? Identify a situation when following this rule might not be preferable or wise.

2. What arguments in favor of this rule can your group identify? At what times would following this rule make good sense?

Be prepared to discuss your conclusions with your classmates.

THINKING—AND ACTING—LIKE A WRITER

As you've just seen, thinking commonsensically about writing can help you understand some of the basic conventions of writing. Later chapters will focus more specifically on ways to increase your rhetorical sensitivity and thus become a more *effective* writer. But you may also wish to improve your *efficiency* as a writer—your ability to manage your time well, to cope with the inevitable frustrations of writing, and to use all your personal energies and resources when you write. Can some commonsense thinking about writing help you in that respect as well?

Writing is a *process*, yet few people stop to think about how their writing process may affect the quality of their writing. Such analysis can prove illuminating, however. One of my students, for example, formulated an analogy that helped us all think very fruitfully about how the writing process works. "Writing," he said, "is actually a lot like sports."

Writing—like sports? Let's see what this comparison reveals about the writing process. (After you read the following discussion, try substituting another activity, such as playing a musical instrument, for sports. The analogy, you'll probably find, holds for a number of similar activities.)

1. *Writing and sports are both performance skills.* You may know who won every Wimbledon since 1950, but if you don't actually play tennis, you're not a tennis player—just somebody who knows a lot about tennis. Similarly, you can know a lot about writing, but to demonstrate (and improve) your skills, you must *write*.

2. *Writing and sports both require individuals to master complex skills and to perform these skills in an almost infinite number of situations.* Athletes must learn specific skills, plays, or maneuvers, but they can never execute them routinely or thoughtlessly. Writers, like athletes, must be resourceful and flexible. You can learn the principles of effective essay organization, for instance, and you may write a

number of essays that are, in fact, well organized. Nevertheless, each time you sit down to write a new essay, you have to
consider your options and make new choices about your
writing.

3. *Successful athletes and writers know that a positive attitude
is essential.* You've read about athletes who "psych" themselves up before a game or competition, sometimes with the
help of a sports psychologist. But any serious athlete will tell
you that's only part of what having a positive attitude means.
It also means running five miles when you're already tired at
three or doing twenty-five repetitions during weight training
when you're exhausted and no one else would know if you
did only fifteen. A positive attitude is also important in writing. If you approach a writing task with a negative attitude—
"I never was good at writing"—you immediately create
obstacles for yourself. Keeping a positive, open attitude is
hard when you're a beginner—at tennis, skiing, or writing.
But it's essential.

4. *To maintain a high level of skill, both athletes and writers
need frequent practice and effective coaching.* This point is
so obvious for sports that it hardly merits discussion. Without frequent practice and an experienced coach who can
help the athlete evaluate his or her performance, an athlete's
skills will inevitably slip. "In sports," a coach once said,
"you're either getting better or worse." Without practice—
which for a writer means both reading and writing—your
writing skills also will inevitably slip (and so will your confidence). Likewise, coaching is essential in writing because it's
hard to distance yourself from your own work. Coaches—
your writing instructor, a tutor in your writing center, or a
fellow student—can help you gain a fresh perspective on
your writing and make useful suggestions about revision as
well.

5. *Successful athletes and writers continually set new goals for
themselves and monitor their own performances.* This point
is actually a variation of the coach's adage mentioned earlier. Athletes know that they are either getting better or
worse, so they set new challenges for themselves and analyze
their performances. They know that coaches can help them,
but that finally they are the ones "performing." Successful
writers know this too, so they look for opportunities to
practice their writing. And they don't just evaluate their
success by an instructor's grade or a supervisor's comment.
Their writing is, they recognize, always work in progress.

Exploration

Freewriting, discussed as a strategy for invention on pages 93–95, is a technique used to generate and explore ideas. In case you are not familiar with freewriting, here is a description of it by Peter Elbow, the professor who first created this technique.

> To do a freewriting exercise, simply force yourself to write without stopping for [a certain number] of minutes. Sometimes you will produce good writing, but that's not the goal. Sometimes you will produce garbage, but that's not the goal either. . . . Speed is not the goal, though sometimes the process revs you up. If you can't think of anything to write, write about how that feels or repeat over and over "I have nothing to write" or "Nonsense" or "No." If you get stuck in the middle of a sentence or thought, just repeat the last word or phrase till something comes along. The only point is to keep writing.

Use this technique to freewrite about your attitude toward writing. Write for five or ten minutes, perhaps beginning with one of the following phrases:

- When I write I feel . . .
- Writing means . . .
- Writing is like . . .

BECOMING PART OF A COMMUNITY OF WRITERS

For many people, one big difference between writing and sports is that athletes often belong to teams while writers, they think, work in lonely isolation—tucked away in a carrel at the library or seated at the kitchen table with only books and notes as companions. But does writing actually require isolation and loneliness? Let's go back to the people described at the beginning of this chapter. Of all these individuals, only the government safety inspectors may actually write together—sitting together and jointly composing their list of problems. Like many in business, industry, and the professions, however, the consulting engineer and the department store manager work as part of one or more teams. Much of the time they compose alone, but their work is part of a group effort: their drafts will be responded to, and probably changed, by the rest of the group or the group leader. Several of the other writers, such as the psychiatric social worker and the students, talk extensively with friends and coworkers before and while writing.

As these examples indicate, the romanticized image of the writer struggling alone until inspiration strikes is hardly accurate. Just consider all the varied activities involved in writing—from first getting an idea or assignment to planning, drafting, and revising. Most writers actually alternate between periods of independent activity, composing alone at the desk or computer, and social interactions, meeting with friends, colleagues, or team members for information, advice, or responses to drafts. These writers may also correspond with others in their field, or they may get in touch with people doing similar work through their reading, library research, or computer networks.

Finally, people who take their writing seriously are just like other people who share an interest. They like to develop social relationships or networks with those who feel as they do. They realize that these networks will help them learn new ideas, improve their skills, and share their interest and enthusiasm. Sometimes these relationships are formal and relatively permanent. Many poets and fiction writers, for instance, meet regularly to discuss work in progress. Perhaps more commonly, writers' networks are informal and shifting, though no less vital. A new manager in a corporation, for instance, may find one or two people with sound judgment and good writing skills to review important letters and reports. Similarly, graduate students working on their M.A. theses may meet informally but regularly over coffee to compare notes and provide mutual support.

Unfortunately, college life generally does not encourage the development of informal networks like these, especially for undergraduates. Besides the barrier of conventional academic competition, most students are so busy with conflicting schedules and demands that they find it difficult to get together or to take the time to read and respond to one another's writing. For these and other reasons, many colleges and universities have established writing centers, places where you can go to talk with others about your writing. Find out if your campus has a writing center. (Your composition instructor will know.) If it does, be sure to take advantage of the opportunity to get an informed response to your work.

Application

If your campus has a writing center, make an appointment to interview a tutor about the services the center provides. You may also want to ask the tutor about his or her own experiences as a writer. Your instructor may ask you to present the results of your interview orally or to write a summary of your discussion.

Whether you have access to a writing center or not, you can still participate in an informal network with others who, like you, are working to improve their writing skills. Because you are in the same class and share the same assignments and concerns, you and your classmates potentially form a natural community of writers. You can benefit a great deal by participating in group activities. Here, for instance, is a statement about the benefits of working in groups by Su Tay, Lisa Brame, Gretchen Clary, and Sean O'Donnel, students in Dr. Deborah Bosley's composition class at the University of North Carolina, Charlotte. "We believe that working in groups is very important. It gives us the chance to share our problems with group members, and it also exposes us to how other people handle the writing process. It helps us to recognize our strengths and weaknesses. It is motivating to know we are not alone in our problems."

Some of the activities in this textbook encourage you to work cooperatively with classmates. Your instructor may even ask you to write an essay collaboratively—a challenge, but good preparation for the team-oriented writing you'll probably do after graduation.

The following guidelines can help you participate effectively in group activities. These suggestions apply whether you work with the same group of students all term or participate in a variety of groups.

Guidelines for group activities

1. RECOGNIZE THAT GROUP ACTIVITIES CAN HELP YOU IMPROVE YOUR EFFECTIVENESS AND PRODUCTIVITY AS A WRITER.

Most college work is competitive and emphasizes individual, not group, achievement. Because of this, some students find it hard to take group activities seriously. "This is okay," they may think, "but my grade's going to depend on the essays I write alone." Your own writing probably will be the major determinant of your grade, but study after study—in business, industry, and education—has demonstrated that most people find learning groups extremely effective for mastering complex performance skills like writing. The responses you get to drafts of essays, for instance, will help you make decisions about revising. And group discussions of assignments and readings will help you generate ideas and topics. Like Dr. Bosley's students, you'll probably find that the group activities were among the most beneficial parts of the course for you—and fun, too.

2. RECOGNIZE THAT BEING AN EFFECTIVE MEMBER OF A GROUP REQUIRES DIFFERENT SKILLS THAN WORKING ALONE.

Good teamwork doesn't come naturally; you may need to develop or strengthen the skills that will contribute to effective group work. As you work with others in your class, keep these suggestions in mind.

- *Remember that people have different styles of learning and interacting.* Some students work out their ideas as they talk; others prefer to think through their ideas before speaking. Effective groups value this diversity and find ways to insure that *all* students participate in and benefit from group activities.
- *Balance a commitment to "getting the job done" with patience and flexibility.* When you participate in group activities you usually have a limited amount of time to respond to a question or problem or to discuss work in progress. Responsible group members will recognize the need to "get the job done," but will also be flexible and patient.
- *Work with your peers to articulate group goals and monitor group processes.* To work together successfully, group members must take the time to clarify goals and procedures for particular tasks; otherwise, valuable time is wasted. Similarly, effective groups develop some means (formal or informal) of evaluating group activities. If you are part of a group that is meeting regularly, you might decide to begin all or some of your meetings by having each person state one way in which the group is working well and one way in which it could be improved. The time spent discussing these comments and suggestions could contribute to better group dynamics.
- *Deal immediately and openly with any problems in the group process, such as a dominating or nonparticipating member.* It's not always easy to discuss problems such as these openly, but doing so is essential to effective group work.

3. DON'T EXPECT TO PLAY THE SAME ROLE IN EVERY GROUP ACTIVITY.

Sometimes you may function as your group's leader, either informally or formally by the group's (or your instructor's) decision. Other times you may act as a mediator or synthesizer, the person who helps the group reach a consensus. Or your main responsibility may be keeping the group on task so you can achieve your goals in the time allotted. In effective groups, members assume the roles most appropriate for the specific task and situation, and they recognize the need for flexibility and variety.

4. DEVELOP WAYS TO ENCOURAGE *PRODUCTIVE* CONFLICT.

"Two heads are better than one," the proverb reminds us—and that's because when two or more people get together to discuss an issue or solve a problem they naturally have different ways of analyzing a topic or of approaching a problem. The diverse perspectives and strategies that people bring to a problem or task are one of the main reasons why group activities are so productive. Capitalize on these differences. Encourage the discussion of new ideas. Experiment with unusual strategies. Don't be afraid to disagree; doing so may enable your group to find a better solution to a problem, to discover a new and stimulating response to a question. Just be sure that your discussion remains both friendly and focused on the task at hand.

5. BE REALISTIC ABOUT THE ADVANTAGES AND DISADVANTAGES OF GROUP LEARNING ACTIVITIES.

No method or strategy is perfect, and group learning activities are no exception. You'll discover that group learning does carry numerous benefits.

- Groups inevitably have greater resources than individuals.
- Groups can employ more complex problem-solving methods than individuals.
- Working in groups can help you learn more effectively and efficiently.
- Participating in group activities can be personally rewarding and also can help prepare you for on-the-job teamwork.
- By responding as writers and readers, groups can give members immediate responses to their writing and numerous suggestions for revision.

But there are potential disadvantages to group learning activities as well.

- Sometimes it can take longer to achieve consensus or solve a problem when people work in groups. (This is usually because the group members examine more options and look at the problem from more angles than a single individual would.)
- Individual group members may not always be prepared, or they may try to dominate or withdraw from discussion.

■ Group members may not share responsibility for a project equitably.

Most of these problems can be avoided if you and the members of your group participate fully in group activities and respond to problems when they occur. Groups are, after all, a bit like friendships or marriages: they develop and change; they require care and attention. Problems can arise, but if you're committed to keeping the group going, alert to signs of potential trouble, and willing to talk problems out, you'll all do fine.

Group Activity

If your instructor has divided your class into groups, meet with the members of your group to discuss how you can most effectively work as a collaborative team. Begin your meeting by exchanging names and phone numbers; take time just to chat and get to know each other. You might also see if your group can formulate some friendly rules to guide group activities. (You might all pledge, for instance, to notify at least one other member if you can't make an out-of-class group meeting.) Try to anticipate some of the problems you may have working together, such as coordinating schedules, and discuss how to resolve them.

Activities for Thought, Discussion, and Writing

1. Now that you have read this first chapter and participated in at least one class discussion, it might be useful for you to set some goals for yourself as a writer. Make a list of five concrete goals you'd like to accomplish in your composition class this term, then write a paragraph or more discussing how you plan to achieve one or two of these goals.
2. Freewrite for five to ten minutes on one or more of the following topics:
   ■ your best writing experience
   ■ your worst writing experience
   ■ how you feel about writing in general
   ■ your strengths and weaknesses as a writer
   Save this freewriting. Your instructor may ask you to use it as the starting point for an essay.
3. Interview one or more students in your current or prospective

major area. Ask questions like these to find out about student writing in this field:

- What kinds of writing are students required to do in classes in this field? Is this writing similar to the writing students might do if, upon graduation, they begin careers in this field? If not, how is it different?
- How is their writing evaluated by their professors?
- How well do the students interviewed feel that their composition classes prepared them for the writing they now do?
- What advice about writing would they give to other students taking classes in this field?

Your instructor may ask you to report the results of this interview to your group so that the group can summarize and present your collective findings to the class. Your instructor may also ask you—working alone or with classmates—to write an essay summarizing the results of your interview or of the class discussion of student writing.

4. After reflecting upon your past experiences with group activities, freewrite for five to ten minutes in response to these questions:

- How would you describe your experience with group activities in the past?
- What factors contribute to making these group activities successful or unsuccessful?
- What strengths do you feel you bring to group activities? What weaknesses?

Your freewrite should give you valuable information that you can draw upon when you work with others in your class. Your instructor may ask you to share your freewrites with other members of your group. The resulting discussion should produce some suggestions that will enable you to work together more productively and efficiently.

CHAPTER 2

UNDERSTANDING THE WRITING PROCESS

THINKING ABOUT WRITING: NONMAGICAL STRATEGIES VERSUS MAGICAL POWERS

Writing is hardly a mysterious activity, yet it is sometimes viewed as if it were. Many people, for instance, seem to think that those who write well possess a magical power or talent. According to this view, people are either born with the ability to write well or they're not. Furthermore, many students believe that those who do write well find writing easy. They just sit down and the words and ideas begin to flow.

My own experiences as a writer, and those of my students, indicate that this popular stereotype simply isn't accurate. Successful writers work as hard on their writing as anyone else—perhaps even harder. Unlike less accomplished writers, however, successful writers develop strategies that enable them to cope with the complexities of writing, and thus to experience the satisfaction of a job well done.

Here are two essays, one by a student writer, Mary Kacmarcik, and one by a professor of English, Burton Hatlen. In different ways, Kacmarcik and Hatlen each discuss what it means to be a writer and comment on their own development as writers. They also each make the point that, as Hatlen says, "writing is a craft, which can be learned by anyone willing to work at it." As you read their essays, ask yourself the following questions:

- To what extent are your own assumptions about writing and experiences as a writer similar to those of Kacmarcik and Hatlen? How are they different?
- Can you recall specific experiences, such as those Kacmarcik and Hatlen describe in their essays, that played a critical role in your development as a writer or your understanding of writing?

Mary Kacmarcik's essay:

A WRITER IS FORMED

The woman at the front of the room hardly resembled my idea of an English teacher. Her raggedy undershirt, heavy flannel jacket, disheveled pants, and braided, stringy hair gave her the appearance of having just returned from a backcountry expedition. And she was huge; she must have tipped the scales at well over two hundred pounds.

"My name is Harriet Jones," she said, "and this is English 111."

This was my introduction to college writing. Ten students had enrolled in this beginning composition class at Islands Community College. Like most of my classmates, I was returning to education after a period in the work force. I had spent one year at Western Washington University but had avoided writing classes. I discovered later, when I sent for my transcripts to apply to Oregon State University, that I had withdrawn from a writing course at Western. I have no memory of this. Did I drop it the first day, or did I struggle with an essay or two before giving up?

At any rate, I went to Alaska that summer to work in the seafood canneries. It was a trip I had planned with two friends

during my senior year in high school. I expected to return to
college in the fall with thousands of dollars in my bank account.
The work was miserable, but I fell in love with remote Sitka, and
I stayed. Time passed with adventures enough to fill a novel. I
eventually landed a job I really wanted at Northern Lights Natural
Foods, a small, family-owned natural foods store. That job inspired me to take a nutrition course at the community college. I
realized during the course that some biology would help me understand nutrition, so I took biology the following semester. I began to consider a career in nutrition which led me to apply to the
Department of Foods and Nutrition at OSU. I wasn't ready to leave
Sitka, however; I would work one more year and take a few more
classes on the side.

That is how I came to be sitting in Ms. Jones's class, preparing myself for a relationship with an English grammar handbook.
We were to respond to short stories, an exercise in which my experience was limited to junior high school book reports. Although I
have always been an avid reader, I had given little thought to
characters, conflicts, plots, and settings. So those early essays
were on topics that did not interest me. I had never heard of a
comma splice either, but Ms. Jones assured us that any paper con-
taining one would be promptly rewarded with an E grade. I would
agonize over blank pages, afraid to begin, afraid of saying the
wrong thing, afraid of committing some technical error. I somehow
managed to fill up the pages and hand in those early essays. Fortunately, Ms. Jones encouraged us to revise after she had graded
our papers.

It turned out that she was also very willing to talk with us
about writing. I discovered that this formidable woman was actu-

ally a caring, humorous person. The writing did not instantly become easier, though. During the second term, we worked on longer papers that required some research. We also did in-class assignments such as freewriting and essay exams. By the end of the term, I had finally become comfortable with putting my ideas on paper.

The year with Ms. Jones was great preparation for my studies at OSU. I learned the importance of editing my work and following conventions. I gained confidence in stating my views. I also learned that teachers are human and that most of them enjoy discussing projects with students outside of class.

In thinking about my history as a writer for this essay, I realized that I have always been a writer--even when I felt unconfident and out of practice. Letters to aunts, uncles, and grandparents were my earliest writings outside of schoolwork, and they have been the main link between my parents' families on the East Coast and my nuclear family here in the Northwest. These letters followed a set format for years:

Dear Aunt _____ (or Grandma),

How are you? I am fine. Thank you for the _____.

Love,

Mary Ellen

My letters have matured with me, and I consider them a sort of
journal except that I mail this journal off in bits and pieces instead of keeping it to read later. My letters describe what I
have been doing, how I feel about things, and what I plan to do.
When I lived in Alaska, letters were my link to family and friends
in Washington.

Another early writing experience was an expanded form of passing notes in school. A friend and I wrote notes to each other
that often went on for pages, much of it nonsense and gossip. We
would work on these packets for days before exchanging them. Now
I can see that we were flexing and developing our writing muscles
as well as building our friendship through the sharing of ideas.

Currently, I write the newsletter for a club I belong to, an
activity I volunteered for to gain experience and to stay involved
with writing. I would like to combine writing with nutrition as a
career. (I considered a major in journalism, but I have a strong
desire to learn everything I can about nutrition.) I would like
to help people improve their health by sharing this knowledge with
them. I still think of myself as someone who is going to write
someday. But I have been writing because I wanted to ever since I
learned how.

Professor Burton Hatlen's essay:

WRITING IS A CRAFT THAT CAN BE LEARNED, NOT AN EFFORTLESS OUTPOURING BY GENIUSES

A writer—that's what I would be when I grew up. I made that
decision in 1952, when I was 16, along with what now seems to be half
the people I knew at the time. We were all going to be "writers,"
whatever we meant by that.

I can't speak for my friends, but in my case, at least, being a writer
meant living a certain kind of life. The setting would be Paris, *la rive
gauche*: a sidewalk café. A man (with a beard, a beret dropping over

his right eye, a turtleneck sweater, sandals, a pipe) is seated at a round table, a half-empty glass of red wine before him. There are other people around the table, but they are a little dim. And there is talk. Jung. Kafka. Anarchism. The decline of the West. But mostly there is that man. Me. Someday.

I didn't need anyone to tell me that the road from a dusty farming town in the Central Valley of California to that Paris café would be a long and difficult one. In fact, it was *supposed* to be long and difficult. "You must suffer, suffer"—so said a cartoon character of my youth to a would-be artist. And I had a real-life example of such suffering. When I was 10, my cousin brought her new husband, George, to town. George had actually been to Paris, and he was going to write a novel before returning there. Later, I heard my aunt tell my mother that she had read the manuscript of his novel. According to her, it was "filthy," and what was more, she whispered, she was sure George "drank." In any case, his novel remained unpublished, and George never made it back to Paris. At some level I realized that his sad story augured ill for my own dreams of living the life of a writer in a 1950's version of Paris in the 20's.

Nevertheless, in 1956, after my junior year at Berkeley, I decided that if I was ever to become a writer, I'd better try to write. I spent five months working at various jobs, and when I had saved $500 I moved into a one-room apartment in San Francisco. By then the "renaissance" there was in full flower, and the city seemed to me a reasonable facsimile of Paris. In North Beach there were real cafés, where real poets—Kenneth Rexroth, Robert Duncan, Lawrence Ferlinghetti (who actually wore a beret)—sat around and talked. If location had anything to do with becoming a writer, San Francisco seemed the right place to be.

For three months, until my money ran out, I spent my evenings in North Beach and my days at the oilcloth-covered kitchen table in my apartment, writing. Or at least that's what I told myself I was doing. In fact, in those three months I managed to write only about three pages of what I called a novel. It was about a young man living alone in a San Francisco apartment, who looked into the sky one day, saw it split open, and went mad. I fussed for the first week or two over those pages, making sure that every word was *juste*. But I had never worked out a plot, and once the young man went mad, I didn't know what else to do with him.

I stopped writing, and devoted my days to reading—all of Dreiser, among other things. What I remember best about that time is not the few paragraphs I wrote, but the wonder I felt as I read the yellowing pages of my second-hand copy of The *"genius."*

In January I went back to Berkeley, and that spring, at the suggestion of one of my teachers, applied to graduate school. Over the next few years, the sidewalk café began to seem no more than an adolescent fantasy, and, before I knew it, I had become not a writer in Paris, but a teacher entangled in committee meetings and bureaucratic in-fighting.

What brought all this back to me was a conversation I had earlier this year with a one-time colleague of mine, the author of a respect-able university-press book on Sir Thomas Browne and, in the days when we taught together, a tenured associate professor and a popular teacher of Shakespeare. A few years ago, at 44, he suddenly resigned his teaching position and moved to Boston, where, I heard later, he was working a couple of days a week as a waiter and spending the rest of his time writing. When I went to Boston last winter I looked him up.

We talked about his novel and my work. Then the conversation turned to our respective children, all of whom, we realized, had not only decided to become artists of one sort or another but, unlike us at their age, were actually *doing* so. I thought about the Paris café, and then I asked him what he had wanted to do with his life when he was 20.

"Actually," he said, "I wanted to live the way I'm living now—working at a nothing job that doesn't take anything out of me, and writing."

That was a pretty fair description of my own dream when I moved to that apartment in San Francisco. What had happened to it? I think the main reason that I never realized the dream was my mistaken notion of what it means to be a writer, which I had picked up partly from media images of Hemingway and Fitzgerald, Sartre and Camus, and partly from my teachers. Those influences had suggested that writing was something geniuses were somehow able to do without thinking about it; ordinary people dabbled at their peril. That writing is also a craft that can be learned, that a young person might decide to write and then systematically learn how to do so, was never so much as hinted at by anyone I knew. So, when the words for my novel did not automatically come pouring out of me, I had concluded that I must not be a writer.

In fact, I have over the years written enough poetry to make a good-sized book, and enough prose—if it were all gathered together—to make two or three. Yet I feel uncomfortable saying I'm a writer who teaches, preferring instead to see myself as a teacher who writes. Nevertheless, writing is clearly a major part of my life. Yes, I do feel some envy of my friend in Boston, who is at last doing what he dreamed of when he was 20. And no, I've never written that novel, because I still don't know how to go about it. If most of what I write is about other people's writing, that's all right, because through it I've found a way to share with others the wonder I felt 30 years ago as I read Dreiser.

Since then, I have gradually come to see that writing takes manifold forms, that the conception of writing as a hermetic mystery, which I picked up from my reading and my teachers in the 1950's, is not only wrong, but pernicious. It dishonors the writing that non-geniuses do and denies the hard work at the craft that is essential to all writing, even the writing of "geniuses." It caused my cousin's husband to decide that if he couldn't be a writer, he didn't want to be anything, and I think it caused me to waste several years chasing illusions.

The myth that real writing is the effortless outpouring of geniuses did not die in the 1950's. There is abundant evidence that it still persists—at least among my students, most of whom also dream that someone, someday, will find a spark of "genius" in what they write. As a teacher who writes (or a writer who teaches), I am becoming more and more convinced that it's my job to nurture the writer in every student, while at the same time making it clear that writing is a craft, which can be learned by anyone willing to work at it.

BURTON HATLEN

Exploration

Now that you have read Kacmarcik's and Hatlen's essays, reflect on your own assumptions about writing and your experiences as a writer. To do so, set aside at least a half an hour to respond (either by freewriting or jotting down notes) to the following questions:

- What do you remember about learning to write?
- How was writing viewed by your family and friends when you were growing up?
- What role have your experiences as a student played in your attitude toward writing?
- Can you recall a particular experience in school or on the job that influenced your current attitude toward writing?
- How do you feel about writing now?
- What images come to mind when you hear the term "writer"?
- Do you think of yourself as a writer? Why, or why not?
- What kinds of writing have you come to enjoy? To dislike?
- What goals have you (or would you like to) set for yourself as a writer?

Application

Using the information generated by the previous exploration, write a letter to your classmates and teacher in which you describe who you are as a writer today—and how you got to be that way. You're writing a letter, so you don't need to worry as much about form and style as you would if you were writing a formal essay. Do keep in mind, however, that your classmates and teacher may actually read your letter, so write with this audience in mind.

Group Activity

Bring enough copies of your letter to class so that you can share it with members of your group. After you have all read each other's letters, work together to answer the following questions. Choose one person to record the group's answers so that you can share the results of your discussion with the rest of the class.

- To what extent are your attitudes toward writing and experiences as writers similar? List three to five statements about your attitudes toward and experiences as writers with which all group members can agree.
- What factors most clearly account for the differences in your attitudes toward writing and experiences as writers? List two or three factors that you agree account for these differences.
- Can you identify any common goals you would like to set for yourselves as writers? List at least three goals you can agree on.

MANAGING THE WRITING PROCESS

Writing is not a magical or mysterious process. Rather, it is a craft that can indeed be learned. But how do writers actually manage the writing process? Notice how differently the following six students say that they proceed.

> My writing starts with contemplation. I let the topic I have chosen sink into my mind for a while. Then I brainstorm on paper, coming up with words, phrases, and sentences that relate to my topic. It is usually during the brainstorming process that I find whether or not I have chosen the right topic. If I am not satisfied with my topic, I start over. Then I make a simple plan for my essay, and then I start on my rough draft. Peer responses, final drafts, and revisions follow, sometimes with more brainstorming in between.
>
> EDITH CASTERLINE

> I have to sit down with pen in hand and just write whatever comes out naturally. I then go back and work with what I've written.
>
> MICHELLE COLLUM

```
    I have to think my ideas out in detail before I begin draft-
ing.  Only then can I begin writing and revising.
                                                    MARSHA CARPER


    When I write, I first brainstorm for an idea.  This may take
only a few minutes or days, depending on the kind of paper I'm
working on.  Once I get an idea, I then sit down and start writ-
ing.  This seems to be the best way for me to get started.  After
I've written the rough draft I then go back and do some major re-
vision.  I revise and have others check for mistakes I might have
missed, and then I type it out.
                                                    DAVE GUENTHER


    As a writer, I am first a thinker and then a doer.  I first
think about my topic carefully, and then I write what I wish to
say.
                                                    GARY ETCHEMENDY


    I write by coming up with a sketchy rough draft and then
filling it in or changing it.
                                                    PAUL AUSTIN
```

On the surface, these students' writing processes seem to have little in common. Actually, however, all involve the same three activities: planning, drafting, and revising. These activities don't necessarily occur in any set order. Michelle Collum postpones most of her planning until after she has generated a rough draft, for example, while Marsha Carper plans extensively before she writes her first word. To be successful, however, all these writers must sooner or later think critically and make choices about words, ideas, and anticipated responses of readers. Then the writers must try out these choices either in their heads or on paper, evaluate the effects of these choices, and make appropriate changes in their drafts. Rather than being a magical or mysterious activity, then, writing is a process of planning, drafting, and revising.

Identifying composing styles

The above description of planning, drafting, and revising may make writing sound neater and more predictable than it actually is. Writing is, in fact, a messy and often unpredictable process. Even though all writers engage in planning, drafting, and revising, they do so in a variety of ways. Furthermore, no one approaches every writing task the same way. (For this reason, it is more accurate to refer to writing proces*ses*, rather than the writing process.) Instead, a writer will decide how to approach a writing assignment based on such factors as these:

- the nature and importance of the writing task
- the writer's own time schedule
- the amount of experience the writer has had with a particular kind of writing

Most successful writers do, however, have a typical or preferred way of managing the writing process. Many people find, in fact, that one of the following three styles of composing describes their own methods of writing.

1. *Heavy Planners.* These people, like Marsha Carper and Gary Etchemendy, generally consider their ideas and plan their writing so carefully in their heads that their first drafts are often more like other writers' second or third drafts. As a consequence, they often revise less intensively and frequently than other students. Many of these students have disciplined themselves so that they can think about their writing in all sorts of places—on the subway, at work, in the garden pulling weeds, or in the car driving to and from school.

    Some heavy planners write in this way because they prefer to, while others develop this strategy out of necessity. Marsha Carper, for instance, says that she simply has to do a great deal of her writing "in her head" rather than on paper because she lives fifty miles from the university and must spend considerable time commuting. In addition, she's a mother as well as a student, and at home she often has to steal odd moments to work on her writing. As a result, she's learned to use every opportunity to think about her writing while she drives, cooks, or relaxes with her family.

2. *Heavy Revisers.* These students, like Michelle Collum and Paul Austin, differ greatly from the heavy planners just described. Heavy planners spend a great deal of time planning (either in their heads or in writing) before they begin to draft an essay. In contrast, heavy revisers need to find out what they want to say through the act of writing itself. When faced with a writing task, they prefer, as Michelle Collum indicates, to "sit down with pen in hand and just write whatever comes out naturally."

Heavy revisers often state that writing their ideas out in a sustained spurt of activity reassures them that they have something to say and helps them avoid frustration. These students may not seem to plan because they begin drafting so early. Actually, however, their planning occurs as they draft and especially as they revise. Heavy revisers typically spend a great deal of their writing time revising their initial drafts. To do so effectively, they must be able to read their work critically and be able, often, to discard substantial portions of first drafts.

As you've probably realized, in both of these styles of composing, one of the components of the writing process is apparently abbreviated. Heavy planners don't seem to revise as extensively as other students. Actually, however, they plan (and, in effect, revise) so thoroughly early in the process that they often don't need to revise as intensively later. Similarly, heavy revisers may not seem to plan; in fact, though, once they write their rough drafts, they plan and revise simultaneously and often extensively.

3. *Sequential Composers.* A third general style of composing is exemplified by Dave Guenther and Edith Casterline. These writers might best be called sequential composers because they devote roughly equivalent amounts of time to planning, drafting, and revising. Rather than trying out their ideas and planning their writing mentally, as heavy planners do, sequential composers typically rely on written notes and plans to give shape and force to their ideas. And unlike heavy revisers, sequential composers need to have greater control over form and subject matter as they draft.

Sequential composers' habit of allotting time for planning, drafting, and revising helps them deal with the inevitable anxieties of writing. Like heavy revisers, sequential composers need the reassurance of seeing their ideas written down; the resulting stack of notes and plans gives them the confidence to begin drafting. Sequential composers may not revise as extensively as do heavy revisers, for they generally draft more slowly, reviewing their writing as they proceed. But revision is nevertheless an important part of their composing process; like most writers, sequential revisers need a break from drafting to be able to critique their own words and ideas.

Each of these three styles of composing has advantages and disadvantages. Heavy planners are often efficient writers; they spend less time at the desk or keyboard than do other writers. But heavy planners must have great mental discipline. An unexpected interruption when they are working out their ideas—a child in tears, a phone call—can cause even the most disciplined thinker to have a momentary lapse. Because so much of their work is done mentally, heavy planners are less likely to benefit from the fruitful explorations and revisions that occur when writers review notes and plans or reread their own texts. And because heavy planners put off drafting until relatively late in the composing process, they can encounter substantial difficulties if the sentences and paragraphs that had seemed so clearly developed in their minds don't look as coherent and polished on paper.

Heavy revisers experience different advantages and disadvantages. Because they write quickly and voluminously, heavy revisers aren't in danger of losing valuable ideas. Similarly, their frequent rereading of their drafts helps them remain open to new options that can improve their writing. Working through numerous drafts can be time-consuming, however, and heavy revisers must learn how to deal with emotional highs and lows that occur as they discover what they want to say through the process of writing itself. As noted earlier, heavy revisers must be able ruthlessly to critique their own writing, discarding large portions of text or perhaps starting over from scratch if necessary. Because they revise so extensively, heavy revisers must be careful to leave adequate time for revision or the quality of their work can suffer.

What about sequential composers? Because they plan to spend time planning, drafting, and revising—and do so primarily in writing, rather than mentally—they have more external control over the writing process than do heavy planners and revisers. Sequential composers are also unlikely to fool themselves into thinking that a quickly generated collection of ideas is an adequate rough draft or that a plan brainstormed while taking the subway is adequate preparation for writing. Sequential composers can, however, develop inefficiently rigid habits—habits that reflect their need to have external control over their writing process. They may, for instance, waste valuable time developing detailed written plans when they're actually ready to begin drafting.

Good writers are aware of their preferred composing style—and of its potential advantages and disadvantages. They take responsibility for decisions about how to manage their writing, recognizing the difference, for instance, between the necessary incubation of ideas and procrastination. Good writers are also flexible; depending upon the task or situation, they can modify their preferred approach. A person who generally is a heavy reviser when writing academic essays, for instance, might write routine business memos in a single sitting because that is the most efficient way to get the job done. Similarly, heavy planners who prefer to do much of the work of writing mentally must employ different strategies when writing collaboratively with others, where a great deal of oral discussion is a necessity.

There is another way of managing the writing process—though it might best be described as management by avoidance.

> 4. *Procrastinators.* All writers occasionally procrastinate, but if you habitually put off writing a first draft until you can only write a *final* draft (and this at 3 A.M. on the day your essay is due), your chances of success are minimal. Though you may have invented good reasons for putting off writing—"I write better under pressure"; "I can't write until I have all my easier assignments done first"—procrastination makes it difficult for you to manage the writing process in an efficient and effective manner.

William Stafford, a noted poet, once commented that "a writer is not so much someone who has something to say as he is someone who has found a process that will bring about new things he would not have thought if he had not started to say them." Stafford's remarks emphasize the importance of developing a workable writing process—a repertoire of strategies that you can draw upon in a variety of situations. Much of this book is designed to help you achieve this goal. Part 2, for instance, presents specific practical strategies, while the following section focuses on general strategies you can use to manage the writing process.

Analyzing—and monitoring—your writing process

Successful writers do not have special powers. They have, however, developed strategies that enable them to respond to—and enjoy—the demands of writing, and they recognize that different writing tasks and situations call for different strategies. They also know that writing is too complex an activity for one-approach-fits-all solutions to problems. Consider, for instance, one very common writing problem, procrastination. Is procrastination always harmful? Can writers always distinguish between inappropriate procrastination and the necessary incubation of ideas? Here's what one thoughtful student writer discovered about her own tendency to procrastinate.

For me, sometimes procrastination isn't really procrastination (or so I tell myself). Sometimes what I label procrastination is really planning. The trouble is that I don't always know when it's one or the other . . .

How do I procrastinate? Let me count the ways. I procrastinate by doing good works (helping overtime at my job, cleaning house, aiding and abetting a variety of causes). I procrastinate by absorbing myself in a purely selfish activity (reading paperbacks, watching TV, going to movies). I procrastinate by visiting with friends, talking on the telephone, prolonging chance encounters. I procrastinate by eating and drinking (ice cream, coffee, cookies--all detrimental). Finally, I procrastinate by convincing myself that this time of day is not when I write well. I'd be much better off, I usually conclude, taking a nap. So I do.

Part of my difficulty is that I can see a certain validity in most of my reasons for procrastinating. There are some times of day when my thoughts flow better. I have forced myself to write papers in the past when I just didn't feel fluid. Not only were the papers difficult to write, they were poorly written, inarticulate papers. Even after several rewrites, they were merely marginal. I would much rather write when I am at my mental best.

I need to balance writing with other activities. The trouble is--just how to achieve the perfect balance!

HOLLY HARDIN

Holly's realistic appraisal of the role that procrastination plays in her writing process should help her distinguish between useful incubation and unhelpful procrastination. Unlike students who tell themselves that they should never procrastinate—and then do so anyway, feeling guilty every moment—Holly knows that she has to consider a variety of factors before she decides to invite a friend to tea, to bake a batch of chocolate chip brownies, or to take a much-needed nap.

Application

The following composing process inventory will help you describe and evaluate your current composing strategies. Respond in writing to each of these questions.

COMPOSING PROCESS INVENTORY

1. What is your general attitude toward writing? How do you think this attitude affects the writing you do?
2. Of the descriptions of the four major composing styles in

this chapter, which best describes the way you compose? If none seems to fit you, how do you compose?

3. How do you know when you are ready to begin writing? Do you have a regular "start-up" method or ritual?

4. How do you procrastinate? (Be honest! All writers procrastinate occasionally.)

5. Think about your writing habits and rituals. What time of day do you prefer to write? What place suits you best? What equipment (pen, pencil, paper, computer, and so on) do you prefer to use? Do any of these habits or rituals interfere with the efficiency of your writing process?

6. What do you find most difficult or frustrating about writing? Easiest and most rewarding? Why?

7. What planning and revising strategies do you use? Do you spend enough time planning and revising? (Many writers don't.) Can you think of at least one concrete way to improve your planning or revising strategies?

Group Activity

Meet with classmates to discuss your responses to the composing process inventory. Begin your discussion by having each person state two important things he or she learned as a result of completing the inventory. (Appoint a recorder to write down each person's statements.) Once all members of your group have spoken, ask the recorder to read these statements out loud. Were any statements repeated by more than one member of the group? Working as a group, formulate two conclusions about the writing process based on your discussion that you would like to share with the class. (Avoid vague and general assertions, such as "Writing is difficult.") Be prepared to discuss your conclusions with your classmates.

Keeping a writer's notebook

Many writers keep journals or notebooks, recording in them whatever seems useful at the time. Sometimes writers may focus on work in progress, jotting down ideas, descriptions, or bits of conversation. But writers also use their journals or notebooks to reflect on their own experiences as writers. Holly Hardin's discussion of procrastination was, in fact, an entry from her notebook. You may want to record your responses to this textbook's explorations and applications in your own writer's notebook.

Whatever is recorded, a writer's notebook serves a single purpose—to help the writer—so if you decide to keep a notebook, it should reflect your own interests and needs. Your notebook may be a nicely bound blank book or a spiral notebook, whatever seems most inviting to you. If you have access to a computer, you might want to take advantage of its speed and flexibility, keeping your notebook on disk and printing copies at regular intervals. Here are some possible uses for your notebook.

USES FOR YOUR WRITER'S NOTEBOOK

- to ask yourself questions
- to reflect on your writing process and on current writing projects
- to brainstorm in response to an assignment
- to record possible ideas for future writing projects
- to note details, arguments, or examples that might be useful in an essay
- to try out various introductions or conclusions
- to play around with imagery or figurative language such as similes or metaphors
- to map out a plan for an essay
- to express your frustrations or satisfactions with your writing
- to make schedules for current writing projects
- to preserve random thoughts about work in progress
- to freewrite about an idea or topic you're working on
- to copy phrases, sentences, or passages that impress you as particularly effective models for imitation or analysis

---

Application

Try keeping a writer's notebook for two weeks. At the end of this period, reflect on the following questions. Did keeping a notebook help you come up with ideas for writing? (Can you locate two or three entries that you could possibly develop into an essay?) Has your notebook helped you better understand how you manage the writing process? Did you enjoy writing in your notebook? What surprised you about keeping a notebook?

Practicing effective time management

Effective time management can make the difference between completing a writing assignment on time (and being satisfied with your work) or having a frustrating, unproductive experience. Something as minor as being careful to organize your notes and drafts for a research paper can save you hours of confusion. Here are some suggestions to guide you as you plan for your writing.

Guidelines for managing your time

1. Begin a writing assignment as soon as possible after you receive it. You may just write down a few ideas, but you'll have focused your mind on your project, if only briefly, and thus will have taken a crucial first step in the writing process.

2. Establish a rough schedule for your writing. You don't have to write down your schedule—though that might help you keep on track. At some point fairly early in the writing process, however, you should consider your assignment in the context of the overall demands on your time. As you do so, ask yourself such questions as these:

   ■ What demands does this assignment make of me? What is likely to be most difficult for me about this assignment? What strengths do I bring to this assignment? How can I minimize my difficulties and build on my strengths?

   ■ How much time should I anticipate spending on planning, drafting, and revising? Is this schedule flexible enough to accommodate such potential problems as a false start or difficulty revising?

   You might not stick exactly to this schedule, but it will help you manage your time more effectively.

3. Develop some way to organize work in progress as you plan, draft, and revise.

4. If you've never done a certain kind of writing before, talk with your instructor or writing tutor about how much time it should take and how best to schedule your time. If the project is lengthy, such as a research paper or technical report, you may want to make regular appointments with a tutor in the writing center so that he or she can help you approach the assignment in an organized manner.

Group Activity

As students, you and your classmates understand better than anyone else the pressures that you face. Working with a group of classmates, generate at least three additional suggestions for effective time management when working on writing projects. (Be sure to select a recorder.) Be prepared to share your advice with classmates.

Avoiding being too easy or too hard on yourself

Be realistic about your writing. Expect that your first drafts won't be as good as you'd like; you'll undoubtedly revise them. Expect to make some errors on your first drafts; you can correct them later. Expect that some kinds of writing will be easier for you than others. When you encounter a major problem, such as uncertainty about how to organize your essay or develop your ideas, ask your instructor, fellow students, or tutor for help. Most importantly, don't let your struggles with a particular essay or report stop your progress. One of the best ways to cope with a writer's block is to relax, take a break, and let your unconscious mind work on the problem while you think about something else.

Developing productive writing habits and rituals

Scratch a writer and you'll discover a person with decided habits and rituals. Professional writers often are particularly conscious of their writing habits and rituals. All writers, however, have some predispositions that affect their writing. Some people write best early in the morning; others, late at night. Some require a quiet atmosphere; others find the absence of noise or music distracting. Some people can compose only by writing longhand; others much prefer the typewriter or computer. People have different ways of telling themselves that they are ready to write. Clearing my desk of its usual rubble is one way that I tell myself it's time to get serious. Here is how two students, Holly Hardin and Tom Grenier, describe their start-up writing rituals. Holly relies on exercise to provide the mental and physical push she needs.

Exercise immediately before assaulting a paper seems to provide me mental, as well as physical, stimulation. After I run,

I tackle a first draft with incredible PMA (positive mental attitude). The head of steam I build during my run (the natural "run-
ner's high") tides me over to at least the second or third page of
my first draft. Finishing most papers after that point is usually
not a big problem. While I exercise, I spend as much time as I
can thinking about new analogies or visualizing the paper's organization and flow. I think about the most basic message that I
want my reader to get. If I were to summarize each paragraph in
one sentence, I think to myself, what would the sentences say? Is
there anything I can eliminate?

Sometimes I think about a chosen audience for the topic. If
I were to tell them about the subject face-to-face would my message change? What would I say? What would they most easily understand?

Near the end of my run, I think about how good the paper will
be--I hone my expectations. This cheerleading pushes me through
the front door and straight to my desk. I can hardly wait to get
started. I'm almost afraid the ideas I generated will escape me
before I can corner them on paper.

I don't know whether the final product of this process is any
better than it might otherwise have been, but it eases the pain of
first-draft compositions. I produce a draft more confidently and
more quickly than I would by sitting down and hacking away at it.

HOLLY HARDIN

As you'll see, Tom Grenier's approach is quite different.

Most of my writing begins at the kitchen sink. After the
dishes are drying in the rack and the living room is in order, I
head for my bedroom--where I do my writing--and make the bed, fold
socks, empty the trash, and straighten anything that looks at all
out of order. Throughout the final stage of this ritual I am spi-
raling inward toward my writing desk, the last place I clean.
When the desk is bare except for a typewriter, a handbook, and two
dictionaries (a paperback for quick spelling references and a hard
cover for bigger jobs), I sit down and begin contemplating the
task at hand. The essence of writing is organizing ideas,
thoughts, gut reactions, or a slew of academic resources into a
coherent expression of words on paper. Following the premise that
the mind will take up the discipline put on the body and sur-
roundings, the process of that organization moves from the outside
inward until I'm sitting in front of the typewriter sharpening a
pencil with my pocketknife. Cleaning house is also a good way to
work out the "prewrite jitters" and let me think casually about
what I want or need to write. With the house straight at a quiet
hour, I sit down and start on the first drafts of an introductory
paragraph. Now the process has moved out again in a form that I

```
can store, mull over, scribble on, and type again in a new draft.
I'm off!
```

TOM GRENIER

Notice how Tom and Holly both emphasize the ways in which their particular rituals help them cope with what Tom calls the "prewrite jitters." Productive writing rituals like these are a very positive way of pampering yourself—of creating the environment most conducive to writing.

WRITING WITH A WORD PROCESSOR

I probably don't have to persuade you of the advantages of writing with a word processor. As a student, you are undoubtedly already aware that computers can do a great deal to ease the labor of writing. Those who find pen or pencil drafting a slow and uncomfortable process often marvel at the ease with which word processing enables them to generate text. Even writers who prefer to write rough drafts longhand insist that simply being able to revise without retyping entire documents more than justifies the time and effort spent learning to use a word processor. And as companies produce increasingly sophisticated and powerful computers and software, word-processing programs offer a variety of options in addition to such traditional features as a spellchecker and thesaurus. A program with window or split-screen capability, for instance, allows you to look at two sections of a text at the same time, while computer graphics programs allow you to include computer-generated charts, graphs, diagrams, and even artwork in your writing.

The following suggestions should make the process of writing with a word processor easier and more productive.

Guidelines for writing with a word processor

1. UNDERSTAND WHAT A WORD PROCESSOR CAN—AND CAN'T—DO FOR YOUR WRITING.

Writing with a word processor can make your writing process considerably more efficient and ease the burdens of revision. But not even the most sophisticated word-processing program has a REVISE function key: you must still wrestle with words and ideas, still determine if your essay is clearly organized and well developed. Your essay may look neat and professional, thanks to your printer, but your readers will finally be persuaded not by fancy typefaces or formats but by the quality of your ideas and the effectiveness of your style.

2. RECOGNIZE THAT DIFFERENT WRITERS USE WORD PROCESSORS IN DIFFERENT WAYS—AND EXPERIMENT TO FIND THE BEST WAY *FOR YOU.*

Some people reserve the computer for entering and printing documents they have already written. They may make minor revisions at the computer, but they generally make major revisions on their printed texts and then enter the changes into the computer. Others actually compose at the computer. A writer might brainstorm at the computer, for instance, and then use the word-processing program's split-screen option to keep these notes on screen as a guide while writing. As you might expect, heavy revisers (people who prefer to generate ideas by writing) adapt particularly easily to composing at the keyboard.

Take the time to explore the options available to you and find those best suited to your own needs. If you're uncomfortable composing at the computer, try drafting brief or less important documents, such as letters or ungraded assignments, on-screen. With time and practice, you may find yourself drawn to the computer for longer and more important assignments—or you may discover that you prefer the slowness of handwritten drafting.

3. RECOGNIZE THE POTENTIAL LIMITATIONS OF ON-SCREEN REVISION.

Computers can make revision easier and faster, but they have potential limitations as well. Sometimes writers can be seduced by the computer's ease of revision into focusing on minor stylistic changes instead of organization or development of ideas. Many writers find that to evaluate these more global aspects of their writing, they must work with hard copy. Because of the small size of the computer monitor's screen, it can be difficult to grasp the big picture—yet effective writing depends on just this ability.

When you print drafts of an essay to read and revise, be sure to save these earlier versions. You may decide that an introduction that you rejected in favor of a later version was best after all. Having a "paper trail" makes it easy to reinsert your original introduction.

4. TAKE ADVANTAGE OF THE SPECIAL FEATURES THAT MANY WORD-PROCESSING PROGRAMS PROVIDE.

Some writers use their computers as glorified typewriters, so that these machines function primarily to ease the burden of producing neatly printed texts. But most computer programs offer a number of features that can make writing easier and more productive. I have already mentioned the window or split-screen option. Some programs allow you to write notes or directions that appear on-screen but not in the printed text; this feature allows you to interact with your own writing without cluttering up drafts with comments that must be deleted later. Your program's MOVE or BLOCK function enables you to move sections of text easily, while the SEARCH function makes it possible to locate every instance of a word or phrase. You can use this function when editing to check that you've not overused a word or to correct a misspelled word used several times in a draft. Finally, if you are fortunate enough to have access to networked computers, you can benefit from electronic collaboration. Such networks enable you to get on-screen responses to work in progress; they also make group writing projects easier and more productive.

Activities for Thought, Discussion and Writing

1. If your college or university has a writing center, interview one or more of the tutors who work there about their writing methods and habits. Do they fall into one of the four patterns described in this chapter? How do they approach their college writing assignments? In what ways are their experiences and writing processes similar and dissimilar to yours? Can they give you any useful tips on how to be a more successful writer? Be prepared to share the results of your interview with your classmates.

2. All writers procrastinate occasionally—some just procrastinate more effectively than others. After brainstorming or freewriting about your favorite ways of procrastinating, write either a humorous or serious essay on procrastination.

3. Many published interviews with professional writers are available. You can learn a great deal about writing from reading these essays. Choose one of the following collections of essays and read two to five interviews. While reading them, try to think of the ways the statements these writers make might—and might not— apply to your own writing.

   ■ *Writers at Work: The Paris Review Interviews.* First series. Edited by Malcolm Cowley. New York: Viking, 1958.

   ■ *Writers at Work: The Paris Review Interviews.* Subsequent series edited by George Plimpton. New York: Viking, 1963, 1967, 1976, and 1981.

   ■ *The Writer on Her Work.* Edited by Janet Sternburg. New York: W.W. Norton, 1980.

   ■ *The Writer's Craft.* Edited by John Hersey. New York: Alfred A. Knopf, 1974.

4. The exploration and application on pages 29 and 30 encouraged you to reflect on your assumptions about writing and your experiences as a writer. Drawing on these activities and on the rest of the chapter, write an essay in which you reflect on this subject.

CHAPTER 3

UNDERSTANDING THE RHETORICAL SITUATION

Whenever you write—whether you are jotting a note to a friend or working on a lab report—you are writing in the context of a specific situation with its own unique demands and opportunities. A management trainee writing a memo to her supervisor faces different challenges than does an investigative journalist working on a story for the *New York Times* or a student writing a research paper for a political science class. Successful writers know that they must consider the situations in which they write; they can't rely on formulas or blind luck when they compose. They know that they must use their rhetorical sensitivity—their understanding of the relationships among writers, readers, and texts—to help them make decisions as they write and revise.

In this chapter you will learn how to use your rhetorical sensitivity—your understanding of the elements of rhetoric—to analyze your specific writing situation. By asking yourself questions about this situation and by considering the three Aristotelian appeals (explained in the final section of this chapter), you can determine the most fruitful way to approach your topic and to respond to the needs and expectations of your readers.

LEARNING TO ANALYZE THE RHETORICAL SITUATION

Rhetoric, as introduced in Chapter 1, involves three key elements: a writer, a reader, and a text that makes their communication possible. Even though you may write alone at your desk, computer, or kitchen table, the act of writing inevitably involves you with all the elements of rhetoric. When you think about these elements, you are analyzing your rhetorical situation. Let's suppose, for example, that for some time you've owed a close friend a letter. One aspect of your rhetorical situation, the fact that you owe your friend a letter, is thus external. Once you decide that your friend is too important to lose touch with, you internalize the situation as a problem to resolve. How you decide to "solve" this problem—how you choose to begin your letter, what you write about, how you present yourself, what tone you use—all these decisions are personal, creative, unique.

More than your own creativity as a writer comes into play when you actually compose your letter. In writing to your friend, you will probably follow such conventions of correspondence as dating your letter and providing a salutation. The conventions of correspondence may also influence the content of your letter. You may decide to explain your slowness in responding, for example, by falling back on the much-used phrasing "I know I should have written sooner, but . . ." As you write, you're probably also aware that your friend will expect your letter to be at least several paragraphs long—as most personal letters are—and that you should balance news of yourself with questions or comments about your friend.

Application

Imagine that you must write the following letters:

- a letter of application for a job
- a letter to a friend whose parent has recently died
- a letter to your bank asking for the correction of an error on your current checking account statement

Keeping the elements of rhetoric in mind, spend a few minutes thinking about how you would approach these different writing situations.

- What is your role as writer and your purpose for writing in each situation?

- What image of yourself, or *persona*, would you wish to present in each letter, and how would you vary your language accordingly?
- How would the different readers of each letter influence the form and content of your writing?
- What other factors, such as format, would you need to consider in writing these letters?

Write a brief description of each situation, responding to the questions above.

Using your analysis to guide your writing

Most people don't consciously analyze the rhetorical situation when they write personal letters. They rely on commonsense rhetorical sensitivity to help them determine the most effective ways to present their ideas and to communicate with their readers. When you face the challenge of new and more difficult kinds of writing, however, as you do in college, it often helps to analyze your rhetorical situation consciously. Such analysis encourages you to consider each of the elements of rhetoric when you write.

The following guidelines provide questions you can use to analyze your rhetorical situation.

Guidelines for analyzing your rhetorical situation

WRITER

1. Why are you writing?
2. What do you hope your writing will accomplish? Do you want to convey information? Change the reader's mind? Entertain the reader?
3. How might your goals as a writer influence the eventual form and content of your essay?
4. What role does this rhetorical situation invite you as the writer to play? Is your role fixed (as it is when you write an essay exam)? Or is it flexible to some extent?
5. What image of yourself (*persona*) do you want to convey to your readers? What "voice" do you want readers to "hear" when they read your writing?

READER

1. Who is the intended audience for your essay? How have you envisioned this audience? Is it more accurate or helpful to think of your readers as members of a specific audience (subscribers to a special-interest magazine, for instance) or as a general audience encompassing people with a wide range of backgrounds and interests?
2. What role do you intend for readers to adopt as they read this essay? What kinds of cues will you use to signal this role to readers?
3. If you do envision yourself as writing to a specific audience, do those readers have any demographic characteristics—perhaps their age, sex, religion, income, occupation, education, or political preference—that you need to consider?
4. How will your essay appeal to your readers' interests? Do you expect your audience already to be interested in the subject of your essay? Or do you need to create and maintain their interest?
5. How might the needs and expectations of your readers influence the form and content of your essay?

TEXT

1. If you are writing in response to an assignment, to what degree does the assignment specify or restrict the form and content of your essay? How much freedom, in other words, do you as the writer have?
2. What generic or stylistic conventions does your rhetorical situation require you to follow? Are these conventions rigidly defined (as in the case of lab reports) or flexible to some extent?
3. Does the nature of your subject implicitly or explicitly require that you provide certain kinds of evidence or explore certain issues?
4. Could you benefit by looking at models or other examples of the kind of writing your situation requires?

As these questions indicate, the process of analyzing your rhetorical situation challenges you to look both within and without. Your intended meaning—what you want to communicate to your readers—is certainly important, as is your purpose for writing. But unless you're writing solely for yourself in your journal or notebook, you can't ignore your readers or other situational factors. Analyzing your rhetorical situation helps you to respond creatively as a writer yet keeps you aware of limits on your freedom.

Setting preliminary goals

Before beginning a major writing project, you may find it helpful to write a brief analysis of your rhetorical situation, or you may simply review these questions mentally. This process of analyzing your rhetorical situation is an opportunity to determine your *preliminary* intentions or goals as a writer. (Your intentions will often shift as you write. That's fine. As you write, you will naturally revise your understanding of your rhetorical situation.) Despite its tentativeness, however, your analysis of your situation will help you to begin writing with a sense of direction and purpose.

Here is an analysis of a rhetorical situation written by a student, Lynn Hansen. Also included is Lynn's essay so that you can see the relationship between her description of her rhetorical situation and her essay.

Here is Lynn's analysis of her rhetorical situation.

I'm writing a review or travel essay on Burgdorf Hot Springs, a semiprivate resort thirty-five miles north of McCall, Idaho. My review might appropriately be published in a magazine like Pacific Northwest.

Since Burgdorf offers only primitive accommodations and minimal development of the pool, I expect that the hot springs will attract a certain Bohemian type, so I'm aiming my review for such readers. I am also assuming that my audience will consist mainly of outdoor enthusiasts who appreciate the joys of wilderness hiking, camping, and backpacking. I recognize that a wide range of people read Pacific Northwest; however, those who are already somewhat interested in hot springs and outdoor activities would be most likely to choose to read my essay. Others might read the essay in order to experience Burgdorf Hot Springs vicariously, so I'll try to make my essay interesting for a range of readers.

I want my persona to be pleasant, open, communicative, and appreciative of the fine experiences Burgdorf Hot Springs has to offer. I want my tone or "voice" to be friendly and engaging. I will concentrate in this essay on making the content of my review colorful, interesting, and easy to read. Because I feel that it is important to the success of my article that I convey feelings of adventure, mystery, and romance about the place I am reviewing, I will include some information on the rich historical background of Burgdorf. Since this is a travel review, I must also be sure to include basic information about the resort. The purpose of my review is to increase the audience's awareness that such places exist and to encourage those who are interested to explore and enjoy our natural wilderness areas.

Here is Lynn Hansen's essay.

BURGDORF HOT SPRINGS

You've opened your eyes at the first hint of light and rolled out of your sleeping bag to climb stiffly down from the loft. Shivering in the soft half-light of dawn, you look around the cabin for your towel, swim suit, and sandals, quickly get dressed, and then make a mad dash down the trail to the pool.

At the other end of the meadow, through the pine trees, you see steam rising from the pool and hanging heavy in the cool crisp air. The thought of your body (which is by now covered with goose bumps) easing into the hot water nearly makes you forget that you are walking through the wet grass at dawn in your bathing suit!

At last you are floating in the hot, pure mineral water, hovering at seven thousand feet above sea level. Every muscle relaxed, you forget tense and careworn thoughts of the world and its complicated affairs. All that is left is the blissful environment of sunrise sky, expansive mountains, and the peace and quiet that pervades the forests and wilderness lands of the Northwest.

Welcome to Burgdorf Hot Springs, a rustic, primitive hot-springs resort located thirty-five miles north of McCall, Idaho. The experience just described is common to hundreds of primitive and semiprivate geothermal water flows that can be found throughout the mountainous regions of Colorado, Oregon, Washington, Idaho, Utah, Montana, and Wyoming. The hot springs at Burgdorf is one of the oldest privately developed mineral-water resorts in Idaho. Much of what can be appreciated at Burgdorf-- the large open-air pool, the quaint hand-built log cabins, the

scenic meadows, the clear mountain streams, and an abundance of
peace and quiet--has largely remained unchanged over the past
thirty years.

Burgdorf Hot Springs, and indeed the entire surrounding ter-
ritory, has a rich history which includes gold mining, trapping,
ghost towns, and legendary folk heros. Once sacred Indian cere-
monial grounds, the land around the hot springs was first settled
by an immigrant named Hans Burgdorf in the middle of the 1800's.
During the height of the gold rush, Frank Harris (whose descen-
dants still own Burgdorf) added to the already existing store and
half-dozen cabins by building eight more log-and-chink cabins and
an impressive three-story log hotel which was open for one summer
and then closed due to lack of business. Today the hotel still
stands in the meadow between the cabins and the pool. It is
filled with handmade furniture and an enticing assortment of an-
tiques, junk, and old photographs.

For the past sixteen years Frank Harris's great-great-
grandson and great-great-granddaughter have been in control of the
destiny of the hot springs. There were a few years in the seventies when a community of fifteen or so young people lived in the
cabins year-round, and the hot springs were closed to the public.
In 1975 the springs were reopened to the public but only for
guests staying at three or four of the cabins. The resort's popularity has grown by word-of-mouth. In the past few years the number of permanent residents has dwindled, so more cabins have been
made available for rental. As more people come to stay in the
cabins and soak in the pool, the young Harrises have taken care to
see that the tranquil atmosphere of the resort does not change.

Although it is possible to rent a cabin on a drop-in basis,
it is best to write ahead for reservations. This must be done

through the mail since there is no phone or electric service to Burgdorf. Requests for reservations should be addressed to Burgdorf Warden, Burgdorf Hot Springs, McCall, Idaho, 83611. Only cabin guests are allowed to use the pool, so be forewarned that a one-day trip to enjoy the pool is out of the question.

Costs for staying at Burgdorf are minimal ($5.00 per night per adult, $3.50 per child). Most of the cabins are one-room log structures with sleeping lofts. Each cabin is equipped with a table, a wood-burning cook stove, an easy chair or two, a kerosene lantern, a good sharp axe, and all the dry wood you can use. Besides these necessities, an old broom and dustpan usually lean in the corner. You must provide your own cooking utensils, food, and water. Water is packed in from a clear mountain stream that runs a few hundred feet behind the cabins.

Many people come to Burgdorf, rent a cabin, and use the resort as a base camp for further explorations in the surrounding mountains. Visitors can hike to numerous lakes which afford excellent fishing, swimming, and huckleberry picking. Thirty miles up the road from Burgdorf lies the old mining town of Warren. A classical ghost town by modern standards, Warren has two open saloons and a post office. There are more things to see and do from Burgdorf than can be exhausted in a few days.

But speaking of exhausted, imagine yourself coming back from a ten-mile hike, covered with trail dust and sweat, dragging your aching feet up that final fifty yards to your cabin to stow your gear next to the wood box, shed clothes, boots and all, grab your towel and--once again, there you are, blissfully floating over the white sand bottom in the clear warm turquoise water, watching the clouds turn rose pink as they hang effortlessly in the sky.

Exploration

To what extent does Lynn Hansen's essay achieve the goals she established for herself in her analysis of her rhetorical situation? To answer this question, first reread Lynn's analysis. In your own words, summarize Lynn's goals in terms of the key elements of rhetoric: writer, reader, text. Now reread Lynn's essay. Does Lynn fulfill the goals she established for herself? How? List at least five reasons why Lynn does or does not achieve these goals. Then find at least one passage in the essay that illustrates each of these five statements.

_____ THINKING ABOUT READERS _____

If you look again at Lynn Hansen's description of her rhetorical situation on page 50, you will notice that she carefully considers the expectations and interests of her audience, readers of *Pacific Northwest* magazine. Lynn recognizes that a small number of potential readers would seriously consider visiting Burgdorf Hot Springs, and that an even smaller number might actually do so. Only a "certain Bohemian type," Lynn reasons, would be attracted to a rustic, undeveloped hot springs. But Lynn understands that those with no intention of vacationing at Burgdorf Hot Springs might nevertheless read and enjoy her review.

Some "armchair travelers" might read to vicariously experience a trip to the hot springs. Others might read her review simply because they enjoy reading essays about travel, just as some people enjoy reading mysteries or science fiction. Lynn also recognizes that those who read her review will have expectations based on previous reviews that they have read. They will expect her to provide enough information about Burgdorf Hot Springs so that they could plan a trip there if they wished to do so. They will also expect the review to be interesting, with vivid descriptions of the location, stories about the history of the hot springs, and other details that help them learn more about, and vicariously experience, this rustic, primitive resort.

How was Lynn able to develop such a rich, complex understanding of her readers? In part she drew upon daily interactions with others; her knowledge of people told her that only a "certain Bohemian type" would actually visit Burgdorf Hot Springs. But Lynn also drew upon her experiences as a reader. By reading other travel reviews, Lynn developed a strong if intuitive understanding of the general form and style of such reviews. In analyzing her rhetorical situation, Lynn drew upon the rhetorical common sense she has developed as a writer, reader, speaker, and listener.

Like Lynn, you have naturally developed considerable rhetorical common sense. As a student, for instance, you undoubtedly recognize the importance of teachers as readers of student writing. What students sometimes call "psyching out the teacher" actually is an example of rhetorical common sense in action. When you are working on an assignment for a class, whether an essay exam or a research paper, it makes sense for you to consider your teacher's expectations. Analyzing your teachers as readers involves more than considering their views on a particular subject, however; it includes understanding the values and intellectual commitments they share with other members of the academic community. Chapter 10, "Understanding Academic Audiences and Assignments," discusses in greater detail these values and commitments, such as the preference that arguments should be supported by evidence that is substantial and appropriate to the discipline and topic.

Your understanding of your readers' expectations and needs can help you make choices as you write. Lynn Hansen chose to begin her review in a dramatic way because she knew that she had to catch her readers' attention quickly. After all, readers of *Pacific Northwest* don't *have* to read her essay; they *choose* to do so. By addressing readers directly ("You've opened your eyes at the first hint of light and rolled out of your sleeping bag to climb stiffly down from the loft"), Lynn invites readers to stop flipping through their magazine and join the world of her essay. Her vivid description also reassures readers that this will be a good travel essay, one that will enable readers to "see" this remote resort in Idaho via the words on the page.

Writers anticipate readers' needs and expectations, and they project their understanding of their readers through subtle textual cues. Lynn Hansen's dramatic, conversational introduction, for instance, cues readers to relax, kick off their shoes, and enjoy a brief textual visit to Burgdorf Hot Springs. Without explicitly saying so, Lynn's introduction lets readers know both the kind of essay they should expect—a travel review, not a dense analysis of a current economic issue—and the role she hopes they will adopt as readers, that of a fellow adventurer who appreciates the wilderness and would enjoy reading about (if not traveling to) an unconventional resort like Burgdorf Hot Springs.

If Lynn were writing an in-class essay exam, her understanding of her teacher as reader would similarly influence her choices. Teachers may find all or some of their students' essays interesting, and they may learn new things from their students—I certainly have. Nevertheless, teachers read students' writing primarily to determine what students have learned about a subject and how effectively they can express this understanding to others. Teachers also often read under considerable time pressure; a pyschology teacher may take sixty essay exams home on a Tuesday, knowing they must be returned the following Thursday. A dramatic, attention-getting introduction, such as Lynn wrote for her review of Burgdorf Hot Springs, would irritate, not entertain, a psychology teacher reading an essay exam. Such a teacher would find a concise introductory paragraph—one that clearly specified the writer's main point and indicated how the writer would support this point—much more successful.

As these examples indicate, and as Chapter 9, "Understanding the Reading Process," further emphasizes, the relationship between writers and readers is dynamic, not static. Both writers and readers draw upon the rhetorical sensitivity they have developed through writing, reading, speaking, and listening when they interact with a written text. Similarly, both writers and readers must anticipate and project as they attempt to create meaning through language.

Exploration

Suppose that Lynn Hansen had wanted to write an essay on Burgdorf Hot Springs not for readers of *Pacific Northwest,* but for the Sunday supplement of a major East Coast newspaper such as the *New York Times.* What consequences might this different readership have for her rhetorical situation? How might she have to revise her essay in response to the interests and expectations of these readers? Write one or two paragraphs responding to these questions.

As a writer, your relationship with your readers is shifting and complex, not fixed and static; this relationship varies with your rhetorical situation. When you consider the expectations and interests of your readers, you naturally think *strategically,* asking yourself questions such as these:

- To what extent are my readers interested in and knowledgeable about my subject?
- What formal and stylistic expectations will my readers bring to my essay?

- What other aspects of my readers' situations might influence how they respond to my essay?
- How can I use my understanding of my readers' expectations and interests when I make decisions about the content, form, and style of my essay?

By asking yourself questions such as these—by thinking strategically about your writing—you can build upon the rhetorical sensitivity you have already developed as a speaker, listener, reader, and writer.

Later chapters will help you more fully understand the complex relationship between writing and reading, writers and readers. Chapter 4, "Writers Reading" discusses some of the ways that writers provide textual cues for readers—cues that reflect these writers' understanding of their rhetorical situation. Chapters 7 and 8, which focus on "Strategies for Successful Revision," present a number of ways that you can benefit from the responses of others to work in progress while also strengthening your skills as a reader of your own writing. For though others can help you see the strengths and weaknesses of work in progress more clearly, as a writer you must be able to read your own drafts from multiple perspectives, maintaining an internal dialogue between your own intentions and your understanding of the needs and expectations of your readers. Finally, the chapters in Part 3, "Connections: Writing, Reading, and Reasoning," discuss the skills you need to develop to participate effectively in the world of academic readers and writers.

Application

Introductions often help signal the relationship the writer intends to establish with readers. The following excerpts introduce two different discussions of stress, both designed for a general audience. The first excerpt is from the first chapter of a book titled *The Work/Stress Connection: How to Cope with Job Burnout*. The second is from the section called "Work and Stress" in *The Columbia University College of Physicians and Surgeons Complete Home Medical Guide*. As you read these excerpts, think about the differing roles that they invite readers to assume.

> Sally Swanson, a thirty-eight-year-old mother of four, works as a bank teller in Des Moines, Iowa. Like many women, she feels the pressure of running a home, raising children, managing a job, and carving out leisure time for herself. "I did fine until we got a new supervisor last year," she says with an exhausted sigh. "Within two

months I had started to burn out." Sally takes antacid pills several times a day. She worries that she may have an ulcer. "I feel as if he's looking over my shoulder all the time," she says. "He never has a good word to say to anyone. Sometimes the tension at the bank is so thick you could cut it with a knife."

Particular kinds of work seem to cause special stress, and the effects of health are manifested in an all-too-common pattern: fatigue, insomnia, eating disorders, nervousness, feelings of unhappiness, abuse of alcohol or drugs. Stress is often related to the nature of the job or imposed irregularities. Rotating shift work, in which hours are erratic or inconsistent with the normal sleep cycle, produces both physical and mental stress by constantly upsetting circadian rhythms that control specific hormonal and other responses. Jobs that involve little variation but require constant close attention, for example, assembly-line work or jobs requiring repetitive tasks with dangerous equipment, seem to be particularly stressful. In one study in a sawmill, people who ran the equipment had much higher levels of stress-related hormones than workers who did not come in contact with machinery, even though their jobs also may have been boring and repetitive.

Now that you have read these two introductions, describe the writer-reader relationship established in each. What signals or cues do the authors provide for readers to enable them to recognize and adopt an appropriate role? Cite at least three examples of these signals or cues.

RESPONDING TO YOUR RHETORICAL SITUATION: ARISTOTLE'S THREE APPEALS

Analyzing your rhetorical situation can provide information that will enable you to make crucial strategic, structural, and stylistic decisions about your writing. In considering how to use the information gained through this process, you may find it helpful to employ what Aristotle (384–322 B.C.) characterized as the three appeals. According to Aristotle, when speakers and writers communicate with others, they draw upon these three general appeals:

1. *logos:* the appeal to reason
2. *pathos:* the appeal to emotion
3. *ethos:* the appeal to the credibility of the speaker or writer

As a writer you appeal to *logos* when you focus on the logical presentation of your subject by providing evidence and examples in support of your ideas. You appeal to *pathos* when you use the resources of language to engage your readers emotionally with your subject or appeal to their values, beliefs, or needs. And you appeal to *ethos* when you create an image of yourself, a *persona*, that encourages readers to accept or act upon your ideas.

These three appeals correspond to the three basic elements of rhetoric. In appealing to *ethos*, you focus on the *writer's* character as implied in the text; in appealing to *pathos*, on the interaction of writer and *reader*; and in appealing to *logos*, on the logical statements about the subject made in your particular *text*. In some instances, you may rely predominantly on one of these appeals. A student writing a technical report will typically emphasize scientific or technical evidence, not emotional or personal appeals. More often, however, you will draw upon all three appeals in your effort to create a fully persuasive document. A journalist writing an essay on child abuse might begin her discussion with several examples designed to gain the attention of her readers and to convince them of the importance of this issue (*pathos*). Although she may rely primarily on information about the negative consequences of child abuse (*logos*), she will undoubtedly also endeavor to create an image of herself as a caring, serious person (*ethos*), one whose analysis of a subject like child abuse could be trusted.

In the following example, Julia Kohashi, a home economics major, uses Aristotle's three appeals to develop strategies for an argument urging students who have never donated blood in the past to do so. Julia had previously analyzed her rhetorical situation, so she had already thought about her goals for this essay. Determining which appeals to emphasize and how to do so enabled her to develop plans to achieve her goals.

Here is Julia's analysis of her three appeals.

> Logos: Most college students already know the reasons why they should give blood, so it wouldn't make sense to review these reasons at length. I'll mention these arguments quickly--just as a reminder--and I'll provide some information students may not know about the blood drive. But the focus of my argument will not be on logos.
>
> Pathos: Students who haven't donated blood are probably frightened or uneasy about doing so. They might not be willing to admit their fears, so they rely on other excuses for not donating blood (Maybe I'll faint; I don't have enough time). Because I think that these underlying fears are the main cause of students' failure to give blood, I will attempt in this essay to appeal to

the emotions, values, and interests of my readers. I will use a
variety of strategies to achieve this; most importantly, I'll tell
the "story" of my friend, Kim, who donated blood for the first
time last quarter. Kim's story should allow me to address a number of common fears without appearing to lecture students.

    <u>Ethos</u>: If students feel that I'm lecturing or preaching to
them, they'll refuse to pay attention to my message. Consequently, I'll present myself as just another student, someone who
like them has too much to do and too little time. I want my voice
to seem relaxed, friendly, conversational. I do want my readers
to recognize that I'm committed to the importance of giving blood,
however, so there should be a slight tone of urgency as well.

Here is the final version of Julia Kohashi's essay. As you read this
essay, notice how she draws upon the three appeals as she analyzed
them.

THE RED CROSS NEEDS YOU!

Have you ever wondered what would happen if you were in des-

perate need of a transfusion and there wasn't any blood available?

I have, and it scares me. It also scares me knowing that at this

moment there may be someone in need of blood. In fact, according

to the Red Cross, more than nine out of ten persons will have

needed blood or a blood product at some time before they reach

age 72.

In order to meet this need, the Red Cross needs to collect as

many pints of blood as possible. There must always be an adequate

supply on hand for emergency transfusions. Furthermore, once col-

lected, blood cannot be kept indefinitely. It is stored at opti-

mal temperatures to prolong its life span, but if it goes unused,

its quality eventually diminishes, so more is constantly needed.

Once each term the American Red Cross Blood Program team

visits Oregon State University for three days. During these three

days the Red Cross nurses accept approximately fifteen hundred

pints of blood for the Pacific Northwest Blood Program. OSU is the largest single source of donations for this program, which benefits the entire region.

You could help by giving a little of your time, energy, and blood this term. The thought of giving a pint of your blood may concern you, but you can overcome this initial fear. Donating blood is a rewarding experience. Ask Kim.

Kim is a friend of mine who never donated blood until last term. She had all of the qualifications—she is at least seventeen years old, has good health, and weighs over 105 pounds. Like many others, Kim always had excuses for not being able to participate in the blood drive. They ranged from being too busy with classes to not getting out of bed early enough to go to the blood drive.

After a dinner conversation about the blood drive one night last term, Kim began to think again about donating blood and perhaps saving someone's life. The next day she courageously went to give her first pint. Waiting in line took a while, and later Kim told me she had had second thoughts about her decision. As she watched the other students lying on the lounge chairs with tubes connected to their arms, she thought they must be feeling excruciating pain. Kim didn't notice that most of them actually seemed to be resting comfortably.

Kim went through a health station where a nurse took her medical history and checked her body temperature, blood pressure, pulse, and hemoglobin level. Before she knew it, Kim was among those lying on the lounge chairs. The nurses were pleasant, and the "stab" didn't hurt as much as she had expected. In just ten minutes, she was through giving a pint of blood.

Some people, like Kim, feel a little light-headed after donating and need to lie down for a few minutes. Eating something before donating blood will help to prevent dizziness, though it

should not be a high-fat food. The many students assisting the
Red Cross personnel make certain that donors feel fine before they
leave the area. On the way out, each donor is treated to a cookie
or doughnut and something to drink.

You don't get any personal reward or payment from donating
blood, but by helping to keep the blood supply level up, you help
all who may need a transfusion--including yourself, your family,
and your friends. You get a feeling of personal satisfaction from
giving blood, knowing that you are helping someone and perhaps
even saving a life.

The American Red Cross will once again visit our campus this
week, and Kim will donate her second pint of blood. The Red Cross
needs your help, too. See you at the blood drive!

Exploration

In what ways does Julia Kohashi's essay draw upon the three
appeals as she analyzed them? Write one or two paragraphs responding to this question. Be sure to include at least two or three
examples in your analysis.

The strategies described in this chapter—analyzing your rhetorical situation and employing Aristotle's three appeals—are grounded
in commonsense principles of communication, principles that date
back at least to the time of Plato and Aristotle. Understanding these
principles and knowing how to apply them will enable you to respond effectively in a variety of writing situations.

Activities for Thought, Discussion, and Writing

1. The following letter from the United States Committee for UNI-
   CEF (United Nations Children's Fund) is typical of many letters
   requesting charitable contributions for worthwhile activities.

Using this letter as evidence or data, try to determine the assumptions the writer or writers made about this rhetorical situation. (Though Hugh Downs, a popular television personality, signed this letter, he may not have actually composed it.) After you have listed these assumptions, indicate ways in which these assumptions may have influenced the form or content of the letter. What assumptions about the readers, for example, may have led the writer to introduce the letter as he or she did?

Dear Friend:

In the ten seconds it took you to open and begin to read this letter, three children died from the effects of malnutrition somewhere in the world.

No statistic can express what it's like to see even one child die that way . . . to see a mother sitting hour after hour, leaning her child's body against her own . . . to watch the small feeble head movements that expend all the energy a youngster has left . . . to see the panic in a dying tot's innocent eyes . . . and then to know in a moment that life is gone.

But I'm not writing this letter simply to describe an all-too-common tragedy.

I'm writing because, after decades of hard work, *UNICEF*—The United Nations Children's Fund—*has identified four simple, low-cost techniques which, if applied, have the potential to cut the yearly child mortality rate in half.*

These methods don't depend on solving large-scale problems like increasing food supply or cleaning up contaminated water. They can be put into effect before a single additional bushel of wheat is grown, or before a single new well is dug.

They do depend on *what you decide to do* by the time you finish reading this letter. You see, putting these simple techniques to work requires the support of UNICEF's projects by people around the world. In our country, it means helping the U.S. Committee for UNICEF contribute to that vital work.

With your help, millions of children will be given the chance of a lifetime—the chance to live—to grow up healthy and strong.

Without your help, more children will continue to die painfully, slowly and needlessly—children like the nine who have died in the past 30 seconds.

The first method is called *"oral rehydration."* Most children who die of malnutrition don't starve to death—they die because their body weight has been severely lowered by germs that cause diarrhea.

Simple medicines can stop such illness in our own country. But in the developing countries, there are no such medicines—and children may develop a new infection every six weeks. Until recently, there was no easy way of stopping the symptom and saving their lives.

But now, it's known that a mixture of sugar, salt and water in the right proportions will stop the critical loss of fluids and salts that leads to death. The cost of this "miracle" cure—less than ten cents a dose. But for want of that simple mixture, five million children die each year.

With your help, the U.S. Committee for UNICEF can assist UNICEF's projects to provide "oral rehydration salts" to mothers in developing countries around the world—and to teach families how to make the mixture on their own, to save the lives of children.

The second breakthrough method of saving children is to provide *worldwide immunization* against six childhood diseases: measles, polio, TB, tetanus, whooping cough and diphtheria. Together, these diseases kill three and a half million children each year in developing countries—the vast majority of them are malnourished youngsters with little resistance to disease.

It used to be hard to keep vaccines stable in their long journeys from laboratories to remote, often tropical places where children needed them most. But within the last year and a half, a measles vaccine has been developed that does not require refrigeration. The result: measles can now join smallpox on the list of child-killing diseases that have been wiped out—permanently.

The cost of this new measles vaccine is less than ten cents a dose. With it, *the lives of one and a half million children can be saved this year alone.* But without it, they will continue to die—like the child who has died of measles in the past 30 seconds.

With your help, the U.S. Committee for UNICEF can assist in UNICEF's work to deliver the new measles vaccine—and vaccines to fight the five other major child-killers—to youngsters who need them so badly in the developing world.

The third and fourth breakthrough methods of saving children's lives are even simpler. They require no medication at all. But they do require a worldwide education campaign—to promote *breast-feeding* among mothers, instead of the tragic trend toward bottle-feeding in developing lands, and to provide mothers with simple *paper growth charts* to detect the "hidden malnutrition" that can leave a child irreparably retarded in mind and body.

With your help, the U.S. Committee for UNICEF can assist UNICEF in mounting the massive educational campaign needed to teach parents these basic ways of preventing malnutrition—and can save the lives of children for years to come.

There you have it: four easy ways of saving the lives of millions of children for years to come.

Now it's time for you to decide what you're going to do about it.

I know you receive appeals for many good causes. But I can't think of a single cause more important than the life of a child. And in a very real sense, the life of a child somewhere in the world can be drastically changed by what you decide to do right now. You see, UNICEF's good work is supported entirely by voluntary contributions. That means your help does make a critical difference.

That's why I'm asking you to take a moment now to send a gift of $20, $50, $100, $500—as much as you possibly can—to the U.S. Committee for UNICEF in the enclosed reply envelope.

Your gift is tax deductible to the extent allowed by law. And by the time you fill out next year's tax returns, there will be one or more healthy, living children in the world as a result of the gift you send today. You will have given those kids the chance of a lifetime. And I hope that will make you feel very proud, indeed.

We're counting on your help. My personal thanks and best wishes.

Sincerely,

Hugh Downs

2. Lynn Hansen and Julia Kohashi did a good job, you'll probably agree, in anticipating the expectations and interests of their readers. In writing their essays, they focused not just on content (what they wanted to say), but also on strategy (how they might convey their ideas to their readers). Not all interactions between writer and reader are as successful. You may have read textbooks that seemed more concerned with the subject matter than with reader's needs and expectations. Or you may have received direct mail advertising or other business communications that irritated or offended you. Locate an example of writing that in your view fails to anticipate the expectations and needs of the reader and write one or two paragraphs explaining your reasons. Your teacher may ask you to bring your example and written explanation to class to share with your classmates.

3. The following advertisements (Figs. 3-1, 3-2, and 3-3) are from popular magazines. Analyze the ways in which these advertisements draw upon Aristotle's three appeals: *ethos*, *pathos*, and *logos*.

One out of four women over 50 will get osteoporosis.

To help avoid being one of them, call 1 800 333-5447.

After 50, a woman begins losing her natural defense against osteoporosis... estrogen.

Estrogen, together with calcium, can play an important role in keeping your bones strong. As you reach menopause, your estrogen levels begin to drop, and you become increasingly at risk of developing weakened bones and potentially crippling fractures.

Taking low dose **PREMARIN**® (conjugated estrogens tablets) is the single most effective way to prevent osteoporosis after menopause.

Premarin® is estrogen obtained exclusively from natural sources, and has been used and trusted by women and physicians for nearly 50 years.

Call today for free information.
We'll send you a brochure that tells you what you should know about estrogen, menopause, and osteoporosis. Then, we strongly suggest you visit your doctor, since taking any drug may involve some chance of side effects, and only a doctor can tell you whether Premarin is right for you. In fact, we'll even send you a certificate you can redeem for a free exercise videotape after you make that important visit. Just call the toll-free number above or write:
Premarin Osteoporosis Information Center, Box 5201, Miami, FL 33102

W WYETH-AYERST LABORATORIES | WORLDWIDE LEADERSHIP IN FEMALE HEALTHCARE

See the following pages for more information.

Figure 3-1

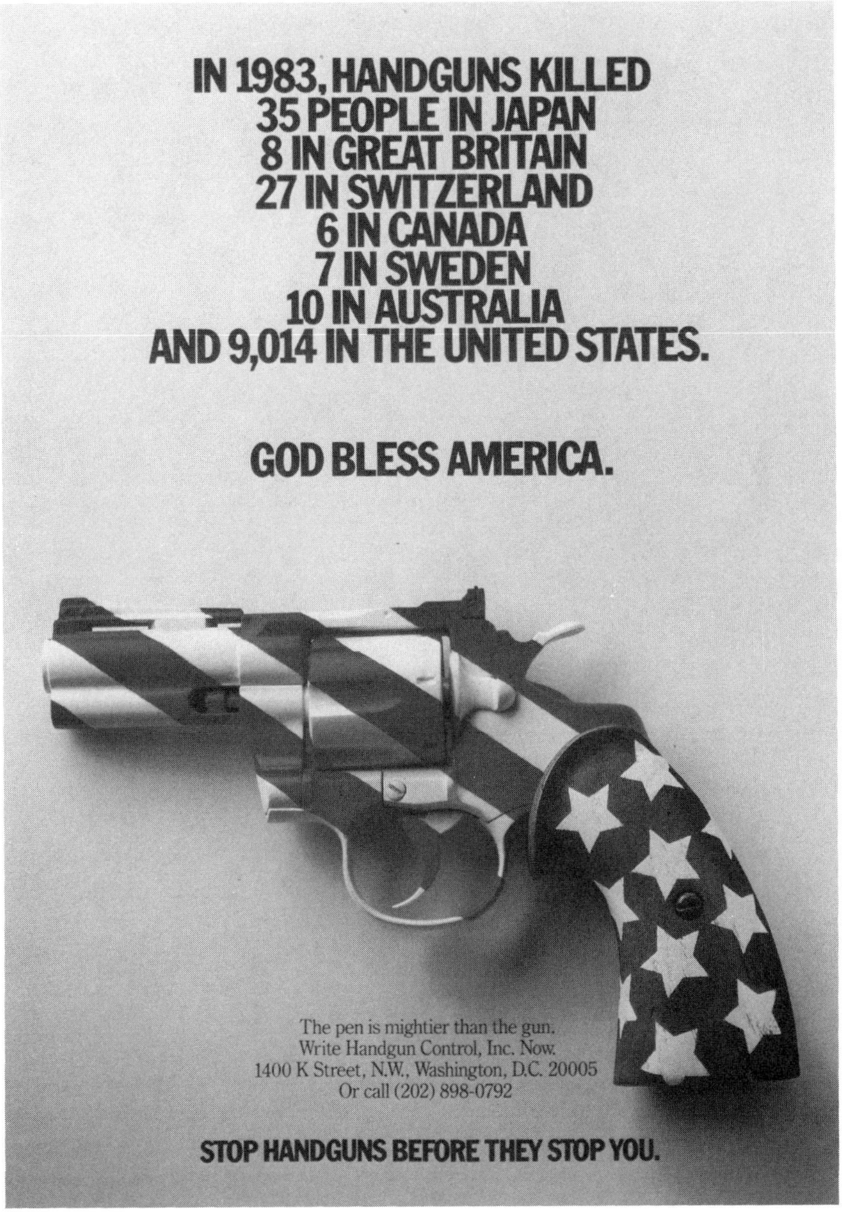

IN 1983, HANDGUNS KILLED
35 PEOPLE IN JAPAN
8 IN GREAT BRITAIN
27 IN SWITZERLAND
6 IN CANADA
7 IN SWEDEN
10 IN AUSTRALIA
AND 9,014 IN THE UNITED STATES.

GOD BLESS AMERICA.

The pen is mightier than the gun.
Write Handgun Control, Inc. Now.
1400 K Street, N.W., Washington, D.C. 20005
Or call (202) 898-0792

STOP HANDGUNS BEFORE THEY STOP YOU.

Figure 3-2

Figure 3-3

CHAPTER 4

WRITERS READING

Writing is hardly a magical or mysterious activity. Rather, writing, like speaking, is a basic form of human communication, a powerful means of self-expression and dialogue with others. Effective writers use their rhetorical sensitivity—sensitivity developed through reading, writing, speaking, and listening—to help them analyze their rhetorical situation and make appropriate choices when they write. Here is how Mary Ann Firmin, a student at Oregon State University, explains the importance of analyzing the rhetorical situation when you write:

> Think of an orchestra playing without the conductor--that is how writers write when they don't understand their rhetorical situation. Without the conductor there are still musicians producing music; when writers don't understand the rhetorical situation there are still writers producing words. But with a conductor, the orchestra produces music that speaks to the audience because the conductor has a clear vision of how the music should sound and can blend the musicians into a group that has a controlling purpose. When writers understand their rhetorical situation, they can use all the elements of writing to have the greatest persuasive effect on the audience. It is difficult to describe how this happens, but the proof is in the product. When you have a conductor, the music can move people. When you understand your rhetorical situation, your words can change people.

In the previous chapter, you learned how to ask yourself questions about your rhetorical situation and to use the results of your analysis to set preliminary goals and make effective choices as a writer. In this chapter you will continue to learn more about the rhetorical situation, but you will do so from the perspective of the reader. By reading to understand not just what writers say but *how* they say it—by reading like a writer—you can learn how to make your own writing more effective.

READING LIKE A WRITER

An analogy may help you understand how reading can contribute to your development as a writer. Consider the musicians described by Mary Ann Firmin. To develop their skills musicians practice often, but they also listen to both live and recorded music. When they do so, they listen not simply to be moved by the music, to experience it, but also to discern how those who are performing achieve particular effects. They listen actively, participating in the music but also asking questions about musical technique and style. When they play, they draw upon this knowledge and experience as they develop their own performance.

Like musicians, effective writers know that they can learn a great deal about how writing works by reading. Reading and writing are, after all, so interconnected that they are, in effect, two sides of the same coin. As Deborah Brandt has said, "Learning to read is learning that you are being written to, and learning to write is learning that your words are being read." By learning to read others' writing more critically and sensitively, by looking for clues to how other writers have analyzed and responded to their rhetorical situations, you can gain valuable insights about how writing works. You can improve your ability to read your own writing as well.

In a general sense, you have already been reading like a writer, for although you undoubtedly acquired some of your current knowledge about writing from formal instruction in English classes, much that you know you have gained by reading. You may never have taken a class in short-story writing, for instance, yet simply by reading stories you have some understanding of how stories work. You can develop your innate rhetorical sensitivity as a reader by consciously asking yourself questions while you read. If you find an essay particularly interesting and effective, for instance, stop to ask yourself why. You might consider the writer's *persona* or voice and the role it plays in the essay. You might reread the essay looking for clues that reveal how the writer has envisioned the intended audience. (Can you locate passages, for instance, where the writer anticipates readers' interests and needs?) Or you might focus on how the writer has used certain generic and stylistic conventions and reflect upon why these conventions are appropriate given the writer's goals and situation. By focusing not just on what writers say but on what writers *do*, you can learn how other writers have responded to their rhetorical situation, and you can apply that knowledge when you work on your own writing.

ANALYZING TEXTUAL CONVENTIONS

When you read, you engage in silent conversation with the writer. As Chapter 9, "Understanding the Reading Process," emphasizes, your role in this conversation is active. You don't simply decipher or decode a writer's messages: rather, you use your own knowledge and experience to understand, interpret, and evaluate texts. As a reader you are not free, however, to interpret texts according to arbitrary or random whims. Textual conventions—shared agreements between writers and readers about how to construct and interpret texts—play an important role in keeping writers and readers on track so that their conversation doesn't turn into a pitched argument or free-for-all.

The phrase *textual convention* may be new to you, but you can understand it easily if you think about other uses of the word *convention*. For example, *social* conventions are agreements among the members of a community or culture about how to act in particular situations. At one time in America, for example, it was acceptable for persons who chewed tobacco to use spittoons in such public places as restaurants and hotel lobbies. (British writer Charles Dickens complained bitterly of this practice when he visited the United States.) Now this behavior is no longer acceptable: this particular social convention has, over time, changed.

If social conventions represent agreements among individuals about how to act, textual conventions represent similar agreements about how to write and read texts. As such, textual conventions are an important component of the rhetorical situation. When you think about the kind of writing that you are being asked to do, for instance, you are thinking in part about the textual conventions that may limit your options as a writer in a specific situation. Textual conventions constrain writers, then. But writers also use textual conventions to signal their intentions and thus increase the likelihood that readers will respond appropriately to their ideas.

Some textual conventions are quite specific. Personal letters always begin with greetings and end with signatures. Sonnets have fourteen rhymed lines, usually consisting of an octave (eight lines) and a sextet (six lines) or three four-line quatrains with a closing couplet. Similarly, lab reports usually include the following elements: title page, abstract, introduction, experimental design and methods, results, discussion, and references. Someone writing a sonnet or a lab report can deviate from these textual conventions, but only at the risk of having readers misunderstand or reject their writing.

Other textual conventions are much more general. You may have read, for instance, that a well-written academic essay has qualities like these.

CHARACTERISTICS OF AN EFFECTIVE ACADEMIC ESSAY

1. An effective essay is well organized and well developed. It establishes its subject or main idea in the introduction, develops that idea in a coherent manner in the body, and summarizes or completes the discussion in the conclusion.
2. An effective essay is logical. It supports its main points with well-chosen evidence, illustrations, and details.
3. An effective essay is clear and readable. It uses words, sentences, and paragraphs that are carefully crafted, appropriate for the writer's purpose and subject, and free of errors of usage, grammar, and punctuation.

These statements summarize some of the most general conventions that govern academic essays. But because these statements are so general and apply to so many different kinds of writing, you may not know just what they mean in specific situations and in your own writing.

Seeing textual conventions in use

To help clarify how general textual conventions operate and to illustrate how you can analyze textual conventions, let's consider just one of the conventions cited above: the statement that an effective essay establishes its subject or main idea in an introduction (which often also serves to draw readers into the essay). This particular textual convention is learned early, for even young children introduce stories, if only with *Once upon a time*. Furthermore, most writers and readers can easily understand why an essay needs an introduction. No one likes to be thrown into the middle of an essay or report without any idea of the subject. Despite understanding the purpose of this convention, however, writers sometimes feel uncertain about what constitutes the best introduction for a specific essay.

Three articles by a well-known psychologist show how one writer tackled this problem (see Figs. 4-1, 4-2, and 4-3 on pp. 74–79). All three articles were written by Dr. John H. Flavell, although the third was coauthored with two colleagues. All of the articles discuss research conducted by Flavell and his colleagues on the ability of young children to distinguish between appearance and reality, a distinction that Flavell argues is "worth studying because it is part of the larger development of our conscious knowledge about our own and other minds."

Figure 4-1 shows the introduction to the first article, "Really and Truly," which was published in *Psychology Today*, a popular magazine designed for members of the general public who are interested in learning about and applying principles of psychology in their own lives. The second article, "The Development of Children's Knowledge about the Appearance–Reality Distinction" (Fig. 4-2), was published in *American Psychologist*. This academic journal is sent to every member of the American Psychological Association whose almost 60,000 members include psychologists and other behavioral and social scientists with quite a broad range of interests. The third article, "Development of the Appearance–Reality Distinction" (Fig. 4-3), was published in *Cognitive Psychology*, a specialized academic journal for researchers in that field. As you read each essay's introduction, think about the impact that the different publications and intended audiences may have had on the form and content of each essay. Pay attention, also, to the format used to present each article.

Exploration

Read the introductions to Flavell's three articles and write one paragraph characterizing the approach of each article. How would you describe the tone of each article and the kind of language used? What can you learn from your paragraphs about the differences among these articles?

Comparing and contrasting textual conventions

You need only glance at the first pages of Flavell's three articles to notice some striking differences. The first two pages of "Really and

Really and Truly

*UNTIL THEY ARE 4 OR 5, CHILDREN
DON'T UNDERSTAND THE DISTINCTION BETWEEN
APPEARANCE AND REALITY;
WHAT YOU SEE IS NOT ALWAYS WHAT YOU GET.*

BY JOHN H. FLAVELL

It looks like a nice, solid piece of granite, but as soon as you squeeze it you know it's really a joke-store sponge made to look like a rock. If I ask what it appears to be, you say, "It looks just like a rock." If I ask what it really is, you say, "It's a sponge, of course." A 3-year-old probably wouldn't be so sure. Children at this age often aren't quite able to grasp the idea that what you see is not always what you get.

By the time they are 6 or 7 years

PHOTOGRAPHS BY WALTER WICK

Figure 4-1

old, however, most children have a fair grasp of the appearance-reality distinction that assumes so many forms in our everyday lives. Misperceptions, misexpectations, misunderstandings, false beliefs, deception, play and fantasy—these and other examples of that distinction are a preoccupation of philosophers, scientists, artists, politicians and other public performers and of the rest of us who try to evaluate what they all say and do.

For the past half dozen years, my colleagues and I have been asking chil-dren questions about sponge rocks and using other methods to find out what children of different ages know about the difference between appearances and reality. First we give the children a brief lesson on the meaning of the appearance-reality distinction by showing them, for example, a Charlie Brown puppet inside a ghost costume. We explain and demonstrate that Charlie Brown "looks like a ghost to your eyes right now" but is "really and truly Charlie Brown," and that "sometimes things look like one thing

Continued on Page 42

It looks like a rock, it feels like a sponge, but to a 3-year-old the distinction between appearance and reality can be quite confusing.

1985 APA Award Addresses

The Development of Children's Knowledge About the Appearance–Reality Distinction

John H. Flavell   *Stanford University*

ABSTRACT: Recent research on the acquisition of knowledge about the important and pervasive appearance–reality distinction suggests the following course of development. Many 3-year-olds seem to possess little or no understanding of the distinction. They fail very easy-looking tests of this understanding and are unresponsive to training. At this age level, skill in solving simple appearance–reality tasks is highly correlated with skill in solving simple visual perspective-taking tasks. This and other findings are consistent with the hypothesis that what helps children finally grasp the distinction is an increased cognizance of the fact that people are sentient subjects who have mental representations of objects and events. It does so by allowing them to understand that the selfsame stimulus can be mentally represented in two different, seemingly contradictory ways: (a) in the appearance–reality case, how it appears to the self versus how it really is; and (b) in the perspective-taking case, how it presently appears to self versus other. In contrast to young preschoolers, children of 6 to 7 years manage simple appearance–reality tasks with ease. However, they have great difficulty reflecting on and talking about such appearance–reality notions as "looks like," "really and truly," and especially, "looks different from the way it really and truly is." Finally, children of 11 to 12 years, and to an even greater degree college students, give evidence of possessing a substantial body of rich, readily available, and explicit knowledge in this area.

Suppose someone shows a three-year-old and a six-year-old a red toy car covered by a green filter that makes the car look black, hands the car to the children to inspect, puts it behind the filter again, and asks, "What color is this car? Is it red or is it black?" (Flavell, Green, & Flavell, 1985; cf. Braine & Shanks, 1965a, 1965b). The three-year-old is likely to say "black," the six-year-old, "red." The questioner is also apt to get the same answers even if he or she first carefully explains and demonstrates the intended difference in meaning, for illusory displays, between "looks like to your eyes right now" and "really and truly is," and then asks what color it "*really* and *truly* is." At issue in such simple tasks is the distinction between how things presently appear to the senses and how or

what they really and enduringly are, that is, the familiar distinction between appearance and reality. The six-year-old is clearly in possession of some knowledge about this distinction and quickly senses what the task is about. The three-year-old, who is much less knowledgeable about the distinction, does not.

For the past half-dozen years my co-workers and I have been using these and other methods to chart the developmental course of knowledge acquisition in this area. That is, we have been trying to find out what children of different ages do and do not know about the appearance–reality distinction and related phenomena. In this article I summarize what we have done and what we think we have learned (Flavell, Flavell, & Green, 1983; Flavell et al., 1985; Flavell, Zhang, Zou, Dong, & Qi, 1983; Taylor & Flavell, 1984). The summary is organized around the main questions that have guided our thinking and research in this area.

Why Is This Development Important To Study?

First, the distinction between appearance and reality is ecologically significant. It assumes many forms, arises in many situations, and can have serious consequences for our lives. The relation between appearance and reality figures importantly in everyday perceptual, conceptual, emotional, and social activity—in misperceptions, misexpectations, misunderstandings, false beliefs, deception, play, fantasy, and so forth. It is also a major preoccupation of philosophers, scientists, and other scholars; of artists, politicians, and other public performers; and of the thinking public that tries to evaluate what they say and do. It is, in sum, "the distinction which probably provides the intellectual basis for the fundamental epistemological construct common to science, 'folk' philosophy, religion, and myth, of a real world 'underlying' and 'explaining' the phenomenal one" (Braine & Shanks, 1965a, pp. 241–242).

Second, the acquisition of at least some explicit knowledge about the appearance–reality distinction is probably a universal developmental outcome in our species. This knowledge seems so necessary to everyday intellectual and social life that one can hardly imagine a society in which normal people would not acquire it. To

April 1986 • American Psychologist
Copyright 1986 by the American Psychological Association, Inc. 0003-066X/86/$00.75
Vol. 41, No. 4, 418–425

Figure 4-2

cite an example that has actually been researched, a number of investigators have been interested in the child's command of the distinction as a possible developmental prerequisite for, and perhaps even mediator of, Piagetian conservations (e.g., Braine & Shanks, 1965a, 1965b; Murray, 1968).

Third, knowledge about the distinction seems to presuppose the explicit knowledge that human beings are sentient, cognizing *subjects* (cf. Chandler & Boyce, 1982; Selman, 1980) whose mental representations of objects and events can differ, both within the same person and between persons. In the within-person case, for example, I may be aware both that something appears to be A and that it really is B. I could also be aware that it might appear to be C under special viewing conditions, or that I pretended or fantasized that it was D yesterday. I may know that these are all possible ways that I can *represent* the very same thing (i.e., perceive it, encode it, know it, interpret it, construe it, or think about it—although inadequate, the term "represent" will have to do). In the between-persons case, I may be aware that you might represent the same thing differently than I do, because our perceptual, conceptual, or affective perspectives on it might differ. If this analysis is correct, knowledge about the appearance–reality distinction is but one instance of our more general knowledge that the selfsame object or event can be represented (apprehended, experienced, etc.) in different ways by the same person and by different people. In this analysis, then, its development is worth studying because it is part of the larger development of our conscious knowledge about our own and other minds and, thus, of metacognition (e.g., Brown, Bransford, Ferrara, & Campione, 1983; Flavell, 1985; Wellman, 1985) and of social cognition (e.g., Flavell, 1985; Shantz, 1983). I will return to this line of reasoning in another section of the article.

How Can Young Children's Knowledge About the Appearance–Reality Distinction Be Tested?

The development of appearance–reality knowledge in preschool children has been investigated by Braine and

Editor's note. This article is based on a Distinguished Scientific Contribution Award address presented at the meeting of the American Psychological Association, Los Angeles, California, August 1985.

Award addresses, submitted by award recipients, are published as received except for minor editorial changes designed to maintain *American Psychologist* format. This reflects a policy of recognizing distinguished award recipients by eliminating the usual editorial review process to provide a forum consistent with that employed in delivering the award address.

Author's note. The work described in this article was supported by National Institute for Child Health and Human Development (NICHD) Grant HD 09814. I am very grateful to my research collaborators, Eleanor Flavell and Frances Green, and to Carole Beal, Gary Bonitatibus, Susan Carey, Sophia Cohen, Rochel Gelman, Suzanne Lovett, Eleanor Maccoby, Ellen Markman, Bradford Pillow, Qian Man-jun, Marjorie Taylor, Zhang Xiao-dong, and other colleagues and students for their invaluable help with this research.

Correspondence concerning this article should be addressed to John H. Flavell, Department of Psychology, Jordan Hall, Building 420, Stanford University, Stanford, CA 94305.

Shanks (1965a, 1965b), Daehler (1970), DeVries (1969), Elkind (1966), King (1971), Langer and Strauss (1972), Murray (1965, 1968), Tronick and Hershenson (1979) and, most recently and systematically, by our research group. In most of our studies we have used variations of the following procedure to assess young children's ability to think about appearance and reality (Flavell, Flavell, & Green, 1983). First, we pretrain the children briefly on the meaning of the distinction and associated terminology by showing them (for example) a Charlie Brown puppet inside a ghost costume. We explain and demonstrate that Charlie Brown "*looks like* a ghost to your eyes right now" but is "*really and truly* Charlie Brown," and that "sometimes things look like one thing to your eyes when they are really and truly something else." We then present a variety of illusory stimuli in a nondeceptive fashion and ask about their appearance and their reality. For instance, we first show the children a very realistic looking fake rock made out of a soft sponge-like material and then let them discover its identity by manipulating it. We next ask, in random order: (a) "What is this *really* and *truly?* Is it *really* and *truly* a sponge or is it *really* and *truly* a rock?" (b) "When you look at this with your eyes right now, does it *look like* a rock or does it *look like* a sponge?" Or we show the children a white stimulus, move it behind a blue filter, and similarly ask about its real and apparent color. (Of course its "real color" is now blue, but only people who know something about color perception realize this.) Similar procedures are used to assess sensitivity to the distinction between real and apparent size, shape, events, and object presence.

How Do Young Children Perform on Simple Appearance–Reality Tasks?

Our studies have consistently shown that three- to four-year-old children presented with tasks of this sort usually either answer both questions correctly, suggesting some ability to differentiate appearance and reality representations, or else give the same answer (reporting either the appearance or the reality) to both questions, suggesting some conceptual difficulty with the distinction. Incorrect answers to both questions occur only infrequently, suggesting that even the children who err are not responding randomly. There is a marked improvement with age during early childhood in the ability to solve these appearance–reality tasks: Only a few three-year-olds get them right consistently, whereas almost all six- to seven-year-olds do (Flavell et al., 1985).

Some illusory stimuli tend to elicit appearance answers to both questions (called a *phenomenism* error pattern), whereas others tend to elicit reality answers to both (*intellectual realism* pattern). The intellectual realism pattern is the more surprising one, because it contradicts the widely held view that young children respond only to what is most striking and noticeable in their immediate perceptual field (Flavell, 1977, pp. 79–80; for a review of other research on intellectual realism, see Pillow & Flavell, 1985). If the task is to distinguish between the real and apparent properties of color, size, and shape, phenomen-

Development of the Appearance–Reality Distinction

JOHN H. FLAVELL, ELEANOR R. FLAVELL, AND FRANCES L. GREEN
Stanford University

Young children can express conceptual difficulties with the appearance–reality distinction in two different ways: (1) by incorrectly reporting appearance when asked to report reality ("phenomenism"); (2) by incorrectly reporting reality when asked to report appearance ("intellectual realism"). Although both phenomenism errors and intellectual realism errors have been observed in previous studies of young children's cognition, the two have not been seen as conceptually related and only the former errors have been taken as a symptom of difficulties with the appearance–reality distinction. Three experiments investigated 3- to 5-year-old children's ability to distinguish between and correctly identify real versus apparent object properties (color, size, and shape), object identities, object presence–absence, and action identities. Even the 3-year-olds appeared to have some ability to make correct appearance–reality discriminations and this ability increased with age. Errors were frequent, however, and almost all children who erred made both kinds. Phenomenism errors predominated on tasks where the appearance versus reality of the three object properties were in question; intellectual realism errors predominated on the other three types of tasks. Possible reasons for this curious error pattern were advanced. It was also suggested that young children's problems with the appearance–reality distinction may be partly due to a specific metacognitive limitation, namely, a difficulty in analyzing the nature and source of their own mental representations.

The acquisition of knowledge about the distinction between appearance and reality is a very important developmental problem for at least two reasons.

1. The distinction arises in a very large number and variety of ecologically significant cognitive situations. In many of these situations, the information available to us is insufficient or misleading, causing us to accept an apparent state of affairs (appearance) that differs from the true state of affairs (reality). We are variously misled or deceived by the information we receive from or concerning people, objects, actions, events, and experiences. The deceit may be deliberately engineered by another person; the person intentionally misleads us—through the use of lies, facades, dis-

This research was supported by NICHD Grant HD 09814. We are most grateful to the children, teachers, and parents whose cooperation made these studies possible. We are also much indebted to Ellen Markman, Marjorie Taylor, Carole Beal, and numerous other colleagues and students for their useful suggestions over the course of this project. Finally, we thank Rochel Gelman and two anonymous reviewers for their helpful critiques of this article. Please send requests for reprints to Dr. John H. Flavell, Department of Psychology, Stanford University, Stanford, CA 94305.

Figure 4-3

guises, and other artifices. Very often, however, there is no intention to deceive. The time or distance seemed longer to us than it really was; the sun looks like it moves around the earth but it really does not; it appeared that S−R theory could explain language development but the reality turned out (appeared?) otherwise. The last two examples make it clear that all systematic pursuit of knowledge presupposes at least some awareness of the appearance−reality distinction (Carey, in press): "the distinction which probably provides the intellectual basis for the fundamental epistemological construct common to science, "folk" philosophy, religion, and myth, of a real world "underlying" and "explaining" the phenomenal one" (Braine & Shanks, 1965a, pp. 241−242). Although we may not know that appearances have in fact deceived us in any specific cognitive situation, we do know as a general fact that such deception is always possible. That is, although always susceptible to being deceived by appearances, we have acquired the metacognitive knowledge that appearance−reality differences are always among life's possibilities. There are also many situations in which we are aware of an existing appearance−reality discrepancy. In the above examples, for instance, we may subsequently discover the discrepancy of which we were initially unaware. Dreams constitute a frequent case in point: the events seem real during the dream; we know they were apparent rather than real when we wake up. We also deliberately create or seek out appearance−reality differences as well as discover them. Examples are as diverse as pretense and other forms of play, fantasy, the creation of imaginary or possible worlds (by philosophers, scientists, other adults, and children), magic, tricks, costume parties, jokes, tall tales, metaphor, and the arts (e.g., drama). Some differences between appearance and reality are unwanted and painful; for instance, the apparently "sure-fire" investment (financial or emotional) that really is not. Others, however, are sought after and pleasureful; good magic shows and well-crafted "whodunits" are two examples.

2. The development of knowledge about the distinction between appearance and reality is probably a universal development in human beings. The distinction seems so necessary for everyday adaptations to the human world that one can scarcely imagine a society in which normal children would not acquire it. Developments that are both ecologically significant and universal within the species seem particularly worthy of scientific investigation.

How might young children think and act if, as seems likely, their knowledge about the appearance−reality distinction were not as fully developed as our own? In situations where appearance and reality differ they might not consistently attend to both and keep the difference between them clearly in mind, even when evidence is available to indicate

Truly," the *Psychology Today* article, have a great deal of white space and several large illustrations. The title doesn't actually state what the essay is about, but it does pique the reader's curiosity. The article begins informally with an attention-getting image: "It looks like a nice, solid piece of granite, but as soon as you squeeze it you know it's really a joke-store sponge made to look like a rock." Addressing readers directly, the writer quickly establishes the contradiction that the article will explore: "If I ask what it appears to be, you say, 'It looks just like a rock.' If I ask what it really is, you say, 'It's a sponge, of course.' A 3-year-old probably wouldn't be so sure." The final sentence of the first paragraph clearly indicates the main subject that the essay will explore, but its revision of a popular saying—"what you see is not always what you get"—insures that the reader's interest will be maintained.

The second article, published in *American Psychologist*, includes little white space and no illustrations or photographs. It does state prominently that this essay is an APA Award Address; readers of this journal would recognize the importance of this award. The title is straightforward but complete and easy to understand. The article begins not with an attention-getting introduction but with an abstract, which summarizes the findings of the research reported in the article. The first paragraph of the article opens with a concrete incident but quickly moves to a more theoretical discussion: "At issue in such simple tasks is the distinction between how things presently appear to the senses and how or what they really and enduringly are, that is, the familiar distinction between appearance and reality."

The final article, which appeared in *Cognitive Psychology*, the most specialized of these publications, presents the most cramped and least inviting first page. The title is abbreviated. As with the *American Psychologist* article, an abstract summarizes the article. The article itself begins abruptly with a general statement: "The acquisition of knowledge about the distinction between appearance and reality is a very important developmental problem for at least two reasons." The numbered paragraphs that follow this statement are dense; the authors use a number of technical terms, such as *ecologically significant cognitive situations* and *S-R theory*, without defining them.

Analyzing these first few pages supplies important clues about these three publications and the expectations shared by their writers and readers. One fact is clear from these introductory pages: the less specialized the publication, the greater the expectation that the writer will attempt to interest readers in the article. Those who subscribe to *Psychology Today*, the most general and popular of these journals, often don't have a clear purpose when they read;

they're broadly interested in psychology, but they may read only the articles that most pique their curiosity. A writer who hopes to be read will consequently attempt to gain these readers' attention.

Those who read *American Psychologist* are, like Flavell, all professionals in that field. Because psychology is such a broad field with so many subdisciplines, Flavell can't assume that everyone who subscribes to the journal will be interested in his essay. Not even all the readers who subscribe to *Cognitive Psychology*, a more specialized journal that publishes only research in Flavell's area, will read the article by Flavell and his colleagues, though proportionately more are likely to do so.

Given this situation, why doesn't Flavell attempt to gain the attention and interest of readers in the introductions to these more specialized journals, as he does in his *Psychology Today* article? As you may have already realized, readers of *American Psychologist* and *Cognitive Psychology* read with different purposes and in different ways than readers of *Psychology Today*. They read these journals not so much for pleasure or curiosity but because they want to keep up with advances in their field. Most readers of these two journals probably subscribe to many professional publications. They don't have the time to read every article in these journals, so they skim the tables of contents, noting articles that directly affect their own research or have broad significance for their field. Reviewing an article's abstract helps these psychologists determine not only if but *how* they will read an article. Some will read only an article's conclusion, for instance, while others will be more interested in how an experiment was designed and conducted.

These psychologists would find an engaging introduction like that of the *Psychology Today* article a waste of time. Instead, they want a straightforward, to-the-point approach. Their needs are best met by an abstract that allows them to judge for themselves if they should read an article. Furthermore, whereas most readers of *Psychology Today* discard issues after reading them, readers of *American Psychologist* and *Cognitive Psychology* save theirs. They know that an essay that seems unimportant today may need to be read later. They don't read articles in these journals just once, as readers of *Psychology Today* probably do. They may reread important articles a number of times as they work on similar studies or experiments.

Although these three articles report the same research, they differ dramatically in structure, tone, language, and approach to readers. Textual conventions play an important role in these differences. As shared agreements about the construction and interpretation of texts, textual conventions enable readers and writers to communicate successfully in different rhetorical situations.

Application

Answer the following questions about the introductions to the three Flavell articles to analyze further the differences and similarities among these three excerpts.

1. What kinds of examples are used in these excerpts? What function do they serve?
2. What relationship is established in each article between the writer and the reader? What cues help signal each relationship?
3. How do the abstracts of the *American Psychologist* and *Cognitive Psychology* articles differ? How do you account for these differences?
4. How would you characterize the styles of these three excerpts? Point to specific features that characterize each style. What is the effect of these stylistic differences?
5. What assumptions does Flavell make in each article about what readers already know? Try to point out specific instances that reflect these assumptions.
6. How would you describe the persona, or image of the writer, in each article? What specific factors presented contribute to the development and coherence of this persona?

Putting it all together: understanding the demands of academic writing

Some textual conventions are easy to identify. After reading just a few lab reports you recognize that this form of writing adheres to a set format. Other textual conventions are less easy to discern, and to understand. When you first read the introductions to Dr. Flavell's three essays, for instance, you may have noticed that the introduction to the *Psychology Today* essay differed considerably from the introductions to the next two, which were published in scholarly journals. You may not, however, have noted the differences between the latter two introductions.

To recognize, and certainly to understand, these differences you need to have some knowledge not only of the journals in which the essays were published, but also of the readers of these journals. The authors' decision to use technical terms, such as *phenomenism* and

S-R theory, in the introduction to the *Cognitive Psychology* essay reflects their recognition that readers would not only understand these terms but would expect them. Additionally, using terms such as these subtly informs readers that the writers are "insiders," privy to the terminology used by those in this field.

As this example indicates, recognizing and understanding textual conventions can require considerable knowledge not only of the forms of writing but of the situations of writers and readers. When you join a new community of writers and readers, as you do when you enter college, you can find it difficult to understand the demands of the writing you are expected to complete. Look again, for instance, at the characteristics of an effective essay on page 72. When you first read these characteristics, they probably made sense to you. Of course essays should be well organized, well developed, and logical.

When you sit down at your desk or computer and begin working on an essay for a history, sociology, or economics class, however, you may find it difficult to determine how to embody these characteristics in your own writing. Just what will make your analysis of the economic impact of divorce on the modern family logical or illogical, you might ask yourself. What do economists consider to be well-chosen evidence, illustrations, and details? And does your economics teacher value the same kind of logic, evidence, and details as your American literature teacher?

Exploration

Freewrite for five or ten minutes about your experience thus far with academic writing. What do you find productive and satisfying about such writing? What seems difficult and frustrating? Does your ability to respond to the demands of academic writing vary depending on the discipline—do you find writing essays about literature easier, for instance, than lab reports and case studies? What do you think makes some kinds of academic writing harder or easier for you?

Part 3 of *Work in Progress*, "Connections: Writing, Reading, and Reasoning," will address these and other issues. You already know enough about rhetoric and the rhetorical situation, however, to realize that there can be no one-size-fits-all approach to every academic writing situation. To respond successfully to the challenge of academic writing, you must explore your rhetorical situation; you must also draw upon the rhetorical sensitivity you have gained as a reader, writer, speaker, and listener.

The rhetorical approach to writing described in *Work in Progress* provides the tools you can use to respond appropriately to the challenges of academic writing. A rhetorical approach to writing emphasizes, first, the futility of two common student writing strategies: attempting simply to mimic a form you think the teacher expects or to determine the teacher's own biases about a subject and repeat these in writing. Each of these strategies represents a *partial* understanding of academic writing. As a student you do need to be concerned about the textual conventions or forms characteristic of academic writing; you also need to consider the expectations of your reader—in this case your teacher. But you cannot do so effectively unless you have a clear understanding of your larger rhetorical situation; otherwise, you are like a violinist trying to play a symphony single-handed.

A rhetorical approach to writing suggests a number of common-sense strategies that you can use when writing in an academic context. For writing to be successful, rhetoric emphasizes, you must have something to say, something to communicate with others. There is thus no substitute for direct critical engagement with the subject matter of your courses. As Chapter 10, "Understanding Academic Audiences and Assignments," emphasizes, your teachers share an intellectual commitment first to the concept of education as inquiry and then to their own discipline. When teachers read your writing they are looking for evidence that you have *learned* (not simply memorized) something.

Becoming critically engaged with a subject and communicating the result of that engagement with others are not necessarily the same thing, however. What can you do when you are unfamiliar with the textual conventions of academic writing in general, or of a particular discipline? A rhetorical approach to writing suggests that one important way to learn about textual conventions is to read examples of the kind of writing you wish to do. Discussing these models with an "insider"—your teacher, perhaps, or an advanced student in the field—can help you understand why these conventions work for these readers and writers. Forming a study group with others in your class, or meeting with a tutor in your writing center, can also help you increase your rhetorical sensitivity to the expectations of your teachers and the conventions of academic writing.

Finally, a rhetorical approach to writing encourages you to think *strategically* about writing, whether personal, professional, or academic, and to respond creatively to the challenges of your rhetorical situation. As a writer you have much to consider: your own goals as a writer, the nature of your subject and writing task, the expectations of your readers, the textual conventions that your particular situation requires or allows for. The rhetorical sensitivity you have already developed can help you make appropriate choices in response to these and other concerns. But you will also need to draw on other resources—textual examples, discussions with teachers, writing assistants, and other students—as you work on a variety of writing tasks. As a writer, you are not alone. By reaching out to other writers, in person or through reading their work, you can become a fully participating member of the academic community.

Application

Arrange to interview a teacher in another course you are taking this term, preferably one in which you have done some writing, so you can learn more about your teacher's expectations of student writing. You may wish to ask some or all of the following questions:

- What do you look for when you read students' writing? (Or, alternatively, how would you characterize effective student writing in your discipline?)
- In your experience, what is the difference between an "A" and "C" student essay (or lab report or case study)?
- What are the major weaknesses or limitations of the writing produced by students in your classes?
- What advice would you give to students in an introductory class in your field who want to understand how to write more effectively?
- Do you think your discipline values particular qualities in student writing not necessarily shared by other fields, or is good writing good writing—no matter what the discipline?
- Could you suggest some examples I could read that would help me understand the conventions of effective writing in your discipline?
- How would you characterize the differences between effective student writing and effective professional writing in your field?

- What role do you see yourself as playing when you read student writing?
- Is there anything else you can tell me that would help me better understand the kind of student writing valued in your discipline?

After your interview, write a summary of your teacher's responses. In addition, write at least two paragraphs reflecting on what this interview has taught you about academic writing.

Group Activity

Once you have completed your interview and written your summary, meet with a group of students. Begin by reading your summaries out loud. Then working together—be sure to appoint a recorder—answer these questions:

- Can you locate at least three statements or beliefs shared by all those interviewed?
- What were some major points of disagreement? Did some faculty members feel, for instance, that good student writing is good student writing, whatever the discipline, while others believed that their discipline valued particular qualities in student writing?
- What surprised you in the interviews? Agree upon at least two examples and briefly explain why you were surprised.
- What did these interviews help you better understand about academic writing? Include at least three statements that reflect your group's discussion of your interviews.

Be prepared to share the result of your discussion with the rest of the class.

Activities for Thought, Discussion, and Writing

1. Recall a particular experience in high school or college when you successfully responded to an academic writing assignment. What factors contributed to your success? Spend five minutes brainstorming a list of these factors.
2. Now recall a particular experience in high school or college when you were unable to respond successfully to an academic writing

assignment. What factors contributed to your difficulties? Spend five minutes brainstorming a list of these factors.

3. From a newspaper or magazine, choose an essay, editorial, or column that you think succeeds in its purpose. Now turn back to the Guidelines for Analyzing Your Rhetorical Situation on pages 48–49 and answer the questions *as if you were the writer.* To answer the questions, look for evidence of the writer's intentions in the writing itself. (To determine what image or persona the writer wanted to portray, for instance, look at the kind of language the writer uses. Is it formal or conversational? Full of interesting images and vivid details or serious examples and statistics?) Answer each of the questions suggested by the guidelines. Then write a paragraph or more reflecting on what you have learned from this analysis.

4. Writers can follow appropriate textual conventions and still not be successful. Most textbooks follow certain conventions, such as having headings and subheadings, yet undoubtedly you have found some textbooks helpful and interesting, while others have seemed unhelpful and boring. Choose two textbooks—one that you like and one that you dislike—and make a list of at least four reasons why the former is successful and the latter is not.

PART TWO

PRACTICAL STRATEGIES FOR WRITING

CHAPTER 5

STRATEGIES
FOR
SUCCESSFUL
INVENTION

Writing is a messy, complex, but rewarding process. Few rules for writing apply in every case, and different writing tasks and situations call for different approaches and strategies. Furthermore, two individuals responding to the same task and writing in the same general situation may well proceed in different ways. You might begin working on a writing assignment for your geology class by quickly jotting three pages of notes, while another person in your class might sit quietly, thinking out her ideas carefully before writing.

Even though writing can't be reduced to a series of rules or recipe-like directions, it does involve activities that you can understand, practice, and improve. As Chapter 2 notes, the writing process generally involves planning, drafting, and revising. Successful writers employ a variety of strategies as they work on these activities. The chapters in Part 2 present a number of these strategies.

Read the chapters in Part 2 with a writer's eye. Which of these strategies do you already use? Could you use these strategies more effectively? What other strategies might extend your range or strengthen your writing abilities? As you read about and experiment with these strategies, remember that your needs and preferences as a writer and the situation in which you are writing should influence your assessment of their usefulness.

UNDERSTANDING HOW INVENTION WORKS

Like many people, you may feel that the activity of discovering ideas to write about is the most mysterious part of the writing process. Where do these ideas come from? How can you draw a blank one minute and suddenly know just the right way to support your argument or describe your experience the next? Is it possible to increase your ability to think and write creatively?

Writers and speakers have been concerned with questions such as these for centuries. The classical rhetoricians, in fact, were among the first to investigate this process of discovering and exploring ideas. The Roman rhetoricians called this process *inventio*, for "invention" or "discovery." Contemporary writers, drawing upon this Latin term, often refer to this process as *invention*. Invention is part of the larger activity of planning, discussed further in Chapter 6. Because of the importance of invention, however, this chapter will focus specifically on this process of discovering and exploring ideas.

When you think of invention, you may imagine a writer thinking and writing in isolation. Popular stereotypes encourage this view of invention. Creative writers and artists are often depicted as inspired individuals working alone in their garrets (or, to use a more contemporary image, at their computers), scorning involvement in the lives of ordinary people.

In practice, invention usually involves both individual inquiry and dialogue with others. In writing this textbook, for instance, I spent a great deal of time thinking and working alone. I even experienced a few moments of what might be described as inspiration. For instance, the original outline for this textbook came to me while my husband and I were camping. (I'd been reading a novel, but I quickly grabbed the note card I was using as a bookmark and wrote my ideas down.) As my long list of acknowledgments in the prefatory note to instructors indicates, however, I could not have written this book without the help of many people. In the earliest stages of this project—long before I had written an outline or decided on a title—I spoke with textbook editors as well as with colleagues who had already written textbooks. They helped me understand the intricacies of writing a textbook and the rhetorical situation to which a textbook generally responds. Once I had an outline, I spent many hours talking with both students and fellow composition instructors. By reading articles and books on the teaching of writing, I expanded these conversations. My silent but intense dialogues with these writers were just as important as face-to-face conversations in helping me refine my ideas and troubleshoot potential problems.

Most people don't write textbooks. But most writers—whether they are working on essays, reports, or research papers—generate and explore ideas not only by sitting quietly and thinking or by brainstorming at the computer but by reading, conducting research, and exchanging ideas with friends and colleagues. The following strategies will enable you to invent more successfully, whether you're working alone or talking about your writing with classmates or friends.

USING INFORMAL METHODS OF DISCOVERING AND EXPLORING IDEAS

You may already use several of the methods of discovering and exploring ideas that are described in this chapter: freewriting, looping, brainstorming, and clustering. These methods are informal, natural mental activities. You don't need extensive training or practice to learn to brainstorm or cluster, for instance. Yet these methods can help you discover what you do—and don't—know about a subject. They can also enable you to explore your own ideas and to formulate productive questions that can guide you as you plan, draft, and revise your writing.

Freewriting

Introduced in Chapter 1, freewriting is the practice of writing as freely as possible without stopping to criticize or censor your ideas. This strategy is a simple but powerful means of exploring important issues and problems. Freewriting may at first seem *too* simple to achieve very powerful results: the only requirement is that you must write continuously without stopping. But freewriting can help you discover ideas that you couldn't achieve through more conscious and logical means. Because you generate a great deal of material when you freewrite, freewriting is also an excellent means of coping with the nervousness that all writers feel at the start of a project. (Freewriting can, by the way, be done quite effectively on the computer.)

Freewriting is a potentially powerful strategy you can use in a variety of writing situations. If you are writing a research paper for your political science class on the low voter turnout, you could employ freewriting as a means of exploring and focusing your own ideas. Here, for instance, is one student's freewriting on this issue.

```
    I just don't get it.  As soon as I could register I did--it
felt like a really important day.  I'd watched my mother vote and
my sisters vote and now it was my turn.  But why do I vote; guess
I should ask myself that question--and why don't other people.  Do
I feel that my vote makes a difference?  There have been some
close elections but not all that many, so my vote doesn't liter-
ally count, doesn't decide if we pay a new tax or elect a new sen-
ator.  Part of it's the feeling I get.  When I go to vote I know
the people at the polling booth; they're my neighbors.  I know the
people who are running for office in local elections, and for
state and national elections--well, I just feel that I should.
But the statistics on voter turnout tell me I'm unusual.  In this
paper I want to go beyond statistics.  I want to understand why
people don't vote.  Seems like I need to look not only at research
in political science, but also maybe in sociology.  (Check jour-
nals in economics too?)  I wonder if it'd be okay for me to inter-
view some students, maybe some staff and faculty, about voting--
better check.  But wait a minute; this is a small college in a
small town, like the town I'm from.  I wonder if people in cities
would feel differently--they might.  Maybe what I need to look at
in my paper is rural/small town versus urban voting patterns.
```

This student has not only explored her ideas; she has also identified a possible question to which her paper will respond and sources she will draw upon as she works on her project.

You can employ freewriting to investigate complex academic issues, such as the causes of low voter turnout. But freewriting can also help you to explore your personal experience, enabling you to gain access to images, events, and emotions that you have forgotten or suppressed. If you were writing an essay about your sense of family—how you developed this sense, what it is, and what it means to you now—freewriting could help you recall details and images that would lend a rich specificity to your essay. Here, for example, is my own freewriting about my sense of family. (You may understand this freewriting more easily if you know that I grew up in a family of twelve children, two of whom died in infancy.)

Family. Family. So strong. So many children. Ten. But really twelve. Brian and Anthony dead, both babies. The youngest kids don't even remember—they know but don't remember. Odd. Our own family so enormous, but so little extended family. Mom's parents dead—I do remember Nana, though—one sister. Dad's parents dead too, one sister. Some of my brothers and sisters don't remember any grandparents. Older kids spread out. Leni and Robin in Florida. Sara in Virginia. Andy in Mass. Younger kids closer: Laurie, Shelley, Jeff, Robbie, Julie—all in Ohio, close to Mom and Dad. Me in Oregon, the farthest. Have I forgotten anyone? The list, run down the list. (Memory: amazing friends with how quickly I could say the names, but only in order.) Leni, Lisa, Andy, Sara, Jeff, Robin, Michelle, Laurie, Julie, Robbie. The photo from last summer's reunion: thirty people, Mom and Dad, brothers, sisters, spouses, children. Could be a photo of a company's annual picnic—but it isn't. Families like this just don't exist any more. When did it change? People used to smile at us when we all went out and ask how many. Now a friend with four children tells me people are shocked at the size of her family. I have no children, but I have family. Family—an invisible web that connects.

My brief freewrite did more than generate concrete images and details; it gave me a new insight into my sense of family. Rereading my freewriting, I am surprised at the strong sense of loss that appears as I comment on my infant brothers' deaths and those of my grandparents. I also notice a potential contradiction between my strong sense of family and my recent experience of living a great distance from my family.

Looping

Looping, an extended or directed form of freewriting, alternates freewriting with analysis and reflection. Begin looping by first establishing a theme or topic for your freewriting, then freewrite for five or ten minutes. This is your first loop. After you have done so, reread what you have written. In rereading your freewriting, look for the center of gravity or "heart" of your ideas—the image, detail, issue, or problem that seems richest or most intriguing, compelling, or productive. Write a sentence that summarizes this understanding; this sentence will become the starting point of your second loop. In looking back at my previous freewriting, I can locate several potential starting points for an additional loop. I might, for instance, use the following question to begin another freewriting session:

> What does it mean that my family includes a number of people—my brothers and grandparents—that my younger brothers and sisters never knew, can't remember?

When you loop you don't know where your freewriting and reflection will take you; you don't worry about the final product. My final essay on my sense of family might not even discuss the question generated by my freewriting. That's fine; the goal in freewriting and looping is not to produce a draft of an essay but to explore your own ideas and to discover ideas, images, and sometimes even words, phrases, and sentences that you can use in your writing.

Application

Freewrite for five minutes, beginning with the word *family*. Then stop and reread your freewriting. What comments most interest or surprise you? Now write a statement that best expresses your free-writing's center of gravity or "heart." Use this comment to begin a second loop by freewriting for five minutes more.

After completing this second freewriting, stop and reread both passages. What did you learn about your own sense of family? Does your freewriting suggest possible ideas for an essay on some subject connected with your family? Finally, reflect on the process itself. Did you find the experience of looping helpful? Would you use freewriting and looping in the future as a means of generating and exploring your experiences and ideas?

Brainstorming

Like freewriting and looping, brainstorming is a simple but pro-ductive invention strategy. When you brainstorm, you list as quickly as possible all the thoughts about a subject that occur to you with-out censoring or stopping to reflect on your ideas. A student as-signed to write an essay on child abuse for a sociology class would brainstorm by listing everything that comes to mind on this subject from facts to images, memories, fragments of conversations, and other general impressions and responses. Later, the student would review this brainstorming list to discover those ideas that seem most promising or helpful.

To brainstorm effectively, take a few moments at the start to formulate your goal, purpose, or problem. Then simply list your ideas as quickly as you can. Don't stop to analyze or criticize your ideas; that activity will come later. You are the only person who needs to be able to decipher what you've written, so your brain-storming list can be as messy or neat as you like. You can also brainstorm at the computer.

Brainstorming can enable you to discover and explore a number of ideas in a short time. Suppose, for instance, that after freewriting about my family, I decided to explore the possibility of writing an essay about the potential contradiction between my sense that family is "an invisible web that connects" and the fact that I live so far away from my family. In the five minutes after I wrote that last sentence, I used brainstorming to generate the following list of ideas and suggestions:

- Think about role of place (geography) and family
- The house on Main St.—home since the 4th grade
- Mom's letters: so important in keeping us all in touch!
- Images: Laurie, Shelley, and Sara all with new babies at Julie's wedding
    Andy pulling the same joke on me for 30 years
    The old house on Corey St. Why do I always remember the kitchen?
    My sadness at missing Robin's, Shelley's, and Laurie's weddings because we were in Oregon
    The wonderful, friendly, comfortable chaos at our reunion (the grandkids getting confused by all the aunts and uncles)
- Am I fooling myself? Is the tie I feel with my family as strong as I think it is? Greeting-card sentiments versus reality?
- Special family times: birthdays, Christmas, cooking and baking together. How to evoke these without making it all seem sentimental and clichéd?
- Maybe it's the difficult times that keep families together. The hard times that (especially when you're a teenager), you think you'll never get beyond
- Families change over time. So does your sense of family. How has mine changed?

I certainly would have a long way to go before I could write an essay about my sense of family, but even this brief brainstorming list of ideas and questions has raised important issues I'd want to consider.

Application

Reread your earlier freewriting about your sense of family, assigned on page 96, and then choose one issue or question you'd like to explore further. Write a single sentence summarizing this issue or question, and then brainstorm for five to ten minutes. After brainstorming, return to your list. Put an asterisk (*) beside those ideas or images that hadn't appeared in your earlier freewriting. How do these ideas or images add to your understanding of your sense of family?

Clustering

Clustering shares a number of features with freewriting, looping, and brainstorming. All four strategies emphasize spontaneity. The goal of all four is to generate as many ideas as possible so that you can discover both what you know and what you might want to explore further. Clustering differs from brainstorming, freewriting, and looping, however, in that it uses visual means to generate ideas. Because clustering is nonlinear, some writers find that it frees them from their conventional patterns of thinking and enables them to explore their ideas more deeply and creatively.

To begin clustering, choose a single word or phrase as the starting point or stimulus for your discovery. If you are responding to an assigned topic, choose the word that best summarizes or evokes that topic. If your assignment is broad and you are unsure of your topic or thesis, choose a word that seems suggestive or fruitful. Place this word in the center of a page of blank paper, and circle it. Now fill in the page by expanding on or developing ideas connected with this central word. Don't censor your ideas or force your cluster to assume a certain shape. Simply circle your key ideas and connect them either to the first word or to other related ideas. Your goal in clustering is to be as spontaneous and as natural as possible.

Figure 5-1 presents a cluster that I created shortly after freewriting and brainstorming about my sense of family. Notice that even though I wrote this only a short time later, the cluster reveals new details and images. As with brainstorming, looping, and freewriting, after clustering you must distance yourself from the material you've generated so that you can evaluate it. In doing so, try to find the heart or center of gravity of the cluster—the idea or image that seems richest and most compelling.

Application

Drawing upon your experience freewriting, looping, and brainstorming about your sense of family, assigned on pages 93–97, choose a word to use as the center of a cluster. (If you wish, just use

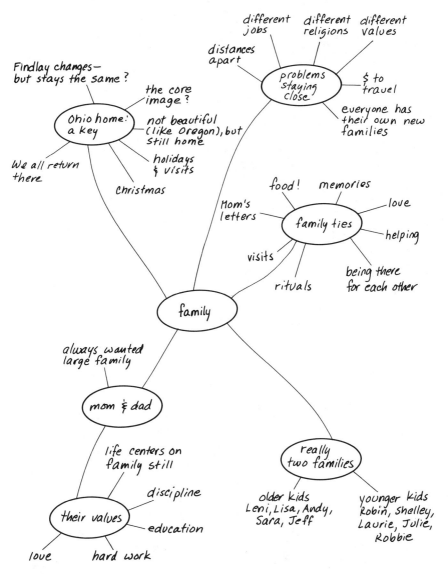

Figure 5-1

the word *family*.) Without planning or worrying about form, fill in your cluster by branching out from this central word. Just include whatever comes to mind.

Group Activity

Meet with classmates to discuss the informal methods of discovering and exploring ideas that you have employed in the preceding Applications. Begin your discussion by having group members briefly describe the advantages and disadvantages they experienced when they experimented with freewriting, looping, brainstorming, and clustering. (Appoint a recorder to summarize each person's statements.) Then as a group discuss your responses to these questions:

1. How might different students' preferences for one or more of these strategies be connected to different learning and composing styles?
2. What influence might such situational factors as the nature of the assignment or the amount of time available for working on an essay have on the decision to use one or more of these strategies?

Be prepared to discuss your conclusions with your classmates.

_____ USING FORMAL METHODS OF _____ DISCOVERING AND EXPLORING IDEAS

The informal methods of discovering and exploring ideas have a number of advantages. They are easy to employ, and they can help you generate a reassuringly large volume of material when you're just beginning to work on a paper. These strategies also help you become interested in and committed to your work in progress. Sometimes, however, you may find more formal and systematic methods of discovering and exploring ideas helpful. The strategies discussed in this section—the journalist's questions, tagmemics, and the topical questions—provide a variety of questions you can use to explore a topical issue, consider it from a variety of perspectives, and generate ideas about it. Because they *systematically* probe a topic, these strategies can help you discover not just what you know about a topic, but also what you *don't* know, and thus alert you to the need for additional reading and research.

The journalist's questions

The journalist's questions—who, what, when, where, why, and how—are perhaps the easiest to understand and apply of the formal methods of discovering and exploring ideas. If you have taken a journalism class or written for your school or community newspaper, you know that journalists are taught the importance of answering these six questions in articles they write. By answering these questions, journalists can be sure that they have provided the most important information about an event, issue, or problem for their readers.

You may find the journalist's questions particularly useful when you are describing an event or writing an informative essay. Suppose that your political science instructor has assigned an essay on the political conflict in the Middle East. Using the journalist's questions as headings, you could begin working on this assignment by asking yourself the following questions:

- *Who* is involved in this conflict?
- *What* issues most clearly divide those engaged in this dispute?
- *When* did the troubles in the Middle East begin, and how have they developed over time?
- *Where* does the conflict in this region seem most heated or violent?
- *Why* have the countries in this region found it so difficult to resolve their difficulties?
- *How* might this conflict be resolved?

Although you might discover much the same information by simply brainstorming, using the journalist's questions insures that you have covered all these major points. Furthermore, using the journalist's questions as headings automatically organizes information as you generate it, whereas a brainstorming list would need to be analyzed, unscrambled, and reorganized.

Tagmemics

The name for this method of discovering and exploring ideas may sound strange or formidable. But tagmemics, the method presented by Richard Young, Alton Becker, and Kenneth Pike in *Rhetoric:*

Discovery and Change, is not difficult to understand and apply. The basic principle underlying tagmemics can be easily stated: an object, experience, or idea can be viewed as a particle (a static unit), a wave (a dynamic unit changing over time), or a field (a unit seen in the context of a larger network of relationships). Each of these perspectives encourages you to ask different kinds of questions about your subject (represented here as X).

- particle perspective   What is X?
- wave perspective   How has X changed over time?
- field perspective   How does X relate to _____?

If you view something as a *particle*, you focus on it as a *static* entity. For example, if you were exploring ideas for a sociology paper on the transformation of the American nuclear family, you could use a particle perspective to ask questions like the following:

- What does the term *nuclear family* mean?
- Who formulated the term *nuclear family*?
- What features characterize the nuclear family?

If you look at a subject from the *wave* perspective, you view it as *dynamic* or *changing over time*. The wave perspective would encourage you to ask such questions as these:

- How long has the nuclear family characterized family structure in America?
- When did the nuclear family begin to change?
- What factors have caused the nuclear family to change?
- How might these factors affect the American family in the future?

Finally, if you look at a subject from the *field* perspective, you ask questions about the way that the subject functions as *part of a larger network of relationships*. This perspective would encourage you to ask questions like the following:

- How are changes in the structure of the American family related to other changes, such as those in the work force, organized religion, the educational system, and divorce rates?
- What are the consequences of changes in the nuclear family for American life in general? For politics? For social services? For education?

Tagmemics is a formal method of discovering and exploring ideas because its three perspectives of particle, wave, and field encourage you to examine your subject *systematically*. Don't be intimidated by the formality of tagmemics; adapt this method to meet *your* needs. Sometimes, for instance, you may use the three perspectives of tagmemics to determine how you might best approach or limit a general subject or problem, like the breakdown of the nuclear family. In other cases, you may use tagmemics to generate a long list of details, examples, and ideas in support of a clearly defined thesis.

Application

Choose a subject of interest to you, such as the impact of computers on business (or education), the debate over the importance of preserving wilderness lands, or the increasing commercialization of college football. Using the journalist's questions and tagmemics, systematically explore the subject you have chosen.

Once you have employed each of these methods, take a few moments to reflect on this experience. To what extent did each strategy help you organize and systematically review what you already know, and to what extent did each define what you still need to find out?

The topical questions

The last formal method for discovering and exploring ideas is based on the topics of classical rhetoric. In his *Rhetoric*, Aristotle describes the topics as potential lines of argument or places (*topos* in Greek means "place") where speakers and writers can find evidence or arguments. Aristotle defined twenty-eight topics, but the list is generally abbreviated to these five: definition, comparison, relationship, circumstance, and testimony.

The classical topics represent natural ways of thinking about ideas. When confronted by an intellectual problem, we all ask such questions as these:

- What is it? (Definition)
- What is it like or unlike? (Comparison)
- What caused it? (Relationship)
- What is possible or impossible? (Circumstance)
- What have others said about it? (Testimony)

Aristotle's topics build on these natural mental habits.

You may use the questions listed above to discover and explore ideas about a subject. To do so, simply pose each question in turn about your subject, writing down as many responses as possible. You may also find helpful the following list of topical questions, adapted by Edward P. J. Corbett from the work of Richard L. Larson. These questions from Corbett's *The Little Rhetoric and Handbook* are organized according to subject matter.

QUESTIONS ABOUT PHYSICAL OBJECTS

1. What are the physical characteristics of the object (shape, dimensions, materials, etc.)?
2. What sort of structure does it have?
3. What other object is it similar to?
4. How does it differ from things that resemble it?
5. Who or what produced it?
6. Who uses it? For what?

QUESTIONS ABOUT EVENTS

1. Exactly what happened? (who? what? when? where? why? how?)
2. What were its causes?
3. What were its consequences?
4. How was the event like or unlike similar events?
5. To what other events was it connected?
6. How might the event have been changed or avoided?

QUESTIONS ABOUT ABSTRACT CONCEPTS (e.g., DEMOCRACY, JUSTICE)

1. How has the term been defined by others?
2. How do you define the term?
3. What other concepts have been associated with it?
4. What counterarguments must be confronted and refuted?
5. What are the practical consequences of the proposition?

Like the other formal methods for discovering and exploring ideas, the topical questions can help you pinpoint alternative approaches to the subject or probe one subject systematically, organizing what you know already and identifying gaps that you need to fill.

Application

Use the topical questions to continue your investigation of the same subject that you explored with the journalist's questions and tagmemics (page 103).

What new information or ideas did the topical questions generate? How would you compare this method to the other two formal strategies?

INVENTING COLLABORATIVELY: LEARNING WITH AND FROM OTHERS

Invention includes not only individual inquiry, such as that stimulated by freewriting, brainstorming, or tagmemics, but dialogue with others. Much of this dialogue occurs naturally as you go about your daily affairs. While riding the bus or subway home after class, for instance, you might talk over a writing assignment with a friend. Or you might brainstorm about an essay topic with your spouse or roommate after dinner. The ideas you gain through such exchanges can contribute a great deal to your understanding of your subject.

The final section of this chapter presents four strategies you can use to learn with and from others as you write. The first two strategies, group brainstorming and group troubleshooting, build upon the informal exchanges you already have with friends, classmates, and family members. The final two strategies, interviewing and conducting research, are more formal methods of discovering and exploring ideas through dialogue with others. You may not have viewed these last two methods—particularly research—as collaborative activities. But they are part of the larger intellectual conversation that your instructors are encouraging you, as a student, to join.

Group brainstorming

You have already experimented with brainstorming alone, so you are aware of its basic procedures and benefits. You can also brainstorm as part of a group, however. In fact, Alex Osborn, the person generally credited with naming this technique, originally envisioned brainstorming as a group, not an individual, activity. Osborn believed that the enthusiasm generated by the group helped spark ideas.

Group brainstorming can be used for a variety of purposes. If your class has just been assigned a broad topic, for instance, your group could brainstorm a list of ways to approach or limit this topic. Or your group could generate possible arguments in support of or opposition to a specific thesis.

Because more than one person is involved, group brainstorming is more complicated than brainstorming alone. When working in a group, follow this procedure.

Guidelines for group brainstorming

1. Carefully define the problem or issue to be addressed at the start of your group session.
2. Appoint someone to act as a recorder. This person can write group members' ideas on the board or on a piece of paper, ready to be reproduced and distributed to group members later.
3. Encourage group members to contribute freely and spontaneously to the discussion. Don't stop to discuss or evaluate ideas; your goal is to generate as many ideas as possible.

Group troubleshooting

Group troubleshooting is a simple but often productive means of helping group members identify and resolve writing problems by discussing work in progress with peers who respond with questions and advice. To troubleshoot effectively, your group should follow this procedure.

Guidelines for group troubleshooting

1. Decide how much time to spend on each person's writing, and appoint a timekeeper to enforce these limits.
2. Begin by having the writer describe the issue or problem he or she would like discussed. The writer also should try to identify particular questions for group response. These questions may be very general. ("This is what I'm planning to do in my essay; can you think of any problems I might run into?" "Do you have any suggestions about how I might develop my thesis?") Or the questions might be quite specific. ("I've only been able to think of two potential objections to my thesis; can you think of others?" "I like these four ideas, but I don't think they fit together very well. What could I do?")
3. Let the writer facilitate the resulting discussion. If the writer needs a moment to write an idea down, for example, he or she should ask the group to pause briefly. The writer

should feel free to ask group members to clarify or elaborate on suggestions.

4. Try as group members to respond to the writer's request for assistance as carefully and fully as possible.

You will probably find group troubleshooting most productive in the early stages of writing when you are still working out your ideas and determining your approach to your subject.

Interviewing

If you've met regularly with a tutor or fellow students to discuss your writing, you have already learned how useful it can be to talk with others about work in progress. There's another way in which talking with others can be useful; you can interview people whose views or experiences might enable you to understand your subject better. If you are writing an essay for your economics class about the job-related problems of clerical workers, for example, you might interview secretaries working on campus. To find out background information for an argument in favor of increased financial support for cultural events on campus, you might interview the person responsible for such programs to find out why current support is so low. Even if you don't use any quotations from such interviews, the information you have gained, as well as your personal involvement with someone knowledgeable about your subject, will enrich your discussion.

Interviews are more formal than most conversations, so be sure that you do not underestimate the importance of carefully preparing for and conducting them. If you wish to interview someone for your writing, follow these suggestions.

Guidelines for interviewing

1. Call or write to request an interview in advance. Carefully explain why you want the interview, how long it will take, and what you hope to accomplish.
2. Come prepared with a list of written questions.
3. If you wish to tape the interview, remember to ask permission first.
4. Take notes during the interview, even if you use a tape recorder. Your notes will help refresh your memory when you don't have time to review the entire tape; they can also help you identify the most important points of discussion.

5. Be flexible. Don't try to make the person you are interviewing answer all your prepared questions if he or she doesn't find some of them appropriate or interesting. If your interviewee shows more interest in a question than you had anticipated or wants to discuss a related issue, just accept this change in plans and return to your list of questions when appropriate.
6. Develop a variety of questioning techniques. People are sometimes unable or unwilling to answer direct questions. Suppose you want to write about your grandmother's experiences during World War II. If you simply ask her what life was like then, she may not respond very fully or specifically. Less direct questions—"Where did you live during the war?" "What effect did rationing have on how you ate?" "Did Grandpa have to fight?"—may elicit more detailed answers.

Conducting research

What does it mean to conduct research? You may think immediately of searching for articles and books in the library, and libraries certainly are a valuable source of information about many subjects. But research is actually a much more common activity in all of our lives. You are conducting research, for instance, if you consult *Consumer Reports* to discover which compact disk player you should purchase. You are conducting research if you read *Bride's* magazine to help you plan your own or a friend's wedding. You are conducting research if you write to the chamber of commerce of a city to which you might move to request information about local businesses, property values, and taxes. And you are conducting research if you volunteer to work with a committee of concerned citizens charged with investigating the adequacy of your community's services for the homeless.

As these examples indicate, we all conduct research to make decisions and become better informed about the world around us. As a student, you will be more effective in the various kinds of research you do for your classes—from preparing a questionnaire or conducting a case study to consulting an electronic data base in the library—if you remember that research is a natural human activity. Though you do need to learn certain skills, such as how to use your library's card catalog or circulation computer, you already understand many basic research methods.

In-depth coverage of research methods and related issues, such as using source materials and documenting sources, is outside the scope of this book. You may wish to consult a college writing handbook if you need further information on these subjects. The rest of this chapter will provide a number of useful suggestions about conducting research, however. Additionally, Part 3, "Connections: Writing, Reading, and Reasoning," focuses on a number of issues directly connected to research. Much of your research in college involves reading; Chapter 9, "Understanding the Reading Process," will help you develop the critical reading skills necessary for effective research. You can't conduct effective research unless you understand your assignment and have developed strategies that enable you to analyze and argue effectively: Chapter 10, "Understanding Academic Audiences and Assignments," and Chapter 11, "Understanding Academic Analysis and Argument," discuss these issues.

Perhaps the most important thing to understand when you conduct research is that the question you want to answer—your purpose—should govern your inquiry. If you are investigating the media's coverage of the AIDS crisis, you will proceed differently than if you are analyzing the impact of cutbacks in federal support for basic research in science or exploring the major causes of pollution in the Los Angeles Basin. The nature of your project will also influence how you conduct research. If you are simply following up leads in an essay because you find the subject interesting, you may limit your research to a brief examination of the essay's bibliography. If you are embarking upon a major research project, you will naturally employ a more extensive, systematic review of relevant research.

When you conduct research, as when you write, you are engaged in a process, one that can vary depending upon the situation. Sometimes when you go to the library you will already have a clear idea of the general topic you wish to explore; in this case you may systematically begin the process of locating materials appropriate for your topic. On other occasions, you will have a less well-developed sense of your subject. You may know that you want to write something about recent political changes in Eastern Europe, for instance, but you may need to do considerable exploratory reading before you can determine a more specific focus and purpose. Attempting to short-circuit your research process, to look for "answers" before you have clearly defined the question you wish to investigate, will only create difficulties in the long run.

Conducting research can be one of the most productive and satisfying parts of the writing process—but only if you understand the purpose of research. Some students view research as nothing more than the process of locating authorities whose words and ideas they can string together in their essays like beads in a necklace. For these students conducting research is little more than a dreary hunt for evidence hidden in books and periodicals. No wonder these students view research as tedious and uninteresting. In actuality, conducting research—like the informal and formal methods of invention discussed earlier in this chapter—is a crucial means of discovering and exploring ideas. Although you should respect the achievements of the authors of the essays, reports, and studies that you read, the process of consulting published materials is more like a conversation than a lecture. Your role is active, not passive. An author is not right just because he or she has published an article or book. After all, scholarly research is an ongoing collaborative activity. One scholar states a position, only to be answered by another. And then a third responds to both. Your job is to enter into that conversation by reading various researchers' works and then coming to informed conclusions about them.

Conducting library research is a complex activity. Although the following brief guidelines cannot tell you how to master your library and understand all its research materials, they can provide some useful suggestions.

Guidelines for library research

1. *Learn how to use your college or university library.* If you are familiar with the process of conducting research, this step will involve little more than observing where materials are located in your library and discovering what special services, such as computerized data bases, are available to you. But if you are less experienced at research, you will need to spend more time learning about all the resources provided. Even though you are busy with regular course work, take the time to get to know your library. Many academic libraries offer tours or educational programs for students. Take advantage of these if they are available.

2. *Establish an appropriate search strategy.* Before going to the library to do research for a project, even a minor one, you should work out a search strategy. Such a plan insures that you will consult appropriate sources; it also helps you avoid frustration and wasted time. Often, for instance, you will want to get a broad overview of your subject before you read more specialized studies. Determining what materials to consult for this overview might be the first step in your search strategy. In other cases, especially when you already have some knowledge of your subject and have been assigned or have developed a limited topic, you may consult specialized materials from the start. The important thing is to have a plan—to figure out what you need to know and how

you can best locate that information. If you have difficulty establishing an appropriate search strategy, ask a reference librarian for help.

3. *Recognize that your research may take longer than you expected.* You may be surprised and frustrated when you discover that books you had counted on finding in the library are checked out or that a resource you had expected to be helpful is not. Be sure to budget not just adequate but *extra* time for research in case you run into unexpected difficulties.

4. *Recognize the importance of evaluating sources.* Not every book or essay you find in the library is accurate, up-to-date, and authoritative. When you conduct research, you must evaluate the usefulness and authoritativeness of your sources. To do so, ask yourself questions like the following:

   ■ Who is the author? Is he or she a recognized expert in the field? Have other sources referred favorably to this author's work?

   ■ Who published this? Does this publisher (whether of books or periodicals) have a solid reputation in the field?

   ■ To whom is the author writing? Is this a work intended for general readers or specialists?

   ■ When was this published? If it was not published recently (within the last three to five years), is it current or outdated? How rapidly is information in this field changing?

   ■ How relevant is this work to my topic? Have I skimmed a book's table of contents and preface or reviewed an article's introduction, section headings, and conclusions to determine if it merits a more careful reading?

At times, especially at the start of a research project, you may not be able to answer these questions because you just don't know enough about your subject. When that occurs, you have several options. The first is to consult the reference librarian. Large academic libraries generally have one or more librarians who specialize in each of the major disciplines and thus are especially well qualified to help you. If your library doesn't have specialized reference librarians, consult one of the general reference librarians. A second option is to discuss your sources with your instructor. After you have completed some preliminary research, for instance, you might ask your instructor's advice about the appropriateness of your sources and your search strategy. Finally, you can follow up leads in works you have already read. When researchers cite other scholarly works, they are not only acknowledging their use of the ideas of others but also indicating those whose work seems important to them. By consulting studies cited in footnotes or bibliographies, you will discover those researchers most qualified and likely to comment on the work you are attempting to evaluate.

This chapter has described a number of strategies you can use to discover and explore ideas. Your preferred composing style, the nature of your subject, and the situation in which you are writing will influence your choice of strategies. In deciding how to generate ideas for an essay, take a pragmatic, goal-oriented approach. Don't waste time freewriting if you already have lots of ideas and a sense of how you want to approach your subject. Instead, see if you can develop a workable plan—as discussed in the next chapter—and then start writing. You may decide to stop and freewrite later, but then you'll have a clear purpose and thus will use your time more effectively. In some instances, even making a plan may seem unnecessary. If you're full of ideas and just want to write, you may want to explore your ideas by writing a draft and seeing, in effect, what you think. That's fine, too. Just remember that *all* of these methods of invention require you to evaluate the ideas you have generated, whether they take the form of a brainstorming list, a cluster, or a first draft.

Activities for Thought, Discussion, and Writing

1. Earlier in this chapter you used freewriting, looping, brainstorming, and clustering to investigate your sense of family. Drawing on these materials, write an essay in which you explore just what the word *family* means to you.

2. Observe some of your classmates working together on group brainstorming or group troubleshooting. Don't participate in the group activities; simply observe the group interaction. As you observe, make notes about what you see. You may find it helpful to record how often each member of the group participates in the discussion, for example. Pay attention, too, to group dynamics. Is the group working effectively? Why, or why not? What could group members do to insure more effective interaction? Summarize the results of your observations in a report to group members. Be sure to suggest several ways the group could work more effectively in the future.

3. Choose one of the strategies discussed in this chapter that you have not used in the past. Experiment with the strategy as you work on your current writing assignment. If there is time, discuss this experiment with some of your classmates. Then write a brief analysis of why this strategy did or did not work well for you.

CHAPTER 6

STRATEGIES FOR SUCCESSFUL PLANNING AND DRAFTING

Planning is an important part of the writing process. People plan in different ways, depending on how they prefer to compose. Some develop detailed written plans; others rely primarily on mental plans to guide them as they draft and revise. Still others plan by freewriting a draft of their essay and determining their goals by interacting with their own written text. Other factors can affect the process of planning. A student who usually develops extensive written plans for major academic writing assignments may rely on just a few speedily jotted notes when writing a brief weekly sales report to her supervisor. Similarly, as a student you naturally use different strategies when planning how to respond to an in-class essay examination question than you do when beginning a lengthy research paper.

People plan in different ways and at different times in the writing process, but planning always involves the following related activities:

- analyzing your rhetorical situation
- discovering and exploring ideas
- establishing a controlling purpose
- developing a workable plan

Earlier chapters already discussed strategies you can use to analyze your rhetorical situation and to discover and explore ideas. This chapter will focus on the remaining two activities in the list: establishing a controlling purpose and developing a workable plan. It will also present a number of strategies for effective drafting.

UNDERSTANDING THE PROCESS OF PLANNING

You may find it helpful to think of planning as involving cycles or waves of "play" and "work." When you are discovering and exploring ideas, for example, you are in a sense playing. When you freewrite, loop, brainstorm, or cluster, your major goal is to be creative—to push your ideas as far as you can, without worrying about how useful they may turn out to be later. Even more formal methods of invention, such as tagmemics or the topical questions, encourage mental play and exploration.

Most people can't write an essay based on a brainstorming list or thirty minutes of freewriting, however. At some point, they need to settle down to work, considering questions like the following:

QUESTIONS FOR PLANNING YOUR ESSAY
1. What main point do I want to make in this essay?
2. Who might be interested in reading this essay?
3. How might my readers' expectations influence the form and content of this essay?
4. How can I structure my essay to communicate my ideas most effectively to readers?
5. What kinds of examples and details should I use to support my main point?

Questions such as these require you to work on your ideas—to determine just what point you not only want to make but *can* make in your essay, to decide if you have all the information you need to support your assertions. These planning activities generally require more discipline than the informal or formal play of invention. Because much of the crafting of your essay occurs as a result of these activities, however, this work can be intensely rewarding.

Exploration

How do you typically plan when you are working on a writing project? Do you rely on written plans, or do you use other means to determine goals and strategies for your writing? How might you make your process of planning more efficient and productive? Free-write for five or ten minutes in response to these questions.

ESTABLISHING A
CONTROLLING PURPOSE

The planning activities discussed in this chapter are *goal-oriented* activities. You can't establish a controlling purpose or a workable plan for your essay without having at least a tentative sense of the goals you hope to achieve by writing. These goals may change as you work on your essay, but they represent an important starting point or preliminary set of assumptions for guiding your work in progress.

How can you determine appropriate goals for your writing? Whether you are writing a brief memo to your supervisor, a term paper for your history class, or an application for your first job, you can best understand and establish goals for writing by analyzing your rhetorical situation. This process, described in Chapter 3, encourages you to ask questions about the elements of rhetoric: writer, reader, and text. Once you have analyzed your rhetorical situation, you should have a clearer understanding not only of your reasons for writing but of the most appropriate means to communicate your ideas to your readers.

Your *controlling purpose* for an essay reflects your essay's topic but differs from it in important ways. Unlike your topic, your controlling purpose is both action- and content-oriented. Your controlling purpose reveals not just what you want to write about but also the point you intend to make and the effect you wish to have on your readers. It is an *operational* statement of your intentions. Suppose that you are writing a guest editorial for your campus newspaper. "What are you going to write about?" a friend asks. "Library hours," you reply. You have just stated your topic—the subject you're going to write about—but this statement doesn't satisfy your friend. "What about library hours? What's your point?" "Oh," you say, *"I'm going to argue that students should petition the vice president for academic affairs to extend the library hours. Current hours just aren't adequate."* This second statement, which specifies not only the point you want to make but its desired effect on readers, is a good example of a clearly defined controlling purpose.

If you and your friend had time for a longer conversation, you could elaborate on the rhetorical situation for this guest editorial.

You could discuss your own intentions as the *writer* more clearly, and you could note how you intend to anticipate and respond to *readers'* needs and interests. Your friend might be able to give you good advice about how your *text* should reflect one of the most important features of editorials—their brevity. Your friend may be too busy for such extended conversation, however. Your controlling purpose briefly and succinctly summarizes the goals you have in writing this guest editorial.

An effective controlling purpose limits the topic you will discuss and helps you clarify and organize your ideas. Once you have established a controlling purpose, you should be able to develop a number of questions that can guide you as you work on your writing. Here, for example, are just some of the questions you might ask in response to the controlling purpose in the previous example.

- What arguments will most effectively support my position? How might I most effectively structure these arguments?
- How can I focus my discussion so that I can make my point in the limited space typically given to editorials?
- Do I know enough about the reasons why current library hours are limited? Should I interview the director of the library or the vice president for academic affairs?
- Am I correct in assuming that other students find current hours a problem? Should I talk with a number of students to get their reactions to this problem?
- Should I conduct research to find out how our library's hours compare with those at similar colleges and universities?
- Assuming that current library hours are a problem—and I'm convinced they are—how can I persuade students to go to the trouble of signing a petition?
- Given my rhetorical situation, how formal should my language be? And what image of myself should I try to create in my editorial?

As this example indicates, establishing a controlling purpose encourages you to be pragmatic and action-oriented. You may revise your controlling purpose as you work on your essay. In the meantime, you can use the insights gained by formulating and analyzing your controlling purpose to set preliminary goals for writing.

Once you have established a preliminary controlling purpose, you can test its effectiveness by asking yourself the questions listed below. (Or you may wish to discuss these questions with classmates or members of your writer's group.) If you can't answer one or more of these questions, you may not have analyzed your rhetorical situation carefully enough or spent adequate time discovering and exploring ideas.

QUESTIONS FOR EVALUATING YOUR CONTROLLING PURPOSE

1. How clearly does your controlling purpose indicate what you want this essay to do or to accomplish? Is your controlling purpose an *operational* statement of your intentions, not just a description of your topic?

2. How realistic are these expectations, given your rhetorical situation, the nature of the assignment, and your time and page limitations?

3. How might you better prepare yourself to accomplish this controlling purpose? Should you do additional reading or clarify your ideas by talking with others or by spending more time discovering and exploring ideas?

4. In what ways does your controlling purpose respond to your understanding of your rhetorical situation, particularly the needs and expectations of your readers?

5. What questions, like those listed on page 116, does your analysis of your controlling purpose indicate that you need to consider as you work on your writing?

Application

For an essay you are writing for this or another course, use the questions listed here to evaluate your current controlling purpose. Then write a paragraph evaluating the effectiveness of your controlling purpose and suggesting ways to improve it. Finally, list the questions your evaluation indicates you need to consider as you work on this essay.

In some cases, you may be able to establish a controlling purpose early in your writing process. In many other instances, however, you will have to nurture your controlling purpose by thinking about your rhetorical situation and by employing informal and formal methods of invention. You will, in other words, think and write your way into understanding what you want to say. You may even decide that the best way to determine your controlling purpose is to write a rough draft of your essay and see, in effect, what you think about your topic. This strategy, which is sometimes called *discovery drafting*, can work well as long as you recognize that your rough draft will need extensive analysis and revision.

You should always view any controlling purpose as preliminary or tentative—subject to revision. After you have worked on an essay for a while, your controlling purpose may evolve to reflect the understanding you have gained through further planning and drafting. You may even discover that your controlling purpose isn't feasible. In either case, the time you spend thinking about your preliminary controlling purpose is not wasted, for it enables you to begin the process of organizing and testing your ideas.

FORMULATING A WORKABLE PLAN

A plan is a written representation that enables you to explore and organize your ideas and establish goals for your writing. Plans can take many forms. Some writers develop carefully structured, detailed plans. Others find that quick notes and diagrams are equally effective. The form that a plan takes should reflect your own needs, preferences, and situation.

As mentioned earlier, writers don't always make written plans. A very brief writing project, or one that follows clearly defined textual conventions (such as a routine inventory update for a business firm), may not require a written plan. Some writers defer planning until they have written a discovery draft, while heavy drafters prefer to do much of their planning mentally rather than on paper. Nevertheless, as a college student, you will often find written plans helpful. Plans are efficient ways to try out your ideas. As Linda Flower has noted in her book *Problem-Solving Strategies for Writing*, "One of the virtues of a plan is that it is cheaper to build than the real solution would be. Therefore, architects start with blueprints rather than concrete, and writers plan a twenty-page paper before they write." Developing a plan—whether a jotted list of notes or a formal outline—is also a good way to engage your unconscious mind in your writing process. Finally, many students find that by externalizing their goals, by putting them on paper or on-screen, they can more effectively critique their own ideas, an important but often difficult part of the writing process.

There is no such thing as an ideal one-size-fits-all plan. An effective plan is a *workable* plan—a plan that works for you. Plans are utilitarian. They are meant to be used—and revised. In working on an essay, you may draw up a general plan only to revise this plan as you write. Nevertheless, by enabling you to begin drafting, your first plan has fulfilled its function well.

You may better understand how plans work by examining three students' actual plans. These plans vary significantly, yet each fulfilled the author's needs. The first plan, shown in Figure 6-1, is by Lisa DeArmand, a freshman majoring in business. It is a plan for a brief essay reviewing three popular pizza parlors near campus. Lisa had already decided to target an audience of fellow students who might naturally be interested in her subject. As you can see, Lisa's plan, which consists of little more than a few notes about each pizza parlor, is both brief and simple. But in this case it was all that Lisa needed. Lisa already had spent considerable time analyzing her rhetorical situation, and she had recognized that the most effective way to organize her essay would be to compare the three restaurants. She also had detailed notes about these restaurants, including interviews with students, which she planned to use in her essay. Because Lisa had such a clear mental image of what she wanted to say and how she wanted to say it, she didn't need a complex or highly detailed written plan.

Now look at the second plan (Figure 6-2 on page 120). This is a plan by Dodie Forrest, a junior English major, for a take-home midterm in an American drama class. This plan is much more complex than the one for the pizza-parlor review. It includes two diagrams that helped Dodie visualize how the essay might be organized, several quotes from the play that Dodie thought were important, reminders to herself, definitions of terms, and many general comments about the play. Dodie's task was more complex than Lisa's, so it makes sense that her plan should be more complex. Her task was also more open-ended. The question that Dodie was required to answer was this: "Explain why it is necessary for Arthur Miller to create wide sympathy for his character Willy Loman in *Death of a Salesman*. Does he create sympathy for Willy, or is the audience too tempted to

BOBBIE'S PIZZA	PIZZA-IN-A-HURRY	PIZZA ROMA
$4.00	$6.55	$6.10
close	coupons	best pizza!
limited hours	crust thin & soggy	unusual sauce
delivery charge	tastes like frozen	two kinds of crust
pizza ok, but not	pizza	more toppings
great. Little		
variety		

Figure 6-1

judge him morally to be sympathetic?'' Dodie used her plan to help explore her ideas and to determine the best organization for her essay. Although probably no one but Dodie could develop an essay from the various diagrams and notes on this page, this plan fulfilled Dodie's needs. And that's what counts.

Figure 6-2

Here is a third plan, this one by Dave Ross, a returning student intending to major in natural resource economics. Dave began by writing about the "feel" he wanted his essay to have, then developed a detailed plan:

> This will be a personal essay about my experiences working at Urban Ore, a business that sells salvaged building materials. I want the reader to share my pleasure at working among all that great recyclable junk. The interesting "finds," the colorful characters, my own satisfaction at organizing the chaos. The essay should feel crowded with odds and ends, just like the salvage yard is: strange bits of description, stories, humorous observations. I guess "funky" is the word.
>
> I. Description of the yard.
>   -- Among one-family underclass homes, rusting railroad tracks, corrugated sheet metal auto body shops: a weedy, dusty scrapyard surrounded by eight-foot cyclone fence, filled with doors, windows, kitchen cabinets, lamps, toilets, sinks, bathtubs, faucets, pipes, bricks, stoves, coils of wire.
>   -- A real business: this junk generates nearly $200,000 a year in sales to construction workers, contractors, or just weekend fixer-uppers.
>
> II. People working there.
>   -- Joe, the owner: Urban Studies Ph.D., abstract painter, two-time candidate for mayor.
>   -- Webb, looks like Jerry Garcia but with a rhino's strength.
>   -- Charles, lives on brown rice and has a passion for snakes.
>   -- Vagrant cats and a German shepherd named Ripthroat who melts when you scratch his butt.
>
> III. Me working there.
>   -- My first big job, organizing the windows and doors. First big rush of satisfaction: being able to tell a customer exactly where to find the bottom half of a double hung window, 36" by 28".
>   -- First Law of Urban Ore: "The more organized we are, the more we sell." But that's not the only reason I liked doing it. Bringing order out of chaos. An artist of the junkyard.
>
> IV. Treasure Island: Found among the weeds and blackberry brambles: Art Deco bathroom tiles, mint-condition platform heels, bottles of all shapes and colors, a Three Stooges coffee mug (think of more).

V. Not all fun. Sometimes punishing work.
    -- No electricity, heat, running water or toilet. Only one
shack, crowded when it rains.
    -- Winter: cold, stiff hands, wet gloves. Summer: pounding
sun, dust.
    -- rusty nails, metal or glass edges
    -- hauling cast-iron bathtubs, six-burner ranges: hernia city!

VI. Conclusion: honest, constructive work and creative in its
way. Great when a customer found just what he/she wanted--or
something they'd never dreamed of.
    -- One evening, local skid-row types formed a band with stuff
they'd found lying around. Played "Working on the Chain Gang"--
sounded pretty bad, but a lot of spirit. A certain strange beauty
amid the disorder--sums up Urban Ore for me.

Dave's plan is more detailed than Lisa's; it is also more clearly organized than Dodie's. Dave's approach to planning probably reflects his preference for detailed, well-organized plans. It also reflects the nature of the essay he had envisioned: he wanted to include such a profusion of material that a detailed plan would help to ensure a coherent structure. Dave probably couldn't have worked efficiently from a freer, less clearly organized plan, like Dodie's; Dodie, however, might find Dave's more structured approach equally difficult.

Plans play an important role in writing. They help you explore, organize, and try out your ideas; they also enable you to set goals for your writing. You might think of plans as notes, reminders, or directions that you write to yourself. No one else needs to be able to understand your plans, just as no one else needs to be able to shop from your grocery list. This analogy points out, however, that your plan won't work unless you have a clear understanding of the reminders and directions that you have written. The usefulness of any plan will reflect the thoroughness of your *planning* as you think and talk with others about your writing.

Exploration

What kind of plans do you typically draw up? Do you formulate detailed, carefully structured plans, or do you prefer to develop less structured ones? Do you use diagrams or other visual elements in planning? Are your plans workable? Do they work, in other words, for you? Can you think of one or more suggestions that might enable you to develop more useful plans?

Use these questions to think about your plans. Then spend ten minutes writing down your most helpful observations about them.

Group Activity

Meeting with a group of classmates, take turns reading your responses to the previous Exploration. After each person has read, work together to answer these questions. (Be sure to appoint a recorder.)

1. What planning strategies do those in your group most often employ?
2. How often do group members develop written plans? What kinds of plans do you most often develop? How formal and detailed are your plans, for instance? Do group members often use diagrams and other visual means to plan your writing?
3. Did any group members suggest planning strategies that other members think they might like to experiment with? If so, briefly describe these strategies and explain why group members believe they might be useful.
4. Make a list of three conclusions about planning with which all group members can agree. Make another list of at least three suggestions on how group members can plan more efficiently and productively.

Be prepared to share the results of your discussion with your classmates.

DEVELOPING EFFECTIVE STRATEGIES FOR DRAFTING

Drafting—inscribing words on paper or typing them into your computer—is only part of the writing process. You actually begin writing an essay when you first spend ten minutes freewriting or brainstorming in response to an assignment. Revision, too, often occurs before you complete a rough draft: If you make a list of possible titles for an essay, cross out two, and circle one as your best current choice, you have revised. Drafting is nevertheless an important component of the writing process, for it is through drafting that you create a text that embodies your preliminary intentions. Once you have a rough draft, you can begin the rewarding process of developing and refining your ideas through revision.

Overcoming resistance to drafting

When you first sit down at your desk or computer to begin drafting, it can be hard to imagine the satisfaction of completing a rough draft. Indeed, just picking up pen or pencil or beginning to type at the computer can seem impossible; suddenly you can think of a hundred things you'd rather do. All writers experience some resistance to drafting; productive writers, however, have developed ways to overcome this resistance.

Many writers rely upon rituals, such as those described on pages 40 and 41, to help them deal with what Tom Grenier calls the "prewrite jitters." There are other strategies you can use to overcome resistance to drafting. If you've already spent time discovering and exploring ideas and making one or more tentative plans, you will have the reassuring knowledge that you're not starting from scratch. Reading through early notes and plans is a very effective way to begin a drafting session.

Another way to motivate yourself to start drafting is simply to remind yourself that you're only working on a draft; it doesn't need to be perfect. When you begin drafting, your initial goal should simply be to *get words on paper*. If you can't think of a way to begin your essay, for instance, don't try to do so; simply begin writing a section that you are ready to write. As you reread what you've written, you'll eventually discover an introduction that works for you.

Many writers find it helpful to discuss their ideas with others when they're having trouble getting started. If you do this, be sure to have pen and paper ready so you can write down important points that come up in your discussion. If no one is available to discuss your writing, try composing a "letter" to someone you know and trust about your difficulties. Such a letter might begin like this: "Dear Mom, I need to draft a report for my biology class, but I just can't get started. I'm supposed to be writing about _____, but the only thing I'm sure I want to say about this subject right now is. . . ." Before you know it, you're off and running!

Finally, freewriting, a strategy for discovering and exploring ideas, can also help you overcome resistance to drafting. When I first began this second edition of *Work in Progress*, for instance, I tried for several days to begin writing and simply couldn't. Finally, I sat down and scribbled this freewriting.

> Well, it's Tuesday, August 7th, 1990, and I've still not begun working on revising WIP. What happened to all my good intentions? I thought by this time in the summer I'd have been working at least two to three weeks. But then my expectations of summer are always unrealistic. Why am I surprised when the usual happens? Unexpected guests, unanticipated house problems (ant invasion, broken dishwasher). And of course the other work that I was positive I'd have done by May 1st took longer than I'd expected.
>
> Why do I let all this get to me so? Why can't I be more flexible? Already I've gone through my pre-major-writing-project ritual of cleaning my study, throwing out old papers, catching up on correspondence, and just fussing and fidgeting. Even now I don't know if that's time wasted or a ritual that I need. And I still haven't been able to get started. I have to face up to the fact that I've got a lot of resistance to this project; after all, I feel like I just wrote WIP. I'm glad it's going into a second edition, but I'm as human as the next person. Beginning a big writing project intimidates me, makes me feel overwhelmed. And it's so beautiful outside. . . .
>
> I guess I'll just have to do what I did when I wrote WIP in the first place—make myself begin writing and count on the act of writing itself to make my anxieties go away. After all, I don't have to revise the book overnight. If I work steadily, the pages will add up eventually.

Once I did this freewriting, I was able to begin working on the revision itself. I needed to express my emotions and fears before I could begin drafting.

Managing the drafting process

Once you get past the initial hurdle of getting started, you'll probably experience the drafting process as a series of ebbs and flows. You may write intensely for a short period, stop and spend time reviewing what you've written, make a few notes about how you might best proceed, and then draft again more slowly—pausing now and then to reread what you've written. The process of rereading your text as it develops is an important part of the drafting process. Research shows that experienced writers not only reread their writing often while drafting but that they reread with an eye to such major concerns as the extent to which their draft responds to the needs and expectations of readers. Chapter 8, "Strategies for Successful Revision: Revising for Structure and Style," will present a number of strategies you can use to strengthen your ability to read work in progress. Here are some suggestions that should help make the *process* of drafting more efficient and productive.

Guidelines for drafting

1. DON'T TRY TO CORRECT—OR PERFECT—YOUR WRITING AS YOU DRAFT.

When you are drafting, your goal should be to get enough words on paper so that you can reflect on and revise your writing. The easiest way to produce a rough draft is to work at an even pace so the momentum of drafting helps you move steadily toward your goal. Stopping to worry whether a word is spelled correctly or to fiddle with a sentence can interrupt your momentum and throw you off balance. (If you're drafting at the computer, you may want to turn off the monitor so you can't edit.) Furthermore, most writers find that it's easier to delete unnecessary or repetitive material when they revise than to add new material. When drafting, your goal should be to get words on the page, not to make decisions more appropriate to revision. If you can't quite articulate an argument or formulate an example, write yourself a note and keep drafting. When you return to your draft you can fill in these gaps and omissions.

2. TRY TO KEEP IN TOUCH WITH YOUR "FELT SENSE," YOUR AWARENESS OF WHAT YOUR WRITING IS *DOING*, AS YOU DRAFT.

When drafting you naturally attend to many things. You stop and reread the words on the page. You reflect about your topic and assignment; you think about your readers. Additionally, particularly if you are an effective writer, you look at what you have written not just to see what is on the page or on-screen but also what is *not* there or *might be* there. Some writers call this kind of attention to their writing as it develops keeping in touch with their "felt sense" as writers.

You might think of "felt sense" as inspiration—and it is, in the sense that many writers, if interrupted while drafting, would find it difficult to articulate why they are writing a particular sentence or paragraph. The ability to develop "felt sense" does not require magical or mysterious gifts, however. Rather, writers develop "felt sense" when they are deeply immersed in their writing—when they are intensely involved not only with meaning (what they want to say) but with their entire rhetorical situation. Here, for instance, is a freewriting I did shortly after that on page 125.

It's amazing. Two days ago I was so blocked that I could only deal with my anxiety by freewriting. That loosened up the logjam and I was able at least to start. Then late yesterday something clicked: I realized that at last I'm back in WIP. I can't describe it very specifically, but suddenly I can see some of the issues I need to think about with the early chapters, can feel how the changes I want to make will affect the form of these chapters. I wouldn't call this inspiration—boy did I struggle for two days to get to this moment—and I know it won't last forever. But I'm sure grateful to have this feeling now.

To develop and maintain your "felt sense" while drafting, you need to draft for long enough periods—an hour, minimally, but longer if possible—so that you can become immersed in your writing. And though you are of necessity writing words, sentences, and paragraphs, you need to think about such issues as the clarity and appropriateness of your organization while drafting. Reflecting on concerns such as these—asking yourself questions like "Where am I going; am I still following my plan?" or "Will readers be able to understand the example I just wrote; do I need to elaborate on it?"—and jotting down notes about your current thoughts are good ways to keep in touch with your "felt sense" as you draft.

3. LEARN WHEN—AND HOW—TO STOP DRAFTING.

As mentioned earlier, a drafting session should last at least an hour, and *considerably* longer if possible. But how do you know when it's time to call it a day? Only you can determine the answer to this question, but here are some factors to consider. You don't want to interrupt your writing if you're really "hot," if words and ideas are flowing. But you don't want to write so long that you're exhausted, "written out," when you stop writing.

Ideally, you will naturally come to a stopping point, a moment when you feel you've solved a problem you've been wrestling with, concluded the section of your essay you've been working on. At this point it's a very good idea to take a few moments to jot down not just what you think you've accomplished in that drafting session, but what you need to do when you return to your writing. You may also wish to pose a few questions to yourself. "What's the best transition into this next major section of my essay?" you might write. "Which of the examples I've gathered should I use next?" If you're like many writers, your subconscious mind will reflect on these questions and present appropriate answers to you when you next sit down to draft.

If you get so frustrated or blocked with your writing that you feel you must stop or explode, try to make the best of a difficult situation by calling on your subconscious mind for help. Don't just crumble your paper and toss your pencil (or turn off your computer) in disgust. Spend a few moments jotting down the reasons you're having this problem, and then propose at least a few strategies you will try if you encounter these difficulties at the start of your next session. You may be relieved to discover when you next sit down to work that you suddenly know how to resolve your problem.

4. DRAFT WHEN YOU'RE NOT DRAFTING.

As the previous discussion illustrates, you can draw upon your mind's subconscious ability to see connections and to resolve problems through the process of incubation. When you incubate ideas, you stop thinking consciously about them and just let them develop in your mind while you relax, sleep, or occupy yourself with other projects. As a result of this period of incubation, you will often spontaneously recognize how to resolve a problem or answer a question.

You can't draw upon your mind's subconscious powers, however, if you don't build time for incubation into your drafting process. And don't confuse productive incubation with procrastination. Procrastination means avoiding or denying the writing process; incubation means recognizing and using the fluctuations of the process to your advantage.

Exploration

How do you typically draft an essay? How long do your drafting sessions usually last? What do you do when you run into problems drafting? Could one or more of the suggestions presented here enable you to draft more productively? How might you best implement these suggestions?

Spend five or ten minutes freewriting in response to these questions.

Group Activity

Meeting with a group of classmates, take turns reading your responses to the previous exploration. After each person has read, work together to answer these questions. (Be sure to appoint a recorder.)

1. What drafting strategies do those in your group most often employ?

2. How do group members overcome resistance to drafting? How long do drafting sessions typically last? How do you keep in touch with your "felt sense" while drafting?

3. Did any group members suggest drafting strategies that other members think they might like to experiment with? If so, briefly describe these strategies and explain why group members believe they might be useful.

4. Make a list of three conclusions about drafting with which all group members can agree. Make another list of at least three suggestions on how group members can draft more efficiently and productively.

Be prepared to share the results of your discussion with your classmates.

ORGANIZING AND DEVELOPING YOUR IDEAS

The noted British writer E. M. Forster once said: "How can I know what I think until I see what I say?" By working through drafts of work in progress, you gradually learn what you think about your subject. As you move from drafting to revising—an evolutionary process that proceeds differently with each writing project—you also increasingly become engaged with issues of style and structure. The question "What do I think about this subject?" becomes less important; the question "How can I best present my ideas to my readers?" more so.

This final section presents guidelines for organizing and developing your ideas that respond to this second question. As you read these guidelines, remember that they are suggestions only. Remember also that your response to these suggestions should be based on your understanding of your assignment, purpose, and rhetorical situation.

Guidelines for organizing and developing your ideas

1. CHECK TO DETERMINE IF YOU NEED TO EXPAND OR "UNPACK" CODE WORDS THAT MEAN A GREAT DEAL TO YOU, BUT NOT TO YOUR READERS.

If you've spent time employing various invention strategies, begin your drafting session by reviewing the material you've already generated, looking for ideas and details you can use in your draft but also those that need to be more fully developed. Often in rereading these explorations (and early drafts of work in progress) writers realize that they've relied on what Linda Flower calls "code words," words that convey considerable meaning for the writer but not necessarily for readers. Learning to recognize and expand or "unpack" code words in your writing can help you develop your ideas so that their significance is clear to readers.

Here, for instance, is a paragraph from a freewriting a student did when first assigned to write an essay about what the word "family" means to her. Rereading the freewriting at the start of her drafting section, she recognized a number of code words, which she underlined.

```
    When I think of the good things about my family, Christmas
comes most quickly to mind.  Our house was filled with such warmth
and joy.  Mom was busy, but she was happy.  Dad seemed less ab-
sorbed in his business, more the family man than the busy execu-
tive.  In the weeks before Christmas he almost never worked late
at the office, and he often arrived with brightly wrapped presents
that he would tantalizingly show us--before whisking them off to
their hiding place.  And at night we did fun things together to
prepare for the big day.
```

Words like "warmth and joy" undoubtedly evoke many strong connotations for the writer; most readers, however, would find these terms vague. By looking for code words in her freewriting, this writer has learned that in drafting she is going to have to provide readers with a number of concrete, specific details that enable them to visualize what she means.

Sometimes code words are vague words, like "warmth and joy," that need to be made more specific, often through concrete examples. At other times, code words can be professional or technical terms used and understood by "insiders" in a particular field or discipline, but not by others. The terms "rhetoric" and "rhetorical," for example, have a very specific and fully developed meaning for many teachers of writing. When I write articles for others in my field, I can use these terms with little explanation. In writing *Work in Progress*, I realized that I couldn't assume that you would understand these terms, so I had to expand and "unpack" their significance. As this example indicates, depending upon your rhetorical situation, a word may or may not need to be unpacked and expanded for readers.

2. RECOGNIZE THE IMPORTANCE OF SHARING YOUR CONTROLLING PURPOSE WITH YOUR READERS.

Earlier in this chapter, I emphasized the importance of establishing a controlling purpose for your writing. One obvious way to help organize a draft is to share this controlling purpose with your readers. How you can most effectively do so depends upon a number of situational factors. If you are working on a take-home essay examination for your history class, for example, you may wish to include a *thesis statement*, a single sentence that states the main idea of your essay, in your introduction. You may also decide to preview the main lines of argument you will use to support your position. After all, you reflect, your instructor is going to be reading many essay exams—and reading not for enjoyment but to evaluate your understanding of the subject. You don't want to irritate your instructor by making her hunt for your main point.

In other situations, including a specific thesis statement in the first paragraph of your essay may not be necessary, or even desirable. If you are writing an essay about what the word "family" means to you, you might decide that you don't want to reveal the main point of your essay at the start. Instead, you might begin with a specific, detailed example, one that will create interest in your essay and "show," rather than "tell," what "family" means to you.

Readers quickly become irritated if they feel they're reading unorganized, disconnected prose or if their expectations about how a certain kind of writing should be organized are violated. For these reasons, sharing your intentions with readers and providing cues about how you will achieve them is essential. By analyzing your rhetorical situation and by studying how others engaged in similar writing tasks have fulfilled this obligation to readers, you can determine strategies to use to keep in touch with your readers.

3. TAKE ADVANTAGE OF CONVENTIONAL METHODS OF ORGANIZING INFORMATION—BUT BE SURE NOT TO DO SO IN A FORMULAIC OR OVERLY RIGID MANNER.

When you begin drafting, you don't need to start from scratch. Instead, you can draw upon conventional methods of organization, methods that reflect natural ways of analyzing and explaining information. Suppose that you have been studying recent political and economic changes in Eastern Europe and must write an essay about some aspect of this topic. Perhaps in your reading you were struck by the different responses of Polish and Czechoslovakian citizens to a new free-market economy. You could draw upon conventional methods of *comparing and contrasting* to organize your analysis. Or perhaps you wish to discuss the impact that severe industrial pollution in Poland could have on the development of a Western-style economy. After *classifying* the most prevalent forms of industrial pollution, you could discuss the consequences of this pollution for Poland's economy.

As these examples indicate, your subject may naturally lend itself to certain methods of organization. In some cases, you may be able to use a single method of organization—such as comparison, definition, cause-effect, or problem-solution—to organize your entire essay. More often, however, you will draw upon several methods of organization to present your ideas. In considering how you can best draw upon conventional methods of organizing information, remember that you should not impose these methods formulaically, or in an overly rigid manner. Begin thinking about how to organize your draft by reflecting on your goals as a writer and your rhetorical situation. If your analysis suggests that one or more methods of organizing information represent commonsensical, logical ways of approaching your subject, use them in drafting. But remember: form should grow out of meaning, not be imposed on it.

This chapter has discussed a number of strategies for successful planning and drafting. Throughout, it has emphasized the importance of being pragmatic, flexible, and goal-oriented and of asking yourself questions before and while you write. More than anything else, writing is a process of thinking critically and making choices, trying these choices out either in your mind or on paper, and then evaluating their effects and making necessary adjustments. Planning and drafting are essential components of this process.

Activities for Thought, Discussion, and Writing

1. Think of a time when you simply couldn't get your writing going. What did you do to get beyond this block? How well did your efforts work—and why? After reflecting on your experience, write an essay (humorous or serious) about how you cope with writer's block.
2. Choose a writing assignment (for this or another class) that you have just begun working on. After reflecting on your ideas, develop and write a workable plan for this essay. While drafting the essay, keep a record of your activities. How helpful was your plan? Was it realistic? Did you revise your plan as you wrote? What can you learn about your writing process from this experience? Be prepared to discuss this experience with members of your group or with your class.
3. Interview a person working in the field you hope to enter after graduation to discover how he or she plans and drafts on-the-job writing. How does your interviewee's profession and work sched-

ule influence his or her preferred methods of planning and drafting? How often does this person write alone or as a member of a group or team? Does he or she rely upon any technological aids to make these activities easier, such as using a tape recorder for dictation or using a computer network? Write an essay summarizing the results of your interview.

CHAPTER 7

STRATEGIES FOR SUCCESSFUL REVISION: MANAGING THE REVISION PROCESS

What is revision? When does it occur in the writing process, and what does it involve? In the broadest sense, revision occurs throughout the writing process. If you write a tentative first sentence for an essay, decide that it doesn't work, and cross it out, you have revised. Although revision can occur at any time, you will probably revise most intensively after you have written a rough or working draft. At this point, you have managed to articulate at least a preliminary statement of your ideas. Revision challenges you to look at this statement from a dual perspective. You must read your work with your own intentions in mind. But you must also read your work from your reader's perspective so that you can recognize how your discussion may confuse, mislead, or irritate your reader.

Reading thus plays a crucial role in revision. When you read over your work, you attempt to discover weaknesses you can remedy and strengths you can build upon. Consequently, you must think about not just what is actually in your text, but what is *not* there and what *could* be there. You must read the part (the introduction, say, or several paragraphs) while still keeping in mind the whole.

As a writer, you should have a healthy respect for the demands of revision, but you should not be overwhelmed by it. By studying both your own writing process and the products of that process (the essays and other papers that you write), you can develop an awareness of your strengths and weaknesses that will enable you to revise both more effectively and more efficiently. As you write and revise, and as you read and respond to the work of others, you'll discover that revising can be the most rewarding part of the writing process. For when you revise, you have the satisfaction of bringing your ideas to completion in an appropriate form.

Here is how Ellen Goodman, a popular columnist, describes the satisfaction of revising.

> What makes me happy is rewriting. In the first draft you get your ideas and your theme clear, if you are using some kind of metaphor you get that established, and certainly you have to know where you're coming out. But the next time through it's like cleaning house, getting rid of all the junk, getting things in the right order, tightening things up.
>
> *ELLEN GOODMAN*

You don't have to be a professional writer to feel the same sense of satisfaction. Christine Hoekstra, a junior English major, describes her experience of revision in very similar terms.

> Revision is an extremely important part of the writing pro-
> cess for me now. It's really the part of writing where I feel the
> bulk of the work gets done--where the story takes shape, the essay
> is created. I couldn't imagine writing without revising.

For writers like Christine Hoekstra and Ellen Goodman, revision is the heart of the writing process.

Chapters 7 and 8 will enable you to experience the satisfaction of successful revision. Chapter 7 focuses upon revision as a process or activity. It answers questions like the following:

- What is revision? How does revision differ from proofreading or correcting mistakes?
- How can I use responses to work in progress to help establish priorities for revision?
- How can I learn to read my own writing more objectively so that I can recognize strengths and weaknesses?
- How can I develop strategies that will help me revise more effectively and efficiently?

Chapter 8 discusses ways to improve your essay's structure and style. Together, Chapters 7 and 8 should help you understand why writers like Ellen Goodman and Christine Hoekstra can't imagine writing without revising.

_____ REVISING THROUGH RE-VISION _____

You can learn a great deal about revision just by considering the word itself. *Revision* combines the root word *vision* with the prefix *re*, meaning "again." When you revise, you "see again": you develop a new vision of your essay's shape, or of the most emphatic way to improve the "flow" of a paragraph to help readers understand your point.

Revision is very different from proofreading, an activity that generally occurs at the end of the writing process. When you proofread, you are concerned mainly with correctness. Does your essay have any errors of grammar, punctuation, or usage? Are your words spelled correctly? Do you need to fix any obvious problems of word choice or sentence structure? Proofreading is the tidying up that concludes the writing process.

Exploration

Using the preceding distinction between revision and proofreading, think back to previous writing experiences. When, and for what reasons, have you revised your work rather than just proofread it? How would you characterize these revision experiences? Were they satisfying? Frustrating? Why? Freewrite for five or ten minutes about these revision experiences.

Unlike proofreading, revision most typically is a process of discovery, one where much more than correctness is at stake. Because it generates growth and change, revision sometimes requires you to take risks. Often these risks are minor. If you spend three or four minutes attempting to find just the right words to clarify an idea, for instance, you've only lost a little time if you're unsuccessful. Sometimes, however, when you revise you make large-scale or global decisions with potentially more significant consequences.

After writing the first draft of an essay, for instance, Matt Brown, a freshman physics student, met with members of his group to talk about his writing. He was unhappy with his draft, which argued that newspaper carriers work too hard and are paid too little, given the difficulty of their work. The members of his group were sympathetic to Matt's problems, but they couldn't help teasing Matt a bit. After all, how serious are a newspaper carrier's problems in the overall scheme of things? And if delivering newspapers is such a difficult, low-paying job, why do so many young people continue to deliver papers?

Gradually, Matt recognized that he needed to take a different approach to his material. He realized that he could more effectively encourage his readers to empathize with carriers by writing a humorous essay, one that pointed out the problems carriers face but did so in a lighthearted manner. Once he made this decision to revise his approach to his topic, Matt found that he was able to write and revise more quickly with much less frustration. In his case, taking the risk of trying a new approach paid off.

REVISING COLLABORATIVELY: BENEFITING FROM RESPONSES TO WORK IN PROGRESS

As Matt Brown's experience indicates, you can draw upon the responses of others to help you re-see your writing. Talking with others about your writing can also provide crucial social support. You may write alone a good deal of the time, but writing does not have to be a lonely process.

As a student, you can turn to many people for support and for responses to work in progress. Some of these individuals, such as your instructor and classmates, can approach your writing as insiders. They know the assignment you are working on and the standards for evaluation. Others, such as your tutor, friends, or family members, must approach your writing as outsiders. The differences in the situations of these potential respondents will influence how they respond; these differences should also influence how you use their responses. Whether the person responding to your writing is your roommate or your instructor, finally you must decide how to interpret and apply his or her comments and criticisms.

Friends and family members

You can certainly ask friends and family members to read and respond to your writing, but you should understand the strengths and weaknesses they bring as readers. One important strength is that you trust them—or, presumably, you wouldn't ask them to read your writing. Unless you spend time filling them in, however, friends and family members won't understand the nature of your assignment or your instructor's standards for evaluation. This lack of knowledge, as well as their natural desire to see you do well, may cause them to be less critical of your work than other readers might be. Simply saying "It looks good to me" is not a helpful response to work in progress.

Despite these potential problems, friends and family members can provide useful responses to work in progress. When you are considering getting such responses, keep these suggestions in mind.

Guidelines for responses from friends and family

- Choose the person you ask to read your work carefully. Is he or she a competent writer? Have you benefited from his or her response in the past?
- Recognize that this person can't fully understand the assignment or situation, even if you take some time to explain it. Take this lack of knowledge into consideration when evaluating his or her comments.
- Draw upon family members' and friends' strengths as outsiders. Rather than asking them to respond in detail to your essay, for instance, ask them to give a general impression or response. You might also ask such readers to tell you what they think is the main idea or controlling purpose of your essay. If they can't identify one, or if their understanding differs substantially from your own, you've gained very useful information about your essay.
- Ask your friends or family to read your work out loud to you *without having first read it silently themselves*. When you read your own work, you unconsciously compensate to reflect your intentions. Listening to someone else read your work can help you hear problems that you couldn't detect through more conventional analysis. If your reader falters over a phrase or has to read a sentence several times before it makes sense, that may indicate a stylistic or logical problem.
- Don't rely solely on the response of a friend or family member. Try to get at least one other informed response to your work.

Classmates

Chapter 1 discusses some of the ways your instructor may be using groups in your writing class and presents guidelines for effective group participation (pages 17 to 20). If you have been getting responses to your writing from fellow students, you know how helpful their reactions and advice can be. Whenever you ask others to read work in progress, you have one major goal: you want to know how your readers respond to your writing. Does your essay "work" for your readers? How could you strengthen your essay to make it more persuasive and interesting?

Because your classmates know your instructor and assignment as insiders, they can provide particularly effective responses to your writing. Students participating in writing groups typically form strong bonds; they genuinely want group members to do well, to develop as writers. Yet group members can often read work in progress more objectively than can family members and friends, whose judgments can be colored by affection for the writer. When student writing groups function well, they provide a helpful balance of support and constructive criticism.

To insure that *your* writing group works well, follow these guidelines.

Guidelines for responses from your writing group

ADVICE FOR WRITERS

- Learn to distinguish between your writing and yourself. Your classmates are reading your work to help you, not to criticize or discourage you. Don't respond defensively to suggestions for improvement, and don't argue with readers' responses. Instead, use these responses to gain insight into your writing.
- Prepare carefully for group meetings. Identify the areas where you think you need help before you meet with your group. Formulate the questions about your work that you most need to have answered.
- Always bring a *legible* draft to class.
- Be sure that the draft you bring is a working draft, not a jumble of brainstorming ideas, freewriting, and partly detailed planning notes.
- Provide information that will enable readers to understand your goals for your writing. If you are addressing your essay to a specific group of readers—members of a certain organization, for example, or readers of a particular magazine—inform classmates about your rhetorical situation.
- Remember that your fellow students' responses are just that: responses. Treat your readers' responses to your essay seriously, for they are a potentially powerful indication of the strengths and weaknesses of your essay. But maintain

your own authority as the writer. What all this means, finally, is that your readers' responses may be useful evidence about the effectiveness of your essay, but you must always decide how to intepret these responses—what to accept and what to reject.

ADVICE FOR READERS

- Follow the golden rule: respond to the writing of others as you would like them to respond to your work.
- Don't attempt to "play teacher." Your job is not to evaluate or grade your classmates' writing, but to respond to it. Sometimes you may find it most helpful to make teacherlike comments. You may tell your classmate that his or her essay's organization is unclear, for example, or that the evidence provided for an argument is weak. At other times, you may choose to make what Peter Elbow calls reader-based comments about your classmates' work. In *Writing with Power*, Elbow presents three major ways to provide reader-based feedback for writers:
    - [Describe] what was happening to you, moment by moment, as you were reading the piece of writing.
    - Summarize the writing: give your understanding of what it says or what happened.
    - Make up some images for the writing and the transaction it creates with readers.

In giving reader-based feedback to classmates, remember that your major goal is to provide what Elbow calls "movies of a reader's mind." Be honest, but feel free to be creative too. Elbow suggests, for instance, that you use images to convey the persona of the writer:

> What images of the writer come to mind? Hunched over a desk? Sprawled on a divan? Sitting on a beach? How does the writer dress? Hold his body? Wear his hat? Let all images just be intuitive, uncalculated.

You don't need to be an expert to provide responses like these. You simply need to be an attentive, honest, supportive reader.

Group Activity

Take five minutes to think about responses to your work that you have received from classmates. Freewrite for five or ten minutes about these experiences, and then draw up a list of statements describing the kinds of responses that you have found most helpful in the past.

Bring this list to class, and meet with a group of classmates. Begin by having each group member read his or her list. Then, working together, write a series of suggestions for helpful peer response. (You can draw upon comments made in this chapter, but if you do, use your own words to state your suggestions.) Have one student record your group's suggestions. You may wish to copy these recommendations and distribute them to group members to guide future peer responses.

Peer tutors

When students go to a campus writing center, they sometimes misunderstand the tutors' role and situation. They may regard tutors as editors trained to correct their writing. Or they may consider tutors to be faculty aides standing in for "real" instructors who are unavailable or too busy to meet with students. Neither view is accurate.

Tutors are neither editors nor substitute instructors. Many, you may be surprised to discover, aren't even English majors but come from other disciplines: geology, engineering, geography, business, and education (to mention only a few). Whatever their areas of academic interest, tutors are good writers who work well with other students. Like your classmates, your tutor's main job is to *respond* to your writing, not analyze or critique it extensively. But, unlike your classmates, your tutor has been formally trained in peer-response methods. Because tutors work with many students, they have also read and responded to a broad range of writing.

Before you meet with a tutor, you should reread your writing and identify some goals for your conference. (Most conferences are thirty minutes to one hour, so make sure that your goals are realistic given these time limits.) When you do meet with your tutor, discuss these goals. You may also want to provide background information, especially about your assignment. Finally, don't expect your tutor to do your work for you—your tutor's job is to respond and advise, not to correct or rewrite your essay.

Your instructor

Because your instructor is such an important reader for your written assignments, you want to be certain that you make good use of any written comments he or she provides. Use the following suggestions to help yourself benefit fully from these comments.

Guidelines for using your instructor's responses

- Read your instructor's written comments carefully. They are the clearest, most specific indication you have of the degree to which you have fulfilled the assignment.
- Read your instructor's comments *more than once*. When you first read them, you'll be reading mainly to understand your instructor's general response to your writing. That's a useful but limited reading, one that does little to help you set goals for revision. Later, read the comments again several times. In these later readings, see if you can use these comments to help you establish priorities for revision.
- Recognize the difference between your instructor's local and global comments. Local comments indicate specific questions, problems, or errors. For example, *awkward sentence* is a local comment indicating some stylistic or structural problem with a specific sentence. Global comments address broader issues, such as your essay's organization or the effectiveness of your evidence. The global comments, in particular, can help you set large-scale goals for revision.
- Meet with your instructor if you don't understand his or her comments. Even if you do understand the comments, you may wish to meet to discuss your plans for revision.

Friends, family members, classmates, tutors, instructors: all can provide helpful responses to work in progress. None of these responses should take the place of your own judgment, however. Nor should you automatically accept responses (whether criticism or praise) as accurate. Your job as the writer is to *interpret* and *evaluate* these responses, using both them and your own assessment of your rough draft to establish goals for revising.

BUILDING OBJECTIVITY TOWARD WORK IN PROGRESS

As the person who must finally evaluate your own writing as well as interpret the responses of others, you need to develop strategies for objectively viewing your own work in progress. Building such objectivity enables you to achieve the distance necessary to make the hard decisions that revision sometimes requires. The following suggestions should help you develop this objectivity.

Guidelines for revising objectively

1. PLAN AT LEAST A SHORT BREAK BETWEEN WRITING AND REVISING.

It's difficult to critique your rough draft if you've just finished composing it. Your own intentions are still too fresh for you to be able to read your words as they are, not as you intended them to be. Most experienced writers prefer to have at least twenty-four hours between writing and revising. If your schedule won't permit a day's break, spend at least an hour or two away from your draft before revising.

2. PREPARE MENTALLY FOR A REVISING SESSION.

Taking a break from your essay before revising can help you distance yourself from work in progress. But you also need to consider how you can best prepare for—and begin—revising. You may find it helpful, for instance, to review your assignment and your rhetorical situation before you reread your draft. As you do so, ask yourself questions like these:

- To what extent does my draft respond to this assignment?
- To what extent does my draft respond to my rhetorical situation as I have analyzed it?
- What state is my draft in? In other words, how rough or near completion is my draft?
- What goals should I establish for this revising session, and how should I fulfill them? What should I work on first?

By preparing mentally before you begin revising, you will make the most efficient and productive use of your time.

3. REVISE WORK IN PROGRESS FROM TYPED OR PRINTED COPY.

We all grow used to our own handwriting, no matter how awkward or homely our scrawl. Perhaps for this reason, you, like many writers, may find that you're less critical of handwritten than typed or computer-printed drafts. To counteract this tendency, you may find it helpful to type your essays or enter them into a computer as you write and revise. (If you compose at the computer, you're one step ahead.) Once your words appear in neat but anonymous type, you often can see problems that were invisible before. Revising from typed or printed copy can not only help you detect local stylistic problems, it can also help you to recognize global problems of organization and development.

Although some writers prefer to revise on-screen, many people find it easier to revise on hard copy, enter these revisions into the computer, and then print the results. Marsha Carper, a student who revises on the computer, describes this strategy as follows: "When I revise, I make the changes on the printout, then type them in and print another copy. I read this, then make more changes and continue this process until I am satisfied with the product or I have run out of time." Whether you revise using a hard copy or working on-screen, be sure to save copies of all stages your essay goes through. You may wish to save each stage of your revisions on disk as a separate file ("essay 1," "essay 2," etc.). Or you may wish to print revisions as you proceed. Either alternative will work well and will make it possible for you to return to—and use—earlier drafts.

3. USE OUTLINING AND SUMMARIZING TO HELP YOU "X-RAY" YOUR DRAFT.

Determining if your essay is effectively organized—if your ideas build logically and your paragraphs flow naturally—is an important part of revision. Because you are so familiar with your own intentions, you may find it difficult to assess this aspect of work in progress accurately. Two related strategies, outlining and summarizing, can enable you objectively to assess the strengths and weaknesses of your essay's organization and development.

Both processes are quite simple. To outline your essay, for instance, analyze the parts of your essay by converting them to the conventional outline format. To illustrate how you might use outlining when you revise, here is a review of an exhibit of photographs written by a freshman majoring in art.

LIVING COLOR

Living Color is an exhibit of nature photography in color, now on display at the Memorial Union Concourse. The show will be on until December 19. Ray Atkeson, Deborah De Wit, Neil Folberg, William Garnett, Al Hoster, Larry Olson, and Eskire Wood are the photographers listed to be in the show. I couldn't actually find any of Al Hoster's work, but the rest each have three to seven works in the exhibit.

I'm glad I saw the exhibit, but I was not thrilled by it.
The photographs are all classic calendar-type nature scenes and
landscapes--pretty but without depth. They show the diversity and
beauty of nature, but other than that don't make any profound
statements. I was also disappointed with the presentation. Besides the fact that Al Hoster's work was not shown, Wood did not
have a write-up. The other photographers had write-ups describing
their backgrounds, telling of former exhibits and publications,
and in some cases explaining their methods of photography, such as
the cameras, film, and other equipment that they use. Also, the
lighting in the Concourse is bad. The harsh fluorescent lights
glare off the display cases, making it hard to see the photographs. I did appreciate the write-ups on the photographers, especially Larry Olson's, which he wrote himself in the first
person. Olson described his techniques and some of his philosophy
of photography. Here is a brief excerpt: "Photography is an art
form, a means of communication, with unlimited potential. Yet, at
the same time, limitations due to the technical aspects of the
camera, lens, and film must be reckoned with. On one hand, it is
an easy task to set a lens aperture and press a button, but to
capture the essence or inner spirit is a different realm al-
together." (While reading this, I overheard a man with an opinion
different from Olson's. He had just noticed the price on one of
Olson's photographs: "One hundred and fifty bucks? You've got to
be kidding. You could go up to Olympic National Park, buy a camera, take the same picture, and have your film processed for under
that." I didn't point out the photographs across the hall for
$800.)

Although I was not very pleased with the exhibit, I thought
it was worth seeing. The write-ups provided interesting informa-

tion, and it was a nice study break. I didn't need to use my

brain. It was rather like listening to light, pleasant music.

Although you don't gain much intellectually from listening to such

music, it relaxes you and helps clear your mind.

The writer of this draft was aware that it had problems, but he had difficulty pinpointing them. Working with his instructor, the student outlined the basic structure or "skeleton" of his essay. His instructor suggested that he begin with a statement of his controlling purpose and, after outlining, put question marks next to whatever parts seemed to reveal a problem. The student constructed this modified formal outline, using phrases rather than sentences.

OUTLINE OF "LIVING COLOR"

controlling purpose: "I'm glad I saw the exhibit, but I was not

thrilled by it." (?)

   I. Introduction to the exhibit

      A. Place

      B. Artists

      C. Number of works

  II. Quality of the work and its presentation (?)

      A. Photographs

      B. Write-ups by photographers (?)

      C. Presentation of photographs

 III. Usefulness of the write-ups

      A. Larry Olson's write-up

      B. A viewer's comments (?)

  IV. Conclusion

This outline revealed several weaknesses of the draft. The only sentence that the writer could identify as a potential controlling purpose, for instance, is quite vague. Once this passage was isolated from the rest of the essay, the writer could recognize its weakness. The outline also identified organizational problems. The writer could only make the second paragraph fit the outline format by giving it a double title, "quality of the work and its presentation."

Yet the outline heading, like the paragraph it summed up, should refer to one major idea, not two or three. Even given this heading, the writer marked point B about the photographers' write-ups with a question mark because it didn't fully relate to either of the two major ideas organizing this section. The outline did show that the third section focused on just a single idea, the usefulness of the artists' statements, but this idea had no real connection with point B about a passing viewer's comments.

Outlining this essay enabled the writer to recognize that his draft was little more than a loosely organized series of statements about the show and his response to it. When he reviewed the outline with his instructor, he could see that the ideas in his essay needed to be more fully developed. For most of the outline's three main sections, only a single sentence supported each of the subtopics. This draft, as the outline revealed, was itself little more than an outline of an essay. It needed more information to give it depth and force.

If you find the conventions of outlining restrictive or intimidating, you can accomplish the same purpose by writing brief summaries of each paragraph of your essay. Generally, these summaries should indicate the content and purpose of each paragraph. (When you summarize a paragraph's purpose you indicate how it functions for readers—to interest readers in the topic, for example, or to provide support or evidence.) In summarizing the first paragraph of "Living Color," for example, you might note that this paragraph provides readers with basic information about the location of the exhibit and the artists included in it. By analyzing the summaries, you can often identify major problems of organization and development in your writing.

Application

Choose an essay that you are currently working on, and use the outline or summary method to analyze its organization and development. Choose a classmate who has also either outlined or summarized an essay, and trade papers. If your classmate outlined his or her essay, construct your own outline of that essay. If your classmate summarized his or her essay, write your own summary. Once you have completed this activity, look together at your analyses of your essays. To what extent do your summaries or outlines coincide? To what extent do they differ? How did this exchange enable you better to understand the strengths and weaknesses of your essay?

_____ FORMULATING PERSONAL GUIDELINES _____
FOR REVISION

As you gain experience writing and revising, you will better understand your own strengths and weaknesses as a writer. More importantly, you will learn to build on your strengths and diminish or compensate for your weaknesses. One way to express (and heighten) your growing self-knowledge is to formulate your own personal guidelines for revision. These guidelines might include reminders about the problems you typically encounter when you revise and the strategies that you have most successfully used in the past to respond to them. You might also note work habits that encourage successful revision.

The following personal guidelines for revision were developed by students in my freshman composition classes.

BOB DWONCH

1. Write first draft as soon as possible, leaving time to revise.
2. Revise when I feel fresh and motivated; I think more clearly then.
3. Leave time for peer response.
4. When reading a rough draft, watch for complex ideas that I've oversimplified.
5. Check overall organization with a skeleton outline. Does the essay fit together?
6. Check each sentence for clear, concise ideas expressed succinctly.
7. Proofread for punctuation and other final adjustments.

SANDY SMITH

1. Make sure to have the best draft possible when I bring it to class for response.
2. Ask others to read it later if necessary.
3. Before revising try to take the time to outline my paper to see if it's well organized; also ask someone to read my paper to me so I can hear how it sounds.
4. Revise in stages. Work on content, organization, and style before correcting punctuation and spelling errors.
5. Don't do all my revising at once; it helps to take breaks.

JOSH BURGESS

1. Allow more time for revision than for writing.
2. Schedule set times for revision.
3. Be open-minded when others respond to my writing.

4. Don't be afraid to get other people's opinions of an essay before I'm done revising it.
5. Always ask myself the following questions:
   — Is this direct or wordy?
   — Am I sticking to the topic?
   — Could the sentence structure be improved?

KRISTI TRASK

1. Go back to my analysis of my rhetorical situation when I start to lose track of what I want to do.
2. Allow time between drafting and revising so I can get distance.
3. Welcome suggestions for revision; don't be defensive.
4. Look at the whole of the essay first, then the parts.
5. Write down ideas for revision as they occur—don't expect to remember them.
6. Allow enough time!

Application

Take five or ten minutes to reflect upon your previous experiences revising. What aspects of revision have you managed well? How could you improve your abilities as a reviser? After thinking about these questions, write your own personal guidelines for revision.

REVISION IN ACTION: A CASE STUDY

What kinds of changes do writers make as they revise? The following case study, which chronicles the development of an essay by Kira Wennstrom, a freshman biology major, should give you a clearer, more concrete understanding of how revision works.

Kira's assignment was relatively broad and open-ended; it specified only that Kira should write an essay describing some personal experience and explaining the significance of that experience. Kira had few problems coming up with a topic. During the previous summer she had cared for two children while their mother was in the hospital. The experience had taught her a great deal about herself and about the bond between parents and children. She wanted to explore her experience further and to share what she had learned with others.

Kira describes herself as a heavy planner, and her self-assessment seems accurate. She did much of the planning for this essay in her head, rather than on paper. She thought for several days about her experience, and she also discussed it with friends and classmates. By the time Kira sat down to write the first draft, reproduced below, she had thought through her ideas so carefully that she was able to write using only a brief list of major ideas as a guide.

Kira's first draft is reprinted here. Its paragraphs are numbered for ease of reference. Also included are some of the written comments that members of Kira's writing group made in response to her draft.

Kira's first draft

(1)   While my friends swam and tanned at the lake, I ran a household with two incredibly rambunctious and mildly accident-prone children. However, I think in the long run my time was better spent than that of my peers.

1st ¶ seems a bit weak, Kira.

(2)   When Josh and Timmy's mother had to go into the hospital, she asked me if I would be willing to stay with the boys until she could come home. I quickly accepted. However, the few days I had planned on became two weeks, and there was work and trouble and responsibility I never imagined.

Do you really want to emphasize these negative factors so strongly?

(3)   Since the children were only five and eight, I couldn't leave them alone in the house; I had to be there or be with them 24 hours a day. In addition to the normal precautions of making sure I knew where they were, I also had to worry about their father. He and the boys' mother had divorced several years ago, and there were still problems with custody.

Nice concrete details in these ¶'s kira, but do you need them all?

(4)   I spent my days as a housewife: planning

meals, doing laundry, cleaning house. I handled
all the typical minor emergencies. There were
scraped knees to be washed and bandaged, fights to
be settled, Kool-Aid to be cleaned out of the carpet, and once or twice I had to rescue pots and
pans from the sandbox to cook dinner.

The sentence structure flows smoothly here, & during the rest of the essay, too.

(5)   My evenings were spent preparing meals and
dishes and settling disputes as to who was going
to bed when and whose turn it was to choose the TV
channel. After things settled down and the kids
were in their rooms, I was finally left alone to
read or watch the Tonight Show before I hit my own
pillow, exhausted. However, my nights were seldom
complete without being awakened to check out at
least one scary noise or to deny a request for a
midnight snack.

(6)   I had agreed to care for the kids knowing
that it wouldn't be all fun, but I never dreamed
the amount of laundry two active children can go
through. I did a load of wash almost every other
day, and was just barely keeping up. I was also
amazed by the complexities of working out a simple
dinner schedule. There was no single entree that
both boys liked. They would sooner have starved,
I think, than eat anything that didn't come in a
wrapper, a can, or a box. Gradually, as the days
passed, however, I began to realize what it is
about parenting that makes my mother's eyes bug
out at the end of the day. I loved those children
terribly.

whew – this feels abrupt!

(7)   I discovered that perhaps the hardest part of parenting is the loss of privacy. I never had a moment to myself, completely to myself, when I could just let my mind catch up to the rest of me. Having always been used to spending hours alone and enjoying my own company, I found it incredibly difficult sometimes to force a smile when one of the boys interrupted a quiet minute with yet another demand on my time. I learned to treasure the ten or so minutes of silent darkness between the time I shut off the light and the time I went to sleep.

Now that I've read your essay twice, Kira, I can see that you want to balance the work of caring for Josh & Timothy with your love of them. Develop more fully?

(8)   My own mother, whom I telephoned with great regularity, seemed to find enormous delight in the fact that I was going through the same thing that she had been trying (and failing) to explain for seventeen-odd years. She gave me marvelous advice and brilliant suggestions on how to cope with the whole mess and then, I am sure, hung up the phone and laughed her socks off in utter vindictiveness. But I can forgive her this, because although I didn't realize it then, what I was experiencing would prove invaluable.

(9)   I look at mothers, especially mine, with better understanding now, with less scorn. I look at children with a little more appreciation. I use my time alone more carefully now; I spend it wisely, now that I know how crucial it is. Most of all, I value my freedom more highly than ever because I know what it is to lose that freedom. As

esp. nice sentence structure

your conclusion might have more impact if you helped readers

much as I cared about those children, it's not

time yet to give up my claim to my life. I under-

stand now how important it is to live for yourself

before you live for anyone else.

understand how much you came to love Josh & Timmy.

Kira was fortunate when she began revising. Her first draft had many strengths which members of her writing group had acknowledged. But they had suggestions for improvement as well. A number of them commented in their closing notes to Kira that her abrupt shift in paragraph six to a strong statement of her love for Josh and Timmy confused them since it conflicted with her previous emphasis on all the "work and trouble" involved in caring for the two boys. This potential contradiction also made it difficult for Kira's readers to grasp the significance of her final paragraph; several commented that they weren't sure, finally, what point she was trying to make in this paragraph.

After Kira thought about her readers' responses to her draft, she met with a tutor to establish the following priorities for revision:

```
-- work on intro
-- most important: try to show more clearly why Josh and Timmy
   meant so much to me, despite all the work
-- see if all that housekeeping detail needs to stay; cut some?
-- play with style a bit
```

Although Kira's list is (quite appropriately) informal, it nicely identifies several ways that she could improve the focus, organization, and content of her essay. It's not possible to show all the stages that Kira's draft went through, for this process involved many scribbles, inserts, and crumpled papers. But the final draft, reprinted below, demonstrates that Kira's analysis enabled her truly to revise her essay, to "see again" how she could most effectively make her point. Here is Kira's revised essay with comments in the margin pointing out some of her most important changes.

Kira's final draft

THE BOYS OF SUMMER

(1)   Few teenagers get the chance to be parents,

and for those who do, it's usually too late to

change their minds. One summer, though, I was

New introduction gets the reader's attention.

given the opportunity to become a mother--without
the lifetime commitment.

(2)   When Josh and Timmy's mother had to go into
the hospital, she asked me if I would be willing
to stay with them until she could come home. I
quickly accepted, envisioning a few days of playing "mommy" to the kids whose babysitter I had
been for about two years. However, my visions of
happy homemaking paled when the few days became
two weeks and the trouble and responsibility of
being a parent began to hit home.

(3)   Since the children were only five and eight,
I couldn't leave them alone in the house; I had to
be with them twenty-four hours a day. While my
friends swam and tanned at the lake, I spent my
days as a housewife: planning meals, doing laundry, cleaning house. I handled all the minor
emergencies that seem to follow little boys around
like shadows. There were fights to be settled,
Kool-Aid to be cleaned out of the carpet, and once
or twice pots and pans to be rescued from the
sandbox to cook dinner.

Revised paragraph consolidates details on situation from three draft paragraphs.

(4)   My days were whittled away with meals,
dishes, and mountains of laundry. I did a load of
wash almost every other day and just barely kept
up. I was also amazed by the complexities of
working out a simple dinner schedule. There was
no single entree that both boys approved of, and
it was like walking hot coals to try to serve anything new. They would sooner have starved, I

Concise and balanced paragraph combines details on routine work from three draft paragraphs.

think, than eat anything that didn't come out of a
wrapper, box, or can. Most of all, though, I
missed my privacy. Because the children were so
dependent on me, I never had a moment to myself.
I sometimes found it very difficult to force a
smile when one of the boys interrupted a quiet moment with yet another demand on my time.

(5)   As the days passed and I became more profi-
cient at running my little household, I began to
realize a very surprising thing. Despite the
trouble they caused, despite the demands they
made, my two charges were becoming very special
people to me--people who needed me.

Paragraph prepares readers for the shift from responsibilities to emotions.

(6)   I remember taking the boys to the beach one
afternoon and buying them a corn-dog-and-soda
lunch with Gummi worms for dessert. Josh, who was
older than Timmy, loved the lake and delighted in
swimming out just past the dock where the water
was especially cool. Timmy was afraid to follow
his brother and sat beside me on the sand, sucking
on his last Gummi worm and looking wistfully out
to where Josh was laughing and diving. After half
an hour of this, Timmy touched me on the arm and
said, "Take me to Josh, Kira."

New dramatic scene shows readers Kira's deep feelings for the boys.

(7)   "Are you sure, Timmy?"

(8)   "Mm-hm. But hold on tight to me."

(9)   So I held on tight to him, and we waded into
Rainy Lake's cool green water. When we got out
past the point where Timmy could touch bottom, he
locked his arms around my neck and pressed his

face against my shoulder, but he didn't ask me to take him back. As we neared the spot where Josh was playing, I called, and he swam over to us. We splashed each other and giggled, and Timmy clutched me with one hand and Josh with the other. Their bodies were slick like seals, warm against me in the chill lake water. Together we swam out to where none of us could touch bottom, and they held on to me to keep afloat. They trusted me to keep them safe, and I would have drowned before I broke that trust. I loved them.

(10)   Because I loved them, the children had a hold on me like nothing else I know. Simply by going out to play each day, they gave me more hours of worry than I like to admit. Every time one of them was late coming home, I imagined all the dreadful things that might be happening--an angry dog, a child molester, a car accident--until he walked through the door, perfectly safe and wanting supper. When one of them was angry or hurt, I hurt. They were children, and it's so hard to be a child sometimes. Almost as hard as being a mother.

Paragraph adds detail that helps clarify Kira's feelings.

(11)   My own mother, whom I telephoned with great regularity, seemed to find enormous delight in the fact that I was going through the same things she had been trying (and failing) to explain to me for seventeen-odd years. She gave me marvelous suggestions on how to cope with the demands of my new family and then, I am sure, hung

Effective new transition connects paragraphs.

up the phone and laughed her socks off in utter

vindictiveness. But I can forgive her this be-

cause, although I didn't know it then, what I was

experiencing was invaluable.

(12)   I look at mothers, especially my own, with

better understanding now, with less scorn. I

look at children with a little more appreciation.

I use my time alone more carefully now; I spend

it wisely, now that I know how crucial it is.

Most of all, I value my freedom more highly than

ever because I know what it is to give up that

freedom. As much as I cared about those chil-

dren, it's not time yet to let others make such

claims on my life. I understand now how impor-

tant it is to live for yourself before you live

for anyone else.

Conclusion now has greater impact and complexity.

Kira's revision, I'm sure you'll agree, is successful. She combined and deemphasized the details about how hard she worked—details that misdirected some of her readers and were also somewhat repetitive. Kira added paragraph 10 to explain her feelings for Josh and Timmy. And the scene at the beach, another important addition, gave concreteness and immediacy to these feelings. The resulting essay is a penetrating exploration of the rewards, and the demands, of caring for children.

Activities for Thought, Discussion, and Writing

1. To study your own revision process, number and save *all* your plans, drafts, and revisions for a paper you are currently writing. (You could also use materials from a recently written essay if you're between assignments.) After you have completed the paper, go back and review these materials, paying particular attention to the kinds of revisions you made. Can you describe the revision strategies that you followed? Can you identify ways that

you could improve the effectiveness of this process? Your instructor may ask you to write an essay discussing what you have learned as a result of this analysis.

2. In her discussion of revision, Ellen Goodman said that for her revision is "like cleaning house." Take ten or fifteen minutes to make your own list of possible analogies for revision. (Is revision for you like tuning a motor, or pruning a plant, for instance?) Later, return to this list, and decide which analogy best expresses your process of revising. Develop this analogy in one or two paragraphs.

3. Interview two other students in your class about their revision strategies. How do their revision strategies reflect their preferred composing styles? How are their strategies similar to and different from your own? How do these students *feel* about revising—and how do their feelings compare with your own? Can you apply any of the strategies they use in your own writing? What can you learn from these interviews about how revising works and about how you can improve your own revising process? Your instructor may ask you to write an essay summarizing the results of your interviews.

CHAPTER 8

STRATEGIES FOR SUCCESSFUL REVISION: REVISING FOR STRUCTURE AND STYLE

As the previous chapter observed, revision is a process of discovery, one that challenges you to "see again" your writing. When you revise—whether you are restructuring your essay, playing with word choice, or fine-tuning your sentence structure—you are always concerned with the creation of *meaning*. As you work to produce this meaning, you must balance two related objectives: self-expression and communication. When you revise, you attempt to articulate your own ideas as clearly and fully as possible. If you hope to communicate these ideas to others, however, you must be equally attentive to the expectations and interests of your readers.

Revision is a demanding but rewarding process. Chapter 7 presented suggestions that should enable you to manage the process of revision more effectively and efficiently. Chapter 8 continues this discussion of revision by providing strategies for improving the structure and style of your writing. These strategies are designed to help you evaluate, and then revise, your work in progress.

As you read Chapter 8, remember that structural and stylistic decisions, even decisions about a single word, always require you to consider *context*. If you want to decide whether a particular sentence is awkwardly written, for instance, you must look not just at that sentence but also at the paragraph of which it is a part. From the moment you first begin thinking about an essay until you make your last revision, you must be an analyst and decision maker. Even though some decisions you make may seem minor, together they determine the character, and the effectiveness, of your writing.

_____ ASKING THE *BIG* QUESTIONS: _____ REVISING FOR FOCUS, CONTENT, AND ORGANIZATION

When you revise a draft, begin by asking yourself the *big* (or important) questions—questions about your essay's focus, content, and organization. These questions are *big* because they challenge you to consider the degree to which your essay has fulfilled its most significant goals. If you discover—as writers often do—that your essay has not achieved its original purpose or that your purpose evolved as you wrote, you will make major changes in your draft, changes that will significantly affect the meaning of your essay.

Asking the *big* questions first is a *practical* approach to revising. You will only waste your time if you spend half an hour revising a paragraph that you will eventually delete because it doesn't contribute to your essay's main point. Furthermore, once you are confident that the overall focus, content, and organization of your essay are satisfactory, you will be better able to recognize less significant, but still important, stylistic problems.

Use the following questions to assess the effectiveness of your draft's focus, content, and organization.

Questions for evaluating your focus, content, and organization

FOCUS

- What do I hope to accomplish in this essay? How clearly have I defined my controlling purpose? How have I communicated this controlling purpose?
- How does my essay represent an appropriate response to my rhetorical situation? If it is an academic essay, how does it fulfill the requirements of the assignment?
- Have I tried to do too much in this essay? Or are my goals too limited and inconsequential?
- How does my essay respond to the needs, interests, and expectations of my readers?

CONTENT

- How does my essay develop or support my controlling purpose? How does it fulfill the commitment stated or implied by my controlling purpose?
- What supporting details or evidence have I provided for my most important generalizations? Are these supporting details and evidence adequate? Do they relate clearly to my controlling purpose and to each other?
- What additional details, evidence, or counterarguments might strengthen my essay?
- Have I included any material that is irrelevant to my controlling purpose?

ORGANIZATION

- What overall organizational strategy does my essay follow?
- Have I tested the effectiveness of this strategy by outlining or summarizing my essay? (See pages 144–147.)
- To what extent does the organization of my essay flow logically from the commitment established by my controlling purpose?
- Will my organization make sense to my readers and be easy for them to follow?
- To what extent does my essay follow the general conventions appropriate for this kind of writing?
- Could my introduction and conclusion more effectively open and close my essay?

Only after you have answered these questions and used your answers to establish a general plan for revising should you focus on such issues as word choice or sentence structure.

To illustrate how you can analyze the effectiveness of your essay's focus, content, and organization, here is how one student, Todd Carpenter, used these questions to establish goals for revision. Todd was responding to the following assignment: "Write a two- to three-page argumentative essay on a subject of your own choice. You should consider me [Todd's instructor] and your classmates to be the primary readers of your essay." Todd described his rhetorical situation in these terms.

```
       I am writing an argumentative essay for my composition class.
I want to convince my readers--my instructor and my classmates--
that our government should institute a national bottle law.
Oregon is one of the nine states that currently have bottle laws,
so most students in the class may already agree with me about this
```

law's importance. (Since Oregon has had a bottle bill for almost
20 years, students may not realize how important it is.)   But because this is an essay for my writing class, I've got to present
an unbiased view. Even if my instructor agrees that there should
be a national bottle law, she won't give me a good grade unless I
write an effective argument. In class, my instructor has stressed
the importance of looking at both sides of the issue and presenting evidence for my views, so I'll try to do that here.

Here is Todd's rough draft.

WHY ISN'T THERE A NATIONAL BOTTLE LAW?

(1) Our country faces an important problem, yet it's one
that few people take seriously--what to do with the bottles and
cans we use daily. When thrown away, bottles and cans cause pollution, increase the volume of solid wastes, waste energy, and use
up natural resources. To control these problems only nine states
have adopted bottle laws. What a shame.

(2) If you're like me, you're tired of walking down streets
and seeing fast-food wrappers, bottles and cans. Last week I went
to the coast and found a beautiful isolated beach. It was great
until I came upon some hamburger boxes and beer bottles. This
happened with a bottle law. Think how much worse things would be
if Oregon didn't have a bottle law.

(3) Bottle laws are important because they require recycling, and recycling reduces pollution and solid waste. Recycling
aluminum reduces air emissions associated with aluminum production
by 96 percent. Solid waste would reduce as aluminum and glass are
eliminated from landfills. Also, a large percentage of the pollution on and around streets and highways is bottles and cans. If
these cans and bottles were worth some money, people would be less
likely to throw them away.

(4) Extracting aluminum ore requires twenty times as much

electricity as recycling the metal. Therefore, if we recycled more aluminum then less aluminum would have to be extracted. This would save enough energy to provide electrical power for at least two million people annually.

(5) Bottle laws are currently effective in Oregon, Vermont, Maine, Michigan, Iowa, Connecticut, Delaware, Massachusetts, and New York. These laws work largely because of the legislation's support by the people. Of the Americans polled, 73 percent would support such bottle laws. Some people are getting tired of the environment being polluted and abused and now realize that this planet and its resources are finite. Aluminum is a natural resource and without recycling we will eventually run out.

(6) With all the people in favor and the obvious environmental reasons supporting it, one would think that a national bottle law would have started long ago. But some people just don't want to bother with saving their containers, and it is a lot easier to just throw them away, despite the fact that they're worth five cents each. Steel and aluminum companies unfairly attack bottle bill laws--and so do supermarkets. These biased efforts must be stopped now.

(7) Although 54 percent of the aluminum beverage cans made and used in the U.S. are recycled at more than twenty-five hundred recycling centers, this could be increased to as much as 90 percent by requiring a national bottle law. Instead of considering unions' and companies' losses for a basis of decision on the bottle law, we should consider the ecological gains. In the future, a few dollars saved will mean nothing compared to a polluted and destroyed environment society will face without recycling.

Using the questions about focus, content, and organization earlier in this chapter, Todd analyzed his draft. His analysis revealed that his essay would be more effective if he made several important changes. Here is Todd's analysis of his essay:

```
                            FOCUS

     My essay needs to be focused on a single subject, and I think
it is, but I don't indicate my controlling purpose clearly enough
at the start of my essay.  I can also see that paragraph two gets
off track because it talks about litter in general, not just the
need for a bottle law.  I should revise or drop this paragraph.  I
also may need to drop the last sentence of paragraph six.  It may
get off track, too.
     I tried to emphasize evidence in writing this draft, but I
think I need to provide more.  I need to talk more about the rea-
sons why some companies and supermarkets attack bottle bills, and
I should try to present their side of the issue also.


                           CONTENT

     The focus questions already helped me see that I need to re-
vise paragraph two and add more evidence.  I also don't describe
how bottle laws work--and I should.


                        ORGANIZATION

     I think the basic organization of my essay is okay.  I don't
think that I have to make big changes in the structure of my es-
say.  I just have to provide more information and take out some
details that don't fit.
     I'm not sure about my introduction and conclusion--maybe they
could be better.  I'll work on the rest of the essay and decide
later.
```

By using the questions about focus, content, and organization to analyze his rough draft, Todd was able to set priorities for revising. His priorities included the following changes:

- stating his controlling purpose early in his essay
- cutting unnecessary material
- adding additional evidence in support of his position
- explaining how bottle laws work
- checking to be sure he's considered both sides of the argument

In analyzing his essay, Todd also realized that his introduction and conclusion might be more effective. Given the importance of the other changes he needed to make, however, Todd was right to put off working on the opening and closing paragraphs. Once he has made the major changes his analysis calls for, he can look again at his introduction and conclusion.

Application

Here is the revised version of Todd Carpenter's essay. Read the essay carefully, noting the major changes that Todd made as he revised. Write down the two or three most important changes on a sheet of paper. Finally, reread the essay with this question in mind: How could this essay be improved further? Write down one or two suggestions for revision in response to this question.

WHY ISN'T THERE A NATIONAL BOTTLE LAW?

(1) What do you do with your empty cans and bottles? There are two choices, throwing them away or recycling. Throwing away an aluminum beverage container wastes as much energy as filling a can with gasoline and pouring half out. Besides wasting energy, throwing away bottles and cans causes pollution, increases the volume of solid wastes, and uses up natural resources. To control these problems, only nine states have adopted bottle laws. The United States government should require every state to have a bottle law or institute a national bottle law.

(2) To understand how a bottle law can help, you must know how it works. When consumers buy canned or bottled beverages at the store, they pay deposits. This deposit can range from five to twenty cents per bottle or can. In order to get this deposit back, the bottles and cans must be returned to a supermarket after they are emptied. The supermarkets then return the bottles and cans to their manufacturers for either reuse or recycling.

(3) Recycling plays a significant role in reducing pollution

and solid waste. Recycling aluminum reduces air emissions associated with aluminum production by 96 percent. Solid waste is also
reduced as aluminum and glass are eliminated from landfills. Finally, a large percentage of the pollution on and around the
streets and highways is bottles and cans. If these could be returned to supermarkets for cash, people would be less likely to
throw them away.

(4) Extracting aluminum ore requires twenty times as much
electricity as recycling the metal. Therefore, if we recycled
more aluminum, less aluminum ore would have to be extracted. This
could save enough energy to provide electrical power for at least
two million people annually.

(5) Bottle laws are currently effective in Oregon, Vermont,
Maine, Michigan, Iowa, Connecticut, Delaware, Massachusetts, and
New York. These laws work largely because the general public supports them. A recent poll of Americans revealed that 73 percent
support bottle laws. This support undoubtedly results from people's concern about pollution and our planet's limited resources.

(6) Given the large number of people in favor of bottle
laws, you might expect that we would already have a national bottle law. But a vocal minority of people don't want to bother with
saving their containers, so they oppose such legislation. Some
supermarket chains also lobby against bottle laws; they don't want
to have to deal with all the cans that people would bring to them.
I understand these individuals' concerns. Recycling bottles and
cans does require extra effort from consumers and distributors.
The larger economic and ecological issues indicate that this extra
effort is worthwhile.

(7) Finally, steel and aluminum companies and metal workers'
unions oppose bottle laws because they fear they would cause cuts

in their production and therefore affect jobs and wages. EPA and General Accounting studies estimate, however, that a national bottle law would produce a net increase of eighty thousand to one hundred thousand jobs, so these fears are misplaced.

(8) Although 54 percent of the aluminum beverage cans made and used in the U.S. are currently recycled at more than twenty-five hundred recycling centers, we could increase this to as much as 90 percent by requiring a national bottle law. Instead of worrying about the inconvenience and possible economic consequences of instituting a national bottle law, we should consider the ecological gains. In the future, a little time saved will mean nothing compared to a polluted and destroyed environment.

Application

Use the questions for evaluating your focus, content, and organization to evaluate the draft of an essay you are currently working on. Be sure to respond as specifically and concretely as possible. After answering these questions, take a few moments to reflect on what you have learned about your draft. Then make a list of goals for revising.

_____ KEEPING YOUR READERS ON TRACK: _____ REVISING FOR COHERENCE

Most writers are aware that paragraphs and essays need to be unified—that they should focus on a single topic. You know, for instance, that if you interrupt a paragraph on the benefits of walking as a form of exercise with a sentence praising your favorite walking shoes, your readers will be confused and irritated. You may not be aware, however, that a paragraph or essay can be unified and yet still present difficulties for readers. These difficulties arise when a paragraph or essay lacks coherence.

Writing is coherent when readers can move easily from word to word, sentence to sentence, paragraph to paragraph. When writing is coherent, readers are often unaware that writers are giving them signals or cues that enable them to stay on track when they read; the writing just seems to "flow." Writers have various means of achieving coherence. Some methods, such as *repeating key words and sentence structures to reinforce ideas* and *using pronouns to refer back to nouns*, reinforce or emphasize the logical development of ideas. Another method is to *employ transitional words*. Words like *however, although* and *because* function in a sense as directions for readers; they tell readers what to "do" as they read. A sentence beginning with "for example" tells readers, for instance, that this sentence will substantiate or exemplify a preceding point, not introduce a new idea or concept.

The following whimsical paragraph from an essay by Cullen Murphy entitled "Going to the Cats" uses all of these means to help keep readers on track, progressing effortlessly from sentence to sentence. The most important means of achieving coherence are italicized.

> Every decade or so the United States of America crosses some portentous new threshold that symbolizes the nation's evolution from one kind of society into another. *It crossed one* after the Second World War, when for the first time in history American men bought more belts than they did suspenders. *It crossed another* in the mid 1950's, when the number of tractors on American farms for the first time exceeded the number of horses. *Now*, in the 1980's, the country faces a new demographic reality: the number of cats in American households is rapidly overtaking, if it has not already overtaken, the number of dogs. *According to* Pet Food Institute, a Washington-based trade association, *there were* about 18 million more dogs than cats in the United States as recently as a decade ago, *but* today *there are* 56 million cats and only 52 million dogs. *Actually*, because millions of unregistered dogs and cats—the illegal aliens of the animal kingdom—go uncounted, it may be that dogs still maintain a slight edge. *But* sales of dog food are holding steady, *whereas* sales of cat food have been increasing in recent years at an annual rate of five to eight percent. The trend is clear.

Most writers concern themselves with strengthening an essay's coherence *after* writing a rough draft and determining if the essay's focus, content, and organization are effective. At this point, the writer can attend to fine-tuning, making changes that enable readers to move through the writing more easily and enjoyably. Consider the difference in ease of reading between the following two versions of a paragraph from Rachella Edward's essay about her history as a writer.

ORIGINAL PARAGRAPH

I started college, and one of my first classes was freshman composition. Although it was one of my favorite classes, I struggled with the assignments. I liked expressing my ideas in writing, but I knew my instructor would take his green pen and cut the excess from my work. Sometimes he didn't like a favorite line or expression. And when I'd padded my essay to meet page requirements, he usually found me out. At last I was rewarded for my effort. I'd worked long and hard on a paper about my grandmother and my relationship with her. I felt it was my best work. My instructor returned my paper, and I found only a "Yes!" where the grade usually was. It was enough. Knowing that I could write effectively if I worked hard enough was a major step in the process of becoming a writer.

REVISED PARAGRAPH

When I started college, one of my first classes was freshman composition. Although it was one of my favorite classes, I struggled with the assignments. Despite the work the class required, I liked trying to express my ideas in writing--even though I knew my instructor would take his green pen and cut the excess from my work. Sometimes the excess was a favorite line or expression; sometimes it was padding to meet the page requirements. The reward for all my effort finally came, however. I'd worked long and hard on a paper about my grandmother and my relationship with her. I felt the essay was my best work. When the instructor returned my paper, I found only "Yes!" where I usually found my grade. That brief response was enough. Knowing that I could write effectively if I worked hard enough was a major step in the process of becoming a writer.

Application

In the revised paragraph just presented, underline the transitions, pronouns, and repeated words and phrases that contribute to its coherence. Write two or three sentences explaining why the revised paragraph is more effective than the original.

When you read work in progress to determine how you can strengthen its coherence, use your common sense. Your writing is coherent if readers know where they have been and where they are going as they read. Don't assume that your writing will be more coherent if you sprinkle transitions liberally throughout your prose. The logic of your discussion may not require numerous transitions; in such a case, adding them will only clutter up your writing. For example, the following excerpt from an article in *Sunset* magazine about choosing a liquid garden fertilizer proceeds logically from the introduction to a statement of the problem and a series of guidelines. The few explicit transitions, such as "in addition" in the first paragraph, easily keep readers on track.

> The attention-getting labels on liquid fertilizer bottles often seem like the late-night TV commercials of the gardening world. Competing with myriad packages on nursery shelves, they make every claim imaginable. In addition to basic nutrients, they tout everything from vitamins to hormones, extracts, and secret formulas supposed to give bigger blooms or better-tasting vegetables.
>
> How do you know what's best for your plants? From fertilizers, plants can receive nitrogen, phosphorus, potassium, and a variety of micronutrients, including iron, manganese, and zinc. Of these, nitrogen is usually the most important, and for a given price, the fertilizer with more nitrogen is a better value.
>
> Here are some guidelines for choosing liquid fertilizers. . . .

Instead of many unneeded transitions, the few necessary transitional phrases, the pronouns (such as *they* in the first paragraph), and the repeated key words (such as *fertilizer* throughout and *nitrogen* in the second paragraph) supply the logical connections a reader needs.

Revision for coherence proceeds more effectively if you look first at large-scale issues, such as the relationship among your essay's introduction, body, and conclusion, before considering smaller concerns. When you revise for coherence, follow these steps.

Guidelines for revising for coherence

- Read your essay quickly to determine if it flows smoothly. Pay particular attention to the movement from introduction to body and conclusion. How could you tighten or strengthen these connections?
- Now read your essay slowly, paying special attention to the movement from paragraph to paragraph. How do new paragraphs build upon or connect with previous paragraphs? Would more explicit connections, such as transitions, help readers better understand the development of your ideas?
- Finally, read each paragraph separately. How do your word choice and sentence structure help readers progress from sentence to sentence? Would repeating key words or pronouns or adding transitions increase a paragraph's coherence?

_____ EXPLORING STYLISTIC OPTIONS _____

"Proper words in proper places." This is how Jonathan Swift, author of _Gulliver's Travels_, defined style. Swift's definition, though intentionally abstract, is accurate. The style of an essay or story reflects all of the choices that a writer makes—from global questions of approach and organization to the smallest details about punctuation and grammar. In this sense, _all_ of the decisions that you make as a writer are stylistic decisions.

As Swift's definition indicates, style is an elusive yet essential feature of texts. It is difficult to articulate—or consciously to control—all the decisions that influence a writer's style. Yet when proper words _are_ in proper places, not only are readers able to follow the writer's ideas with comprehension and interest, but they sense the person behind the words, the writer's presence.

We often associate style with the personal, referring, for instance, to a person's style of dress or style of interacting with others. And a writer's style does reflect his or her individual taste and sensibility. But just as people dress differently for different occasions, so too do writers vary their style depending upon the rhetorical situation. Just as you may choose to dress conservatively for a job interview, for instance, so too may you decide that in certain rhetorical situations presenting a strong personal style—a style that calls attention to itself—is inappropriate. When you are writing an essay examination, for instance, you know that your instructor is primarily interested in your ability to write intelligently about a subject. A style that calls attention to itself might interfere with, not promote, communication.

Effective writers naturally vary their style depending upon their rhetorical situation. As they do so, they are particularly attentive to the *persona* or "voice" they convey through their writing. Sometimes writers present strong and distinctive voices. Here, for instance, is the beginning of an essay on a Northwest rodeo, the Pendleton Round-Up. The essay is by Ken Kesey, author of *One Flew Over the Cuckoo's Nest*.

> My father took me up the Gorge and over the hills to my first one thirty-five years ago. It was on my fourteenth birthday. I had to miss a couple of day's school plus the possibility of suiting up for the varsity game that Friday night. Gives you some idea of the importance Daddy placed on this event.
>
> For this is more than just a world-class rodeo. It is a week-long shindig, a yearly rendezvous dating back beyond the first white trappers, a traditional powwow ground for the Indian nations of the Northwest for nobody knows how many centuries.

Kesey's word choice and sentence structure help create an image of the writer as folksy, relaxed, down-home, and yet also forceful—just the right insider to write about a famous rodeo.

In other situations, writers don't wish to present a distinctive personal voice. We don't know who wrote the following introduction to *The New Magic of Microwave Cooking*, for instance, but it doesn't really matter. The focus is on microwave cooking, not on the writer.

> Almost everyone knows that microwave cooking is fast. Saving time is generally the first reason for buying a microwave oven. But microwave does a lot more than save cooking time. Foods cooked by microwave retain their natural flavor. You use less seasoning in microwave cooking because seasonings don't cook away.
>
> Microwave cooking saves nutrients: foods with a high natural moisture content need little or no water, others use far less than conventional cooking. Foods cook in their own natural juices, which enhances flavor.

In deemphasizing his or her personal voice, the author of the above passage is not voiceless. Rather, the writer has chosen a relatively anonymous public voice, one appropriate for an introduction to a mass-audience cookbook.

Application

From newspapers, magazines, or books that you are currently reading, choose one passage that presents a distinctive personal voice. Choose another passage that presents a more anonymous public voice. Then answer these questions in writing:

- How would you describe the *persona* or voice evoked by each passage?
- How does the author of each passage succeed in creating this *persona* or voice? In answering this question, be sure to cite specific passages as examples.
- How do you respond personally to each of these passages? Write several sentences explaining your response to each passage.

Work in Progress encourages you to adopt a rhetorical perspective on writing. If you think rhetorically, asking yourself questions about your rhetorical situation, you will naturally consider such major stylistic issues as the *persona* or voice you wish your writing to convey to readers. Look again at the Guidelines for analyzing your rhetorical situation, presented on pages 48–50. These guidelines pose questions that can help you determine the appropriate style for specific situations. You may also find it helpful to review the discussion of Aristotle's three appeals—*ethos*, *logos*, and *pathos* (pages 58–62). When you consider the degree to which you wish to draw upon appeals to reason (*logos*), emotion (*pathos*), and your own credibility as writer (*ethos*), you are led to consider your own *persona* or voice and your relationship with readers.

UNDERSTANDING GENERAL PRINCIPLES OF EFFECTIVE PROSE STYLE

In addition to considering such major stylistic issues as the *persona* or voice they wish to convey to readers, writers must make a number of smaller but no less important stylistic decisions. Some of these decisions are made consciously. When you draft several sentences and study them to determine which provides the most effective transition from one paragraph to the next, you are consciously considering an aspect of style. Other decisions are only partly conscious. When you write a word, strike it out, and write another, you are making a stylistic choice—even if you are only partly aware of the reasons why you prefer the latter word over the former.

The choices you make as you draft and revise reflect not only your understanding of your rhetorical situation but your awareness of general principles of effective prose style, principles that apply to much academic and professional writing. Perhaps the easiest way to understand these principles is to analyze a passage that illustrates effective prose style in action.

Since much of your current reading is of textbooks, here are two paragraphs from the first chapter of a textbook on psycholinguistics, *Psychology and Language*, by Herbert H. Clark and Eve V. Clark. As you read these paragraphs, imagine that you have been assigned to read them for a course in psycholinguistics, an interdisciplinary field that studies linguistic behavior and the psychological mechanisms that make verbal communication possible.

(1) Language stands at the center of human affairs, from the most prosaic to the most profound. (2) It is used for haggling with store clerks, telling off umpires, and gossiping with friends as well as for negotiating contracts, discussing ethics, and explaining religious beliefs. (3) It is the medium through which the manners, morals, and mythology of a society are passed on to the next generation. (4) Indeed, it is a basic ingredient in virtually every social situation. (5) The thread that runs through all these activities is communication, people trying to put their ideas over to others. (6) As the main vehicle of human communication, language is indispensable.

(7) Communication with language is carried out through two basic human activities: speaking and listening. (8) These are of particular importance to psychologists, for they are mental activities that hold clues to the very nature of the human mind. (9) In speaking, people put ideas into words, talking about perceptions, feelings, and intentions they want other people to grasp. (10) In listening, they turn words into ideas, trying to reconstruct the perceptions, feelings, and intentions they were meant to grasp. (11) Speaking and listening, then, ought to reveal something fundamental about the mind and how it deals with perceptions, feelings, and intentions. (12) Speaking and listening, however, are more than that. (13) They are the tools people use in more global activities. (14) People talk in order to convey facts, ask for favors, and make promises, and others listen in order to receive this information. (15) These actions in turn are the pieces out of which casual conversations, negotiations, and other social exchanges are formed. (16) So speaking and listening ought to tell us a great deal about social and cultural activities too.

These two paragraphs, you would probably agree, do embody effective prose style. They are clearly organized. Each paragraph, in fact, begins with a topic sentence which the rest of the paragraph explains. The paragraphs also are coherent. The authors use a number of means—especially repeating pronouns, key words, and sentence patterns—to help readers proceed easily through this explanation. But what most distinguishes these two paragraphs, what makes them so effective, is the authors' use of concrete, precise, economical language and carefully crafted sentences.

Suppose, for instance, that the first paragraph were revised as follows. What would be lost?

(1) Language stands at the center of human affairs, from the most prosaic to the most profound. (2) It is a means of human communication. (3) It is a means of cultural change and regeneration. (4) It is found in every social situation. (5) The element that characterizes all these activities is communication. (6) As the main vehicle of human communication, language is indispensable.

This revision communicates roughly the same ideas as the original paragraph, but it lacks that paragraph's liveliness and interest. Instead of presenting vivid examples—"haggling with store clerks, telling off umpires, and gossiping with friends"—the second, third, fourth, and fifth sentences state only vague generalities. Plus these sentences are short and monotonous. Also lost in this revision is any sense of the authors' personalities, as revealed in their writing. The original examples not only clarify how language is used but also convey to readers a sense of the authors' characters and interests.

As this example demonstrates, effective prose style doesn't have to be flashy or call attention to itself. The focus in the original passage is on the *ideas* being discussed. The authors don't want readers to stop and think, "My, what a lovely sentence." But they do want their readers—students required to read their book for a course—to become interested in and engaged with their ideas. So they use strong verbs and vivid, concrete examples whenever possible. They pay careful attention to sentence structure, alternating sequences of sentences with parallel structures (sentences two, three, and four as well as sentences nine and ten) with other, more varied sentences. They take care that the relationships among ideas are clear. In both paragraphs, for example, the first and last sentences (which readers are most likely to remember) articulate the most important ideas. As a result of these and other choices, these two paragraphs succeed in being economical, yet also emphatic.

Exploring your stylistic options—developing a style that reflects your understanding of yourself and the world and your "feel" for language—is one of the pleasures of writing. The following sections review varied sentences, concrete language, and concise wording, all basic principles of effective style. As you read these guidelines, think of an essay you have written recently. How could you employ these suggestions to strengthen your essay?

Guidelines for revising your style

1. VARY THE LENGTH AND STRUCTURE OF YOUR SENTENCES.

Like most readers, you can undoubtedly recognize extreme examples of monotonous sentence structure. You know immediately, for instance, that the following bit of primary-school prose would bore all but beginning readers:

> Run, Jane, run. See Spot run. Look at Jane chase Spot. How fast Spot runs! Jane is having fun.

On the other hand, if you have to slog your way through sentence after sentence of long, complex prose, your comprehension, not to mention your interest, is likely to decrease.

Few students write only very short or very long sentences. Even though most students use a variety of sentences, however, the sentences often seem randomly presented. Their rhythm may be awkward, or their lengths or structures may work against the ideas the writer is trying to express. Consider, for example, the sentences in the following paragraph from an essay urging students to use coupons when they shop.

> (1) Almost everywhere you look, there are coupons. (2) Daily newspapers are probably the best sources for coupons. (3) The Oregonian and the Barometer have coupons every day. (4) The Gazette-Times has coupons too. (5) The Sunday Oregonian is loaded with coupons. (6) Some of the sources that are not so obvious may be coupon trader bins in groceries and flyers handed out in dorms. (7) The backs of store receipts and coupons on boxes or other items you have previously purchased are also common.

The sentences in this paragraph lack variety. Sentences two, three, four, and five are roughly the same length; they also are structured similarly. Because the information they express is so obvious—each simply indicates a possible source of coupons—these sentences seem repetitive. The final two sentences (six and seven) break this pattern, but they are awkward and hard to follow.

With revision, this paragraph could be much more effective:

(1) You may be surprised by how easy it is to find coupons.
(2) Daily newspapers, such as the Oregonian, the Gazette-Times,
and the Barometer, are probably the best sources for coupons. (3)
If you don't want to purchase a daily paper, the Sunday Oregonian,
which is loaded with coupons, may be the next best choice. (5)
Don't just look for coupons in newspapers, however. (6) You can
also watch for special coupon bins in grocery stores and for
flyers used to distribute coupons in dorms. (7) You can even
discover coupons on the backs of store receipts or on the boxes or
packages from other purchases.

You may have noticed that the revised version of this paragraph changes more than the lengths and structures of the sentences. The wording of the first sentence now is more emphatic. The final two sentences are more direct because they begin with *you*, the subject of the action. Finally, added transitions clarify the relationships among ideas in the paragraph. As this revision shows, even though you may be revising with a particular purpose in mind (in this case to vary the sentences), revision usually involves multiple, not single, changes.

When you revise, you generally want to achieve an appropriate variety of sentence lengths and structures, one that carries readers forward with a clear yet unobtrusive rhythm. The following paragraph from a student essay on salmon fishing illustrates this accomplishment.

Picture yourself in a scenic river setting. The fall colors
are at their peak, and shades of burnt red and copper gold
brighten up the shoreline. The crisp, clean smell of fall is in
the air, and a gentle breeze blows lightly against your face. Off
in the distance you hear the sound of swift white water thundering
over massive boulders until it gradually tames into slower-moving
pools of crystal green. As you look out across the river, the
smooth glassy surface is momentarily interrupted as a large salmon
leaps free of its natural element.

You may at times want to use more dramatic sentence structures to emphasize a point. Here, for instance, is the first paragraph of a chapter called "Some Biographical Statistics" from David James Duncan's novel *The River Why*.

> A fishing prodigy, like a musical prodigy, is perforce a solitary. Because of fishing I started school a year late; because of fishing I was considered a kind of mild-mannered freak by my schoolmates; because of fishing I grew up osprey-silent and trout-shy and developed early on an ability to slide through the Public School System as riverwater slides by the logjams, rockslides and dams that bar its seaward journey. It wasn't that I was antisocial; I simply suffered from that lopsidedness of character typical in prodigies. As young Mozart cared for nothing but keyboards, strings, and woodwinds, so I cared for nothing but lakes, rivers, streams and their denizens. Years before I could have put it into words, I realized that my fate would lead me beside still waters, beside rough waters, beside blue, green, muddy, clear, and salt waters. From the beginning my mind and heart were so taken up with the liquid element that nearly every other thing on the earth's bulbous face struck me as irrelevant, distracting, a waste of time.

Duncan's dramatic sentence structures use repetition and balance to emphasize his character's obsession with fishing.

2. WHEN APPROPRIATE, USE SPECIFIC, CONCRETE LANGUAGE.

Look again at the two paragraphs from the psycholinguistics textbook on page 174. One of the strengths of these two paragraphs is the authors' use of specific, concrete words and examples. Rather than writing that language "is a means of human communication," the authors say that language "is used for haggling with store clerks, telling off umpires, and gossiping with friends as well as for negotiating contracts, discussing ethics, and explaining religious beliefs." This sentence not only interests readers, it also challenges readers to pause and think about just how many ways they use language to communicate.

Specific, concrete words—words that refer to particular items and to objects that you can see, touch, smell, or hear—can give your writing power and depth. Rather than stating "As young Mozart cared for nothing but music, so I cared for nothing but fishing," David James Duncan uses specific, concrete language to make his point:

> As young Mozart cared for nothing but keyboards, strings, and woodwinds, so I cared for nothing but lakes, rivers, streams and their denizens.

Duncan's sentence encourages readers to *visualize* the objects with which these two prodigies were obsessed.

Specific and concrete language isn't always appropriate, however. Sometimes you *need* to use abstract or general terms to convey your meaning. Abstract words—words like *patriotism, love*, and *duty*—refer to ideas, beliefs, relationships, conditions, and acts that you can't perceive with your senses. General words designate a group. The word *computer* is general; the words *Leading Edge Model D* identify a specific machine within that group.

Effective writing usually interweaves the specific and the concrete with the abstract and the general. The sentences in the paragraphs on psycholinguistics, for example, move back and forth from specific and concrete to general and abstract words and statements. After specifying and describing various ways people use language to communicate, the writers close the first paragraph with a much broader statement: "As the main vehicle of human communication, language is indispensable." Good writers use general and abstract language when appropriate—and when you are writing about intellectual problems or ideas or emotions such language often is appropriate. But skillful writers balance abstract generalities with concrete, specific words and examples that give their ideas force and vigor.

Beginning writers, however, sometimes overuse abstract, general words. They may believe that these words sound more intellectual, formal, or official. Or they may assume that they should use abstract or general language when specific, concrete words and examples would be more effective.

Here, for instance, is a paragraph from a student essay analyzing *Sports Illustrated*. Notice how vague much of the language is.

> Sports Illustrated's articles are informative because its
> writers try to get information which nobody else knows. The arti-
> cles explain how the subject is unique and how the subject became
> popular and successful. Articles are rarely negative. Most are
> positive and explain the good things in sports rather than empha-
> sizing the negative aspects, such as drugs.

This paragraph leaves readers with more questions than answers. What does this writer mean when he calls articles in *Sports Illustrated* "informative"? What kind of information that "nobody else knows" are writers for *Sports Illustrated* able to get? Just what kinds of subjects does *Sports Illustrated* cover? (Many magazines feature articles about subjects that are "unique," "popular," and "successful.") Does the magazine emphasize the human drama of competition, for example, or strategy, techniques, and statistics? Those who faithfully read *Sports Illustrated* can probably use their prior knowledge to interpret this paragraph; others can only guess at the writer's intentions.

3. REDUCE WORDINESS.

Most readers are impatient. They are reading for a reason—*their* reason, not yours—and they are irritated if you waste their time with unnecessary words or flabby sentences. Consequently, when they revise, experienced writers read their work carefully to determine if they can prune unnecessary words and sentences from their writing.

In revising to eliminate wordiness, your goal is not necessarily to eliminate every possible word. Rather, your goal should be to insure that *every word serves a purpose*. Repetition for emphasis can justify extra words. Thoughtless repetition does not.

The following suggestions will help you to have "proper words in proper places"—without unnecessary deadwood that reduces the effectiveness of your writing.

■ AVOID MEANINGLESS OR EMPTY PHRASES. When we speak, we often use words that contribute little to our ideas. In responding to a friend, for instance, you might introduce your statement with a phrase like *As a matter of fact*. Or if you are arguing with someone, you might emphasize your views by saying, "The point that I am trying to make is this." In conversations, such empty phrases are harmless; in fact, they can serve as helpful signals to the person with whom you're speaking.

In writing, however, such empty phrases can clog your prose. Below are two sentences with empty phrases; a revision follows each.

> *Because of the fact that* I missed my bus, I was late for school.
> Because I missed my bus, I was late for school.

> For those who oppose abortion, *it is an unquestionable fact* that a fetus is a human being.
> Those who oppose abortion believe that a fetus is a human being.

Many writers find that their first drafts are sprinkled with empty or meaningless phrases. In the rush to express ideas, it's easy to fall back on such familiar, formulaic expressions.

And such phrases do no harm in rough drafts—as long as you delete them later.

■ AVOID THE UNNECESSARY USE OF *IT IS* AND *THERE ARE*. Sometimes you need to begin sentences with the words *it is* and *there are*. (Such sentences are called *expletive constructions*, by the way.) You might begin a paragraph on the disastrous effects of a nuclear winter with the sentence "There are three possible scenarios describing the consequences of a nuclear winter." Because this sentence forecasts the structure and content of your paragraph, it serves a useful purpose. More often, however, writers use this construction needlessly. Consider the following examples and revisions.

> *It is* necessary for anglers to purchase a permit.
> Anglers must purchase a permit.
>
> *There are* fifty-four channels available from our new cable company.
> Our new cable company offers fifty-four channels.

The revised sentences don't force readers to wade through unnecessary words before getting to the point, and they also use active verbs to replace the weaker "is" and "are." The revisions are both more emphatic and more economical than the original versions.

■ AVOID DEADWOOD. Wordiness often results not from a specific problem, such as overusing *it is* or *there are*, but from a more general failure to prune unnecessary words. The resulting deadwood reduces the effectiveness of your writing. While rereading an early draft of the second chapter of this book, for instance, I discovered the following sentence:

> Rather than attempting to determine a sequence of activities that you always follow when you write, you should develop a range of strategies that you can employ at any point in the writing process.

It took only a few minutes to rid this sentence of its deadwood.

> Rather than following a rigid sequence of activities, you should develop a range of strategies that you can employ at any point in the writing process.

This revised sentence communicates the same idea as the original but uses significantly fewer words (twenty-six rather than thirty-four). Like me, you will often discover wordy sentences when you reread your drafts. Don't be surprised at such discoveries. When you're struggling to express ideas, you can't expect to worry about being concise at the same time. Knowing this, however, you should be particularly alert for deadwood—words that clutter up your sentences and lessen their impact—when you revise.

Sometimes you can eliminate deadwood by deleting unnecessary words; in other cases, you may need to revise your sentence structure. The following examples of sentences clogged with deadwood are from early drafts of this textbook; I have underlined the unnecessary words. My revisions follow the original sentence.

> As you *work to improve your* writing, you can *benefit a great deal from* drawing on your *own* commonsense understanding of how people in our culture use language.
> As you write, you can draw on your commonsense understanding of how people in our culture use language.

> Your discussion with your instructor will be most profitable (for both of you) if you *have already done a fair amount of preparation before* the conference.
> Your discussion with your instructor will be most profitable (for both of you) if you prepare for the conference.

> *One traditional way of viewing these disciplines is to see them as falling into* one of the following *major* categories: the sciences, humanities, and social sciences.
> Most academic disciplines fall into one of the following categories: the sciences, humanities, or social sciences.

These examples from my own writing emphasize that even experienced writers need to revise their writing to achieve an effective prose style. Placing "proper words in proper places" does require patience and commitment, but it is also one of the most rewarding parts of the writing process, for it insures effective communication between writer and reader.

Activities for Thought, Discussion, and Writing

1. From an essay you are currently working on, choose a paragraph that lacks adequate coherence. Determine the main reasons why

this paragraph lacks coherence. Then use the strategies discussed in this chapter to revise your paragraph.

2. From the same essay, choose two or three paragraphs that you suspect could be more stylistically effective. Using the discussion of style on pages 171 to 184 as a guide, revise these paragraphs.

3. Here is an essay written by Chris Anderson. Read this essay and then answer the questions that follow it.

RERUNS REDUX

For my son's sixth birthday my wife and I rented a video camera and used up all four hours of tape. I had been against the idea. It seemed too complicated and self-indulgent, too upper-middle-class. But before long I had wrested the camera away from Barb and was directing the drama myself, holding the little minicam against my shoulder and squinting through the viewer at the ebbs and flows of the day, the expressions of my children.

Barb had been right, of course, as she usually is. It was a triumph: our life framed and made present through the square viewfinder, and the rest of us aware of that framing when the camera was pointed at us—aware of ourselves being seen and so aware, too, of everything around us.

I've wondered about the effect of the camera on the people being filmed in a documentary, surprised at their readiness to say things, at how they give themselves away. We, too, got used to the lens eye. At the same time that the camera made us more aware of ourselves, we were also able after a while to relax in front of it, to be ourselves, or an approximation of ourselves. The kids stopped clowning and mugging or pitching their voice for effect. The camera was on long enough to take in big chunks of ordinary time.

It was watching the tape on our VCR later that evening that stopped me in my tracks. I can't get those images out of my mind, the fact of those images. The kids laughed and pointed at themselves at first, then lapsed into their television stare, absorbed. It was as if they didn't take themselves seriously until they appeared on the screen, with the dimensions and the textures of Kermit, Mister Rogers and the Gummi Bears.

The 1980s is the era of the RE generation, some writer in Esquire magazine has said. Because our kids are being raised on reruns of "Leave it to Beaver" and "Star Trek," the fashions and characterizations of their own time will be layered over with the status details of the '50s and '60s. And the VCR gives them the technology to replay scenes over and over again, to re-experience images and dialogue to the point of memorization—manipulating time, not limited, as we were a generation ago, to duration and linear sequence. That Sunday afternoon my children were replaying their own experience of the day, giving it more attention on the screen than they were able to give it as it happened, and I worried a little about the effect of that—like the loss of innocence the Indians or aborigines experienced when they first saw their reflections in a mirror.

But what stopped me, what froze me, was not a sense of being able to control time, but the sense of time passing, of time already having passed. I was looking at the images on the screen through the eyes of the future—say, 20, 30 years ahead, when we would take out the tape and see what life had been before.

The baby is trying to roll a soccer ball, stumbling and stooping in the grass, barely able to walk, huffing and fuming and grinning with the effort of it. Our 4-year-old daughter has just woken up, puffy and frowzy, giggling when the baby throws a ball at her. John, the birthday boy, is racing his two-wheeler up and down the sidewalk in his new, too-big helmet with the lightning bolt decals.

The camera swings, and there is a blob of light from the kitchen window—the impression of leaves outside, and the summer light pouring past them—then the front door and the white walls of the hall, and we are walking toward the bedrooms, the picture and the curtains bouncing on the periphery. There is the sound of a lawn mower in the distance.

My wife is sitting on the couch in a blue sweater, her voice soft among the murmurs of the children. I am walking up the driveway, holding a cup of coffee.

If, as Jean Cocteau said, a photograph is death made visible, what is a four-hour video tape of a 6-year-old's birthday party? But that's not what I want to emphasize, not the sentimental and maudlin. That's not what I've been carrying with me, really. It's more the luminousness of those images, and their ordinariness, as much in my mind's eye as on the screen—the blob of light streaking from the window; Barb with her hands in her lap. It's the movement of the children up and down the hall, the screen door opening and slamming, opening and slamming. The movement and pattern of it that day, any day.

I'm thinking of all the things the camera left out, things we can see only out of the corner of our eye. And the feel of the breeze on the backs of our hands, the smell of the sprinklers watering. That, too, left out.

The next day, after we had returned the camera, we went for a picnic in the woods outside of town, and I remember looking up and seeing the children disappearing down the trail, half hidden by the fir branches and the scrub oak, and I thought of how the camera would have recorded that, the spotting of the leaves, the glimpses of arms and jeans, the shouting. I keep replaying that image in my mind, over and over.

CHRIS ANDERSON

- How would you describe the general style of this essay? Write at least three or four sentences describing its style.
- How would you describe the *persona* or voice conveyed by this

essay? List at least three specific characteristics of the writer's *persona* or voice, and then indicate several passages that you think particularly exemplify these characteristics.

■ Find at least three passages from this essay that you believe demonstrate the principles of effective prose style as discussed on pages 173–182. Indicate the reasons why you believe each passage is stylistically effective.

■ What additional comments could you make about the structure and style of this essay? Did anything about the style of this essay surprise you, for instance? Formulate at least one additional comment about the structure and style of this essay.

4. Find a brief article or essay that you think adheres to the principles of style discussed in this chapter. Bring a copy of this selection to class for discussion. Also bring a list of five specific reasons why you think this essay or article is well written.

PART THREE

CONNECTIONS: WRITING, READING, AND REASONING

CHAPTER 9

UNDERSTANDING THE READING PROCESS

Why do people write? To answer this question, Chapter 1 presented a number of representative writing situations: a psychiatric social worker recording clinical observations, a consulting engineer working with colleagues to draft a proposal, a college student brainstorming ideas for an essay for her history class, a retired teacher writing her recollections of her parents and grandparents. These and other representative writing situations emphasize that whenever we write we do so in a specific context or situation. Because each situation differs, effective writers draw upon their rhetorical sensitivity to make a variety of choices—from global decisions about purpose and audience to local decisions about sentence structure and word choice.

Why do people read? Not surprisingly, people read for as many different reasons and in as many different contexts as they write. People read to gain information—to learn how to program their VCR or to make decisions about whether to invest in the stock market, attend a movie, or purchase a new product. People read for pleasure: they immerse themselves in others' lives and worlds— from serious and humorous tales of romance, suspense, adventure, and travel to poems, fiction, diaries, essays, and social commentaries. People read to engage in extended "conversations" with others about issues or questions of importance to them, such as ecology, America's policy in the Middle East, or women's rights. In these

189

and other instances, people read to enlarge their world, to experience new ways not only of thinking but of being and acting.

As Chapter 4, "Writers Reading," emphasized, you can strengthen your abilities as a writer by learning to read others' writing more critically and sensitively. By focusing not only on what writers say but on what writers *do*, you can learn how other writers have responded to their rhetorical situation, and you can apply that knowledge when you work on your own writing. After studying the introductions that Dr. John H. Flavell wrote to three different articles on the same subject, for instance, you better understand how this writer anticipated the needs and interests of three different audiences—the readers of *Psychology Today*, *American Psychologist*, and *Cognitive Psychology*. By analyzing these introductions, you learned more about how writing works.

Reading and writing are thus mutually reinforcing processes. Perhaps the central reason why this is so is that both are acts of *composing*, of constructing meaning through language. When you first read an essay, for instance, you are engaged in a preliminary or "rough" reading. The process of grappling with an essay for the first time—of attempting to determine where the writer is going and why—is similar to the process of writing a rough draft. When you reread an essay to better appreciate the strategies the writer has used or to critique the writer's arguments, you are revising your original reading, much as you revise a draft when you write.

Both writing and reading challenge you to construct or compose the meaning of a specific text; both also engage you in dialogue with others. Perhaps because writing requires the physical activity of drafting, you are generally aware of the active role you play as writer. You may be less aware of the "work" you do when you read a text. Nevertheless, reading is an equally active process. Here, for instance, is the "Harper's Index" for February, 1991. As you read, notice how you forge connections among these "exotica and telling facts." If you are like most readers, you will discover that certain themes or issues emerge from your reading.

HARPER'S INDEX
A collection of exotica and telling facts from Harper's magazine

Ratio of the average CEO's salary to that of a blue-collar worker in 1980: 25:1

Ratio in 1990: 91:1

Number of years between 1980 and 1990 in which increases in blue-collar wages failed to keep up with inflation: 8

Percentage of U.S. firms with fewer than 100 workers that paid all employee health insurance premiums in 1980: 72

Percentage that do today: 48

Percentage increase, since 1989, in the number of alcohol-related hospitalizations of Boston College students: 100

Convicted drunk drivers in Orange County, California, since 1988, whose sentence included a tour of the morgue: 569

Number of repeat offenders among them: 1

Projected average speed of cars on California's highways in the year 2010, in miles per hour: 11

Maximum speed of a hockey puck in an NHL game, in miles per hour: 96

Minimum amount of time it takes a human sperm to reach an egg, in minutes: 5

Estimated portion of all pregnancies ending in abortion that are the result of contraceptive failure: 1/2

Price of one Homeboy Condom, from Custom Condoms of Somerville, Massachusetts: $1.50

Number of black men in New York state correctional facilities: 24,000

Number enrolled in New York state colleges or universities: 23,000

Chances that an Iraqi male between the ages of 15 and 39 is a soldier: 1 in 3

Number of times that the U.S. Congress has declared war: 5

Estimated number of times that a U.S. president has sent troops into combat situations: 130

Estimated number of times last fall that George Bush told a joke about his dog asking for a wine list with her Alpo: 10

Percentage of Americans who say, "I can't tell a joke to save my life": 99.2

Percentage of preschool children who say that if they were president they would eat ice cream for every meal: 21

Rank of Mr. Rogers, among preschoolers' first choices for president of the United States: 1

Rank of Abraham Lincoln, among the U.S. presidents most often portrayed in films: 1

Number of false noses used by Gérard Depardieu during the filming of *Cyrano de Bergerac*: 100

Average size bra worn by an American woman in 1985: 34B

Average size today: 36C

Percentage increase in pressure on the ball of the foot exerted by walking in a shoe with a three-inch heel: 76

Rank of "acting," "happiness," and "modeling," among ambitions most often cited by *Playboy* centerfold models: 1,2,3

Rank of "honey," among Americans' favorite terms of endearment: 1

Minimum cost of a personalized romance novel, from Swan Publishing of Placentia, California: $45

Percentage of all valentines that are sent by women: 85

Figures cited are the latest available as of December 1990. "Harper's Index" is a registered trademark.

Exploration

Freewrite for five minutes about the experience of reading the "Harper's Index." What strategies did you find yourself using as you read this miscellany of "telling facts"? After freewriting, reread the Index one more time and then list the major themes or issues that your reading stimulated. Reviewing this list, consider the extent to which your own background and experiences influenced your reading of this Index.

Reading, like writing, is a *situated* activity: when you read you draw not only upon the words on the page but upon your own experiences as well. The connections that you perceived among the first three items in the "Harper's Index," for instance, were undoubtedly influenced by your own economic and political views. Reading is situated in additional ways. Just as you approach different writing tasks in different ways depending on your rhetorical situation, so too does your approach to and experience of reading vary depending upon the specific relationship of writer, reader, and text. Without thinking, you naturally read the introduction to a psychology text differently than you read your current mystery or the sports page of your newspaper.

Application

Read the following texts. The first, "Girl," is a very brief short story by the contemporary writer Jamaica Kincaid. The second presents the first two paragraphs of the introduction to Robin Lakoff's book *Language and Woman's Place*, a scholarly work that attempts "to see what we can learn about the way women view themselves and everyone's assumptions about the nature and role of women from the use of language in our culture."

GIRL

Wash the white clothes on Monday and put them on the stone heap; wash the color clothes on Tuesday and put them on the clothesline to dry; don't walk barehead in the hot sun; cook pumpkin fritters in very hot sweet oil; soak your little cloths right after you take them off;

when buying cotton to make yourself a nice blouse, be sure that it doesn't have gum on it, because that way it won't hold up well after a wash; soak salt fish overnight before you cook it; is it true that you sing benna in Sunday school?; always eat your food in such a way that it won't turn someone else's stomach; on Sundays try to walk like a lady and not like the slut you are so bent on becoming; don't sing benna in Sunday school; you mustn't speak to wharf-rat boys, not even to give directions; don't eat fruits on the street—flies will follow you; *but I don't sing benna on Sundays at all and never in Sunday school*; this is how to sew on a button; this is how to make a button-hole for the button you have just sewed on; this is how to hem a dress when you see the hem coming down and so to prevent yourself from looking like the slut I know you are so bent on becoming; this is how you iron your father's khaki shirt so that it doesn't have a crease; this is how you iron your father's khaki pants so that they don't have a crease; this is how you grow okra—far from the house, because okra tree harbors red ants; when you are growing dasheen, make sure it gets plenty of water or else it makes your throat itch when you are eating it; this is how you sweep a corner; this is how you sweep a whole house; this is how you sweep a yard; this is how you smile to someone you don't like too much; this is how you smile to someone you don't like at all; this is how you smile to someone you like completely; this is how you set a table for tea; this is how you set a table for dinner; this is how you set a table for dinner with an important guest; this is how you set a table for lunch; this is how you set a table for breakfast; this is how to behave in the presence of men who don't know you very well, and this way they won't recognize immediately the slut I have warned you against becoming; be sure to wash every day, even if it is with your own spit; don't squat down to play marbles—you are not a boy, you know; don't pick people's flowers—you might catch something; don't throw stones at blackbirds, because it might not be a blackbird at all; this is how to make a bread pudding; this is how to make doukona; this is how to make pepper pot; this is how to make a good medicine for a cold; this is how to make a good medicine to throw away a child before it even becomes a child; this is how to catch a fish; this is how to throw back a fish you don't like, and that way something bad won't fall on you; this is how to bully a man; this is how a man bullies you; this is how to love a man, and if this doesn't work there are other ways, and if they don't work don't feel too bad about giving up; this is how to spit up in the air if you feel like it, and this is how to move quick so that it doesn't fall on you; this is how to make ends meet; always squeeze bread to make sure it's fresh; *but what if the baker won't let me feel the bread?*; you mean to say that after all you are really going to be the kind of woman who the baker won't let near the bread?

JAMAICA KINCAID

LANGUAGE
AND WOMAN'S PLACE

Introduction

Language uses us as much as we use language. As much as our choice
of forms of expression is guided by the thoughts we want to express,
to the same extent the way we feel about the things in the real world
governs the way we express ourselves about these things. Two words
can be synonymous in their denotative sense, but one will be used in
case a speaker feels favorably toward the object the word denotes, the
other if he is unfavorably disposed. Similar situations are legion,
involving unexpectedness, interest, and other emotional reactions on
the part of the speaker to what he is talking about. Thus, while two
speakers may be talking about the same thing or real-world situation,
their descriptions may end up sounding utterly unrelated. The following well-known paradigm will be illustrative.

(1) (a) I am strong-minded.
    (b) You are obstinate.
    (c) He is pigheaded.

If it is indeed true that our feelings about the world color our
expression of our thoughts, then we can use our linguistic behavior as
a diagnostic of our hidden feelings about things. For often—as anyone
with even a nodding acquaintance with modern psychoanalytic writing knows too well—we can interpret our overt actions, or our perceptions, in accordance with our desires, distorting them as we see fit.
But the linguistic data are there, in black and white, or on tape,
unambiguous and unavoidable. Hence, while in the ideal world other
kinds of evidence for sociological phenomena would be desirable
along with, or in addition to, linguistic evidence, sometimes at least
the latter is all we can get with certainty. This is especially likely in
emotionally charged areas like that of sexism and other forms of
discriminatory behavior. This book, then, is an attempt to provide
diagnostic evidence from language use for one type of inequity that
has been claimed to exist in our society: that between the roles of men
and women. I will attempt to discover what language use can tell us
about the nature and extent of any inequity; and finally to ask whether
anything can be done, from the linguistic end of the problem: does one
correct a social inequity by changing linguistic disparities? We will
find, I think, that women experience linguistic discrimination in two
ways: in the way they are taught to use language, and in the way
general language use treats them. Both tend, as we shall see, to
relegate women to certain subservient functions: that of sex object, or
servant; and therefore certain lexical items mean one thing applied to

men, another to women, a difference that cannot be predicted except with reference to the different roles the sexes play in society.

ROBIN LAKOFF

Now that you have read these two texts, use the following questions to analyze your reading experience.

1. What were your expectations when you began to read each of these texts? Did you expect to find one or the other easier or more interesting to read? Why? To what extent did your expectations derive from your own previous experiences as a reader?

2. Each of these texts in a different way comments on the situation of women in society and the role that language plays in women's lives. How did your own assumptions and values about these issues influence your reading? Did you approach these texts as a sympathetic, accepting reader, for instance, or were you resistant to this general subject at the start? Why?

3. Just as writers often shift goals and strategies while writing, so too do readers sometimes revise their goals and strategies while reading. Did you find yourself doing so while reading either the Kincaid or Lakoff passages? Why? What caused these shifts, if they occurred?

4. As you read these two texts, were you aware that the authors' stance toward or relationship with readers differed? How would you describe each author's stance or relationship with readers? Similarly, did these texts invite you to play a different role as reader? How would you describe your role as you read these texts, and how did your awareness of this role influence your reading? Try to list several features of each text that encourage readers to adopt a particular role.

5. What three or four factors most influenced your ease or difficulty of reading these two passages? To what extent did the two texts require you to draw upon different skills and different prior knowledge about the subject matter? Try to rank these factors in terms of the difficulty they posed for you as you read.

6. If you found reading one or both of these texts difficult or unenjoyable, can you imagine someone else who would find them easy and pleasurable to read? What values, knowledge, and skills would this person have—in what ways would he or

she differ from you? If you found one or both of these passages easy and enjoyable reading, can you identify the reasons why?

Now reread each of these two texts. To what extent does this second
reading differ from your first—to what extent, in other words, do
you find youself "revising" your first reading? List several ways that
the second reading differed from the first.

Group Activity

Meet with a group of classmates to discuss your responses to the
preceding application. (Appoint a member of the group to act as a
recorder so you can share the results of your discussion with the
rest of the class.) Begin your discussion by comparing your answers
to each of the six questions on page 195. As a group, formulate two
or three responses to the following two questions.

- In what ways do your answers to these questions differ?
- What do these differences reveal about the nature of the
  reading process?

RECOGNIZING THE NEED
FOR DIVERSE READING STRATEGIES

As a college student, you read many different kinds of texts for a
wide variety of purposes. Sometimes you read primarily for information; you do so when you read your chemistry textbook or when
you scan the screen of your library's circulation computer to determine what references are available for a current project. On other
occasions, you read not simply to gain information or for main ideas
but to engage in the process of inquiry. David Bartholomae and
Anthony Petrosky call this kind of reading "strong reading." To
engage successfully in strong reading, students must understand
that:

> Reading involves a fair measure of push and shove. You make your
> mark on a book and it makes its mark on you. Reading is not simply a
> matter of hanging back and waiting for a piece, or its author, to tell you
> what the writing has to say. In fact, one of the difficult things about

reading is that the pages before you will begin to speak only when the authors are silent and you begin to speak in their place, sometimes for them—doing their work, continuing their projects—and sometimes for yourself, following your own agenda. (*Ways of Reading*, p. 1)

Strong readers evaluate their reading in terms of what they are able to *do* with their reading.

If you are like many students, you may feel more confident reading for information or main ideas than engaging in a strong reading of an essay, poem, political treatise, or engineering, physics, or philosophical problem. And yet the ability to "make your mark on a book," rather than simply allowing it to "make its mark on you," represents one of the most important goals of a college education. Such engaged, critical reading is intrinsically satisfying, for it enables you to engage in genuine inquiry. Strong reading also naturally leads to, and benefits from, writing; one of the best ways to strengthen your writing ability is thus to become adept at strong reading.

Just as successful writers develop a repertoire of writing strategies they can draw upon depending upon their situation, so do successful readers develop a repertoire of reading strategies. The next section of this chapter presents a number of strategies you can use in a variety of reading activities. Whatever reading you do, the following general guidelines for effective reading should make that process easier and more productive.

Guidelines for effective reading

1. RECOGNIZE THAT EFFECTIVE READERS ARE *FLEXIBLE* READERS.

Effective readers understand that different reading situations call for different reading strategies; they also understand that their purpose in reading should help them determine how to approach a text. If you know that you will eventually engage in the strong reading of an essay, you might first employ such strategies as previewing and annotating to get the gist of the text and to understand the author's general values and assumptions. Later you will reread the essay, employing a variety of reading and writing strategies to deepen your engagement with it.

2. ANALYZE A TEXT FOR CUES ABOUT ITS CONTEXT OR SITUATION.

Chapter 3 presents guidelines for analyzing your rhetorical situation as a writer; you can use the same guidelines to analyze the context or situation of an already-published piece of writing. Before and while reading an essay, for instance, you can ask questions like these:

- *Questions about the author.* Why did the author write this essay? What did the author hope the essay will accomplish? How might the author's goals have influenced the form and content of the essay? What voice or image (persona) does the author project in this essay?
- *Questions about the reader.* Who is the intended audience for this essay? Is this essay addressed to a general audience or an audience of specialists? What role does the writer invite readers to adopt as they read this essay? Does the writer assume that readers will already know a great deal about or be interested in this subject?
- *Questions about the text.* When was this text published? By whom? To what specific or general situation or concern might this text be a response? Does the situation in which the author wrote require him or her to follow certain textual conventions? To what extent do these conventions shape this essay? Does the nature of the subject require that the author provide certain kinds of evidence or explore certain issues? Does the author fulfill this obligation? Have I read other examples of similar writing that can help me better understand the goals and strategies of this text?

Your answers to these questions can help you understand the situation or context in which a text was written and thus approach it with a richer appreciation of its assumptions, goals, and strategies.

3. DEVELOP STRATEGIES THAT ALLOW YOU, WHEN APPROPRIATE, TO RESIST OR READ AGAINST THE GRAIN OF A TEXT.

To read critically and actively, readers sometimes choose to resist or read against the grain of a text. While reading an essay on abortion intended for a general audience, for instance, you might decide to consider the essay from the perspective of health-care providers or from that of women who have experienced an abortion. How would they respond to the author's arguments and strategies? You might read the essay paying particular attention to issues the author *doesn't* raise, the kinds of examples that the author *doesn't* use. Or you might focus on the degree to which your own experience does (and doesn't) support the author's arguments. These kinds of probing, inquiring, resistant readings can help you determine not only what an essay says and does but what it doesn't say and do, and thus provide an opening for fruitful questioning, analysis, and dialogue.

4. RECOGNIZE THAT EFFECTIVE READING OFTEN REQUIRES REREADING.

Effective readers understand that rereading a text provides an opportunity for them not only to better appreciate the text but also to better understand their own reading strategies. In rereading an essay on abortion, for instance, you might notice that your agreement with the author's position caused you to downplay problems with some of the arguments. When you begin a second—or third or fourth—reading of the essay, you can bring your previous reading to bear, so that you can read with a fuller appreciation not only of the author's but of your own intentions.

DEVELOPING A REPERTOIRE OF CRITICAL READING STRATEGIES

When you read critically, you read *actively*. You read not just to memorize facts or gather information, but to evaluate, analyze, appreciate, understand, and apply. As a critical reader, you engage in a dialogue with the author. You don't automatically accept the author's perspective or arguments. Instead, you challenge the author and subject his or her ideas to careful examination.

To read critically, you need to develop a repertoire of critical reading strategies. The following discussion will introduce you to a number of strategies for critical reading and provide an opportunity for you to apply these strategies to a specific text, an article on the inappropriate prescription of drugs by doctors.

Previewing

When you preview a text, you survey it quickly to establish or clarify your purpose and context for reading. In doing so, you ask yourself questions such as the following.

QUESTIONS FOR PREVIEWING A TEXT

1. Where and when was this text published? What do this source and date suggest about the accuracy, authority, and currency of this text?
2. What, if anything, do I know about the author of this text?
3. What can I learn from the title?
4. What can I learn by quickly surveying this text? Is the text divided into sections, for example? If so, how do these sections appear to be organized? Can I easily perceive the gist or general approach the author is taking? What predictions

about this text can I make on the basis of quickly surveying it? What questions can I now formulate to guide my subsequent reading of this text?

5. What is my personal response to the text based upon this preview of it?

Application

Using the questions for previewing a text, preview the article from the May 1988 issue of *The Atlantic*, "First, Do No Harm," by Ellen Ruppel Shell, which is reprinted below. Be sure to answer all the questions for previewing a text.

FIRST, DO NO HARM

(1)   Not long ago, more prescriptions for amphetamine were filled in Michigan than in any other state. The reason for this was not clear, but there was informed speculation that assembly-line workers in the automobile industry were probably involved. Assembly-line work is boring, and uppers are known to make time pass quickly. The pusher in many cases was a certain doctor, whose practice was limited to distributing amphetamine in large quantities to anyone who asked for it. People lined up at this door every morning, and the line was said to stretch around the block. These people were weighed and had their blood pressure taken by a nurse, and were then ushered in, seven or eight at a time, to see the doctor. He told them they were looking fine and gave them each a large packet of pills. Some "patients" went through this ritual daily.

(2)   The Michigan doctor, who has since been arrested and is no longer licensed to practice, is said to have distributed more than a million doses of amphetamine a year. His is an extreme example of a problem that the medical profession has been quietly monitoring, and dealing with, for more than a decade. The federal Drug Enforcement Administration (DEA) estimates that about 17,000 of the nation's 650,000 doctors and a fraction of the 50,000 pharmacies dole out prescription drugs purely for financial gain, a clearly illegal practice. But the vast majority of what is called inappropriate prescribing does not involve those unscrupulous "scrip doctors." Hundreds of thousands of dollars' worth of unnecessary and even irrational prescriptions are written every year by doctors acting in a perfectly legal capacity.

(3)   Inappropriate prescription-writing is the most common complaint heard by medical review boards, in some states eclipsing all other

complaints combined. "We have found doctors prescribing fifteen drugs, five of which are contraindicated," says John Ulwelling, the executive director of the Oregon Board of Medical Examiners. "There's no doubt that this is the number-one problem facing medical boards across the country."

(4)   Of all drug-related emergency-room cases, more than half involve drugs that were legally prescribed. Of all drug-related deaths, 70 percent involve prescription drugs (the percentage of deliberate overdoses is unknown). Although the American Medical Association makes a point of loudly condemning the handful of crooked doctors who write thousands of illegal prescriptions for narcotics and other psychoactive drugs, the crux of the problem lies with honest doctors who simply do not know—or, in some cases, care—that the medication they are recommending for a patient is ineffective, needlessly expensive, or dangerous. "The average American doctor is simply writing too many prescriptions," says Dr. Jerry Avorn, an internist and an associate professor at Harvard Medical School. "And, surprisingly, most of the problem is with non-narcotic drugs."

(5)   A classic example, Avorn says, is propoxyphene, a prescription analgesic most commonly known by one of its brand names, Darvon. Propoxyphene is widely prescribed to alleviate mild to moderate pain, yet controlled studies show it to be at best no more effective a pain reliever than aspirin or acetaminophen (Tylenol). The DEA does not consider propoxyphene a particularly dangerous drug, and for that reason many physicians consider it to be relatively benign. But propoxyphene has a number of unpleasant side effects, including dizziness, drowsiness, nausea, and vomiting, and can be dangerous when combined with alcohol. It is also addictive. In a study completed in 1983, overdoses of the drug were blamed for roughly a thousand deaths a year, only about half of which were suicides. Yet doctors continue to prescribe it: Darvocet, a mixture of propoxyphene and another analgesic, is one of the most commonly prescribed drugs in the country.

(6)   Ironically, the main reason propoxyphene is sometimes preferred to aspirin is that it is available only by prescription. There is a strong belief among physicians that patients have faith in prescription drugs and will perceive themselves to be better served if they obtain a prescription during an office visit. The placebo effect of prescription drugs is thought to be greater than that of over-the-counter drugs, and this effect is sometimes considered critical in the treatment of things like arthritis, headache, and chronic back pain, which are extremely difficult to treat.

(7)   "Some patients won't patronize a doctor unless he prescribes drugs," says Dr. Lial Kofoed, of the Department of Psychiatry at Dartmouth Medical School, in Hanover, New Hampshire. "They feel ripped off if all they get is a talking-to. If you go to dinner with doctors in a big city, you'll hear them complain about competition. They don't want to lose a patient to the doctor who will give out a prescription for the latest drug."

(8)   Newer drugs may be perceived as better or safer than older drugs, because they haven't been around long enough for their limitations to show. For example, in the seventies and early eighties doctors widely prescribed Valium (diazepam) for anxiety and tension. Dubbed "mother's little helper" (after a song by the Rolling Stones), the drug was so popular that, doctors reported, patients asked for it by name. But Valium's popularity waned as it became associated with middle-class malaise and as its addictive properties became widely recognized. According to Kofoed, Xanax (alprazolam) is gradually supplanting Valium as the drug of choice for anxiety (Pharmaceutical Data Services reports that Xanax was the fourth most dispensed brand-name drug in 1987). Part of the reason for the change is probably that the patent on the formula for Valium is about to expire, and so Valium is not being heavily advertised in medical journals, whereas Xanax is.

(9)   There is now some concern, however, that Xanax is even more addictive than Valium. "One of the best ways to make a temporary problem permanent is to addict a patient to a drug," Kofoed says. "In the case of Valium or Xanax, you get the original anxiety supplemented by withdrawal anxiety"—that is, people are afraid to give up the drug for fear that if they do, their original symptoms will return.

(10)   Doctors in large practices prescribe more drugs per patient than do doctors in smaller practices. Writing a prescription has in many cases become a tacit way of indicating that the appointment is over—and the sooner the prescription is written, the sooner the doctor can get on to the next case. "It takes a lot less time to prescribe a drug than to explain to a patient why you won't," Kofoed says. "Also, most doctors want to maintain the image of helper, and some doctors will do most anything to keep up that image. So they prescribe a painkiller or a tranquilizer, and the patient is happy."

(11)   This compulsion to please patients at almost any cost is made more dangerous by the fact that many doctors don't know all that much about drugs in the first place. Physicians receive surprisingly little formal training about prescription drugs in medical school. They are expected to learn most of what they need to know during their internship and residency and, later, in medical journals and occasional courses. In reality, however, doctors get the vast majority of their information about new drugs from pharmaceutical sales representatives, known in the industry as detail men, or detailers. Detail men meet with doctors in their offices. They offer free samples, to tide patients over until a prescription is filled. As salesmen, the detailers try to promote the latest and most profitable drugs for their companies, not to give the doctor a balanced presentation. At any rate, many salesmen are incapable of giving one, because they lack the facts to do so. Although a few companies, like Eli Lilly, strive to hire pharmacists to fill their sales slots, most do not. Of 27,000 detailers in the industry, only 4,000 hold degrees in pharmacy. According to T. Donald Rucker, a health economist and a professor of

pharmacy administration at the University of Illinois at Chicago, most detailers are not scientifically trained.

(12)   "When hiring a salesman, some companies figure they're better off with an English or music major than with a pharmacist," Rucker says. "If you are trying to bamboozle a physician into thinking a certain drug is the greatest thing since sliced bread, it helps if you don't know anything about the product beyond what your boss has told you. Besides, pharmacists are in demand, and they are expensive—maybe five or ten thousand more a year than a liberal-arts major."

(13)   Detailing is an expensive process. A study published last November concluded that drug companies spend an average of $81 for every face-to-face encounter between one of their salesmen and a physician. Yet it appears that this approach is cost-effective—every major drug company in the country uses it. In 1977 a vice-president of marketing for a major drug manufacturer told a reporter for *Sales Marketing and Management* magazine, "Dealing with physicians is the best way to sell drugs. . . . All I can say is that every time we've added salespeople, sales have gone up." It is safe to assume that the number of sick people does not correlate with the number of drug salespeople on the road—more drugs are sold because more physicians have been advised to prescribe them.

(14)   Jerry Avorn and his colleague, Stephen B. Soumerai, who has a doctorate in public health, ran a controlled study to see whether doctors' prescribing practices would change if they were provided with unbiased information about particular drugs. In an effort they called academic detailing, they enlisted clinical pharmacists to make office visits and explain the action and limitations of three drugs that are widely considered to be overprescribed: vasodilators, which are prescribed inappropriately for the treatment of senility; cephalexin, an antibiotic that, while effective, is much more expensive than equally effective alternative drugs; and propoxyphene. After spending just over half an hour with a pharmacist, physicians reduced their prescription of these drugs by an average of 13 percent, relative to a control group. Avorn believes that such an outreach program, widely expanded, could reduce the $2.8 billion worth of prescriptions that physicians write each year, and thereby save millions of dollars and many lives. "Nobody's minding the store in academic medicine to systematically inform doctors about drugs," Avorn says. "Industry is very good at this—it does continuing education and marketing that reaches just about every doctor in the country. The bad news is that industry's message is a commercial message. Clearly, industry is not to blame—it's the doctor's fault if this is the only message he listens to, and it is the patient, and society, who is hurt."

(15)   Elderly patients are at particularly high risk of being inappropriately medicated. Ordinarily, the liver or kidneys will clear the body of excess drugs, but in the elderly the efficiency of these organs

lessens and some drugs can build up to toxic levels. On average, people over age sixty-five take twice as many pills as the rest of us (nursing-home patients typically receive from four to a dozen every day, half of them tranquilizers). Often elderly people go to several physicians, each of whom may prescribe one or more drugs without knowing what drugs the other doctors are prescribing or what over-the-counter medications the patient is taking. Hence the risk of dangerous drug interactions is greatly increased. Side effects of overmedication are particularly hard to detect in older people, because they include the very symptoms associated with "normal" old age: incontinence, tremors, loss of facial expression, depression, agitation, confusion, and falls. Often elderly patients are given a long-lasting drug for a short-term problem, such as occasional sleeplessness, which may linger in their systems for up to three days. The result may be permanent listlessness and what looks like symptoms of depression—symptoms that may prompt the prescription of an antidepressant.

(16)   "The problem is that most of us went into medicine because we wanted to help and because we enjoyed science," Avorn says. "Chemical intervention seems to be a scientific way to help people. Drugs represent one of the most effective technologies for ameliorating disease—but they don't always work. You can't fix senility with a pill. Prescription medications are not a substitute for compassion—or common sense."

ELLEN RUPPEL SHELL

Annotating

When you annotate a text, you underline important words or passages and write comments or questions that help you establish a dialogue with the text or remember important points. Different individuals have different styles of annotating. Some people are heavy annotators; they underline many passages and fill the margins with comments and questions. Others annotate more selectively, preferring to write few comments and to underline only the most important passages or key words. In thinking about your own annotating strategies, remember that your purpose in reading should influence the way you annotate a text. You would annotate a text you are reading primarily for your information differently than you would an essay you are reading for an assignment or a poem you are reading for pleasure.

Many readers annotate directly on the text as they read. If you have borrowed the text or prefer not to mark up your own book, you can use a separate piece of paper to copy important passages and to write questions and comments. You may wish to use a reading journal to organize and save your notes and comments on readings.

Use the following questions to help you improve or adapt your preferred method of annotating in different situations.

QUESTIONS FOR ANNOTATING A TEXT

1. What is my purpose in reading this text? What do I need to annotate to accomplish this purpose?
2. Where does the writer identify the purpose and thesis or main idea of the text?
3. What are the main points, definitions, and examples in the text?
4. What questions does this text suggest to me?
5. Can I identify key words that play an important role in this writer's discussion? Does the text provide enough information so that I can understand these key words and appreciate their significance, or do I need to do additional reading or ask another reader for an explanation?
6. Can I identify passages that seem to play a particularly crucial role in this text? What is my response to these passages?
7. Can I identify passages where my personal experience and values or knowledge of the subject cause me to question the author's assertions, evidence, or method?

Application

Annotate "First, Do No Harm" (pages 200 to 204) as you would if you expected to write an essay responding to it for your composition class.

Outlining

Outlining helps you identify both the structure of a text and its essential content, its central informative or argumentative points. Many people make rough outlines when they annotate a text. Simply numbering the main points or drawing up a brief outline in the margin can enable you to understand and assess the effectiveness of a text's organization. Sometimes you will want to outline a text on a separate piece of paper. This can be especially helpful when the material is very complicated or when you need to analyze how a text is structured.

Use the following suggestions as you outline your reading materials.

GUIDELINES FOR OUTLINING A TEXT

1. Determine your purpose in outlining.
2. Based on your purpose and your own preferences, decide how detailed your outline needs to be.
3. Reread the material, noting the main points and their order of presentation. If the thesis is clearly stated, you may want to write it down at the top of the page before your outline begins.
4. Review the main points, deciding which are of the same weight or significance and which are subpoints that develop and follow from main points.
5. Write out the main points and subpoints, indicating their relationships through the levels shown by the numbers and letters of the outline format.
6. When your outline is finished, take a break. Later check it item by item against the sequence of the paragraphs or sections of the text.

Application

Construct an informal outline of "First, Do No Harm" (pages 200 to 204).

Summarizing

Students often underestimate the usefulness of writing clear, concise summaries of essays or books. Writing a summary allows you to restate the major points of a book or essay in your own words. Summarizing is a skill worth developing, for it requires you to master the material you are reading and make it your own. Summaries can vary in length, depending upon the complexity and length of the material being summarized. Ideally, however, they should be as brief as possible.

Here are suggestions to follow as you write your own summaries.

GUIDELINES FOR SUMMARIZING A TEXT

1. Reread the material, trying to identify the main ideas.
2. Underline or number the main points if you have not already annotated or outlined the material.
3. Generally stick to main points, and leave out illustrations, examples, anecdotes, or evidence.
4. Before writing, try to form a coherent mental picture of the most important ideas.
5. State the main ideas in your own words, as briefly and clearly as you can.

Application

Following the guidelines provided above, write a brief summary of "First, Do No Harm" (pages 200 to 204).

Analyzing the argument

Annotating, outlining, and summarizing all can help you determine the central informative or argumentative points made in a text. "First, Do No Harm," for instance, clearly states its thesis or main point at the end of its second paragraph: "Hundreds of thousands of dollars' worth of unnecessary and even irrational prescriptions are written every year by doctors acting in a perfectly legal capacity." This main point constitutes the article's *claim*, and the statements, explanations, and examples throughout the article comprise the evidence or *supports* for this claim.

Whenever you have a claim and a number of supporting statements, you have an argument. Rather than simply accepting an author's assertions and evidence, critical readers attempt to determine for themselves if the evidence provided justifies the author's claim. The first step in analyzing an argument is to figure out precisely what the writer says. The easiest way to do this generally is by making an outline—even a very quick, sketchy one—because this technique reveals how the writer's ideas relate to each other. Once you have outlined an essay or article, you can analyze the effectiveness of its argument by asking yourself the following questions.

QUESTIONS FOR ANALYZING THE ARGUMENT OF A TEXT

1. What is the major claim or thesis of this text? Is it explicitly stated at any point, or is it implicit, there for you to "read between the lines"?
2. What interests or values may have caused this writer to support this particular thesis? (Information about the writer from other sources, as well as clues from the writing itself, may help you determine this.)
3. Does the writer define key terms? If not, what role do these unstated definitions play in the argument?
4. Consider the writer's appeal to *logos*: What kind of evidence does the writer present? Is the evidence used logically and fairly? Has the writer failed to consider any significant evidence, particularly evidence that might refute his or her claims?
5. Consider the writer's appeal to *ethos*. How does the writer establish his or her credibility? What image or *persona* does the writer create for him or herself? How do appeals to *ethos* contribute to the writer's arguments?
6. Consider the writer's appeal to *pathos*: Does the writer attempt to persuade the reader through inappropriately manipulative emotional appeals?
7. What are your values and beliefs about this subject? How might these values and beliefs have affected your response to the writer's arguments?

Application

Using the questions for analyzing the argument of a text, analyze the argument of "First, Do No Harm" (pages 200 to 204). Be sure to answer all of the questions for analyzing an argument.

Group Activity

By comparing your responses to the previous Applications with those of your peers, you can gain a helpful perspective on the effectiveness of your critical reading strategies. You can also better understand how individual students' different purposes and practices influence their reading of and responses to texts.

Bring your responses to the previous Applications in this section to class. (These include your preview, annotations, outline, summary, and analysis of the argument of "First, Do No Harm.") Meeting with a group of peers, compare your responses to one or more of the Applications, as directed by your instructor. After you have shared your responses, work together to briefly describe the extent to which your responses were similar or dissimilar. Then discuss what these similarities and differences have helped you understand about the process of critical reading, coming to two or three conclusions that you are prepared to share with your classmates.

READING TO WRITE: RESPONDING TO YOUR READING

Response is a natural part of the reading process. Some responses are fleeting. While reading an essay on changing demographics in America, for instance, you may find yourself wondering why the writer emphasizes the economic and political consequences of these changes but barely mentions their social and cultural implications. If upon reflection you find that the writer's inattention to the social and cultural consequences of demographic change indicates substantial problems with his or her discussion, you may later write a more formal analysis of this essay in which you point out areas the writer ignored.

Because they are both acts of composing, reading and writing are complementary processes that together can help you not only deepen your understanding of a text but also increase your emotional and intellectual engagement with it. Writing can thus serve several important functions as you respond to your reading. You can use writing to explore a reading and your response to it; you can also express that understanding through writing.

The previous section of this chapter presented a number of strategies you can use to read actively and critically. These strategies encouraged you to attend carefully to the text you are reading—to learn more about how it is structured, the kind of evidence and arguments the writer relies upon. As noted earlier, however, reading involves more than attention to the words on the page. These words represent the writer's intended meaning, but as a reader you construct your own understanding of a text. Your response to a text—the meaning that you make of it, what you *do* with it—is influenced by such factors as your personal interest in and previous knowledge of the text's subject and your familiarity with its textual conventions. If you have never read a sonnet or studied the sonnet form, for instance, you will find it difficult fully to appreciate the difference between a Shakespearean and Petrarchan sonnet. Similarly, if you have never given much thought to the ecological and economic importance of coastal wetlands, you will read an essay on this topic differently than if you have been actively involved in a campaign to protect wetlands in your area.

As a reader, your goal is to get the most out of your reading, to *do* the most with it. To do so, you need to pay attention to your initial response to a reading and to your own reading process. Whatever your response—from interest or confusion to boredom—you can use this response to develop strategies for a second reading. One student who originally found Shell's essay "First, Do No Harm" uninteresting was able to explore the reasons for her response by freewriting:

> I don't know; Shell's essay just doesn't do anything to me.
> I mean the world is so full of problems, especially now, why
> should we care about whether doctors prescribe too many drugs. I
> can see why insurance companies care--my mother complains all the
> time about the cost of our insurance, and somebody has to pay for
> all those prescriptions. But what is this in comparison with the
> problems of the homeless, the cost of war? It's hard to focus on
> overprescribing with these problems going on. Of course if you
> got sick or died from complications of an unnecessary drug, you'd
> probably care. Maybe that's why I can't connect with Shell's es-
> say. She spends a lot of time talking about detailing, the pres-
> sure to prescribe that physicians face, the need for better
> medical training. Why doesn't she emphasize the human costs of
> overprescription more? Does she ignore them or just underempha-
> size them--I'd better go back to the essay.

This student's freewriting enabled her not only to understand why she originally found Shell's essay uninteresting but also to pose a question for a second reading of the essay. Whether you freewrite, brainstorm, keep a journal, participate in an informal or formal discussion group, or use some other means to explore your response to your reading, you are involved in a dynamic process, one that encourages you to use your response as a means of formulating questions and developing strategies for future reading, reflection, and writing.

Activities for Thought, Discussion, and Writing

1. In the advertisement shown in Figure 9-1 on pages 212–213, Jane Bryant Quinn, a well-known business and economics commentator, explains how to read an annual report. Her two-page discus-

sion not only provides useful advice but also considers why someone might want to read a business report and attempts to motivate readers to do so. Working alone, or with a group of classmates, analyze Quinn's discussion. How much of her advice focuses on the textual conventions characteristic of annual reports, and how much focuses on content? Why is it necessary for her to discuss both? What does Quinn's discussion tell you about the kind of knowledge readers must have to make sense of unfamiliar reading material?

2. The discussion by Quinn appeared in a number of national magazines. How do you think that the nature and readership of these magazines influenced the form of her discussion? What textual conventions typical of advertising and news writing characterize her discussion?

3. Analyze the first chapter of two textbooks you are reading this term (including this one, if you like). Do these textbooks share certain textual conventions? How do you think the writers of these textbooks have visualized their rhetorical situation? These textbooks are written for you and other students. How effective are they? How might they be more effective?

4. Here is a brief short story, "Yours," by Mary Robison. Read this story once quickly. Then reread the story, writing down questions, responses, and ideas for a "strong" reading of it. Your teacher may ask you to write an essay responding to or analyzing this story.

YOURS

Allison struggled away from her white Renault, limping with the weight of the last of the pumpkins. She found Clark in the twilight on the twig- and leaf-littered porch, behind the house. He wore a tan wool shawl. He was moving up and back in a cushioned glider, pushed by the ball of his slippered foot.

Allison lowered a big pumpkin and let it rest on the porch floor.

Clark was much older than she—seventy-eight to Allison's thirty-five. They had been married for four months. They were both quite tall, with long hands, and their faces looked something alike. Allison wore a natural-hair wig. It was a thick blond hood around her face. She was dressed in bright-dyed denims today. She wore durable clothes, usually, for she volunteered afternoons at a children's day-care center.

She put one of the smaller pumpkins on Clark's long lap. "Now, nothing surreal," she told him. "Carve just a *regular* face. These are for kids."

In the foyer, on the Hepplewhite desk, Allison found the maid's chore list, with its cross-offs, which included Clark's supper. Allison

(continued on page 214)

How to read an annual report

By Jane Bryant Quinn

International Paper asked Jane Bryant Quinn, business commentator for the CBS-TV Morning News, *columnist for* Newsweek, *and author of* Everyone's Money Book, *to tell how anyone can understand and profit from a company's annual report.*

To some business people I know, curling up with a good annual report is almost more exciting than getting lost in John le Carré's latest spy thriller.

But to you it might be another story. "Who needs that?" I can hear you ask. *You* do—if you're going to gamble any of your future *working* for a company, *investing* in it, or *selling* to it.

Why should you bother?

Say you've got a job interview at Galactic Industries. Well, what does the company do? Does its future look good? Or will the next recession leave your part of the business on the beach?

Or say you're thinking of investing your own hard-earned money in its stock. Sales are up. But are its profits getting better or worse?

Or say you're going to supply it with a lot of parts. Should you extend Galactic plenty of credit or keep it on a short leash?

How to get one

You'll find answers in its annual report. Where do you find *that?* Your library should have the annual reports of nearby companies plus leading national ones. It also has listings of companies' financial

officers and their addresses so you can write for annual reports.

So now Galactic Industries' latest annual report is sitting in front of you ready to be cracked. How do you crack it?

Where do we start? *Not* at the front. At the *back!* We don't want to be surprised at the end of *this* story.

Start at the back

First, turn back to the report of the *certified public accountant.* This third-party auditor will tell you right off the bat if Galactic's report conforms with "generally accepted accounting principles."

Watch out for the words "subject to." They mean the financial report is clean *only* if you take the company's word about a particular piece of business, and the accountant isn't sure you should. Doubts like this are usually settled behind closed doors. When a "subject to" makes it into the annual report, it could mean trouble.

What else should you know before you check the numbers?

Stay in the back of the book and go to

the *footnotes.* Yep! The whole profits story is sometimes in the footnotes.

Are earnings down? If it's only because of a change in accounting, maybe that's good! The company owes less tax and has more money

in its pocket. Are earnings up? Maybe that's bad. They may be up because of a special windfall that won't happen again next year. The footnotes know.

For what happened and why

Now turn to the *letter from the chairman.* Usually addressed "to our stockholders," it's up front, and *should* be in more ways than one. The chairman's tone reflects the personality, the well-being of his company.

In his letter he should tell you how his company fared this year. But more important, he should tell you *why.* Keep an eye out for sentences that start with "Except for..." and "Despite the..." They're clues to problems.

Insights into the future

On the positive side, a chairman's letter should give you insights into the company's future and its *stance* on economic or political trends that may affect it.

While you're up front, look for what's new in each line of business. Is management getting the company in good shape to weather the tough and competitive 1980's?

"Reading an annual report can be (almost) as exciting as a spy thriller—if you know how to find the clues. I'll show you how to find the most important ones here."

Now—and no sooner—should you dig into the numbers!

One source is the *balance sheet.* It is a snapshot of how the company stands at a single point in time. On the left are *assets* — everything the company owns. Things that can

Figure 9-1

quickly be turned into cash are *current assets.* On the right are *liabilities*—everything the company owes. *Current liabilities* are the debts due in one year, which are paid out of current assets.

The difference between current assets and current liabilities is *net working capital,* a key figure to watch from one annual (and quarterly) report to another. If working capital shrinks, it could mean trouble. One possibility: the company may not be able to keep dividends growing rapidly.

Look for growth here

Stockholders' equity is the difference between total assets and liabilities. It is the presumed dollar value of what stockholders own. You want it to grow.

Another important number to watch is *long-term debt.* High and rising debt, relative to equity, may be no problem for a growing business. But it shows weakness in a company that's leveling out. (More on that later.)

"For inside information, an annual report is second only to meeting with the brass behind closed doors. Come on in!"

The second basic source of numbers is the *income statement.* It shows how much money Galactic made or lost over the year.

Most people look at one figure first. It's in the income statement at the bottom: *net earnings per share.* Watch out. It can fool you. Galactic's management could boost earnings by selling off a plant. Or by cutting the budget for research and advertising. (See the footnotes!) So don't be smug about net earnings until you've found out how they happened—and how they might happen next year.

Check net sales first

The number you *should* look at first in the income statement is *net sales.* Ask yourself: Are sales going *up at a faster rate* than the last time around? When sales increases start to slow, the company may be in trouble. Also ask: Have sales gone up faster than inflation? If not, the company's *real* sales may be behind. And ask yourself once more: Have sales gone down because the company is selling off a losing business?

If so, profits may be soaring.

(I never promised you that figuring out an annual report was going to be easy!)

Get out your calculator

Another important thing to study today is the company's debt. Get out your pocket calculator, and turn to the balance sheet. Divide long-term liabilities by stockholders' equity. That's the *debt-to-equity ratio.*

A high ratio means that the company borrows a lot of money to spark its growth. That's okay—*if* sales grow, too, and *if* there's enough cash on hand to meet the payments. A company doing well on borrowed money can earn big profits for its stockholders. But if sales fall, watch out. The whole enterprise may slowly sink. Some companies can handle high ratios, others can't.

You have to compare

That brings up the most important thing of all: *One* annual report, *one* chairman's letter, *one* ratio won't tell you much. You have to compare. Is the company's debt-to-equity ratio better or worse than it used to be? Better or worse than the industry norms? Better or worse, after this recession, than it was after the last recession? In company-watching, *comparisons are all.* They tell you if management is staying on top of things.

Financial analysts work out many other ratios to tell them how the company is doing. You can learn more about them from books on the subject. Ask your librarian.

But one thing you will *never* learn from an annual report is how much to pay for a company's stock. Galactic may be running well. But if investors expected it to run better, the stock might fall. Or, Galactic could be slumping badly. But if investors see a better day tomorrow, the stock could rise.

Two important suggestions

Those are some basics for weighing a company's health from its annual report. But if you want to know *all* you can about a company, you need to do a little more homework. First, see what the business press has been saying about it over recent years. Again, ask your librarian.

Finally, you should keep up with what's going on in business, economics and politics here and around the world. All can—and will—affect you and the companies you're interested in.

Each year, companies give you more and more information in their annual reports. Profiting from that information is up to you. I hope you profit from *mine.*

Jane Bryant Quinn

Today, the printed word is more vital than ever. Now there is more need than ever for all of us to *read* better, *write* better, and *communicate* better.

International Paper offers this series in the hope that, even in a small way, we can help.

If you'd like additional reprints of this article or an 11"x17"copy suitable for bulletin board posting or framing, please write: "Power of the Printed Word," International Paper Company, Dept. 8, P.O. Box 954, Madison Square Station, New York, NY 10010. © 1982 INTERNATIONAL PAPER COMPANY

INTERNATIONAL PAPER COMPANY
We believe in the power of the printed word.

went quickly through the day's mail: a garish coupon packet, a flyer advertising white wines at Jamestown Liquors, November's pay-TV program guide, and—the worst thing, the funniest—an already opened, extremely unkind letter from Clark's married daughter, up North. "You're an old fool," Allison read, and "You're being cruelly deceived." There was a gift check for twenty-five dollars, made out to Clark, enclosed—his birthday had just passed—but it was uncashable. It was signed "Jesus H. Christ."

Late, late into this night, Allison and Clark gutted and carved the pumpkins together, at an old table set out on the back porch. They worked over newspaper after soggy newspaper, using paring knives and spoons and a Swiss Army knife Clark liked for the exact shaping of teeth and eyes and nostrils. Clark had been a doctor—an internist—but he was also a Sunday watercolor painter. His four pumpkins were expressive and artful. Their carved features were suited to the sizes and shapes of the pumpkins. Two looked ferocious and jagged. One registered surprise. The last was serene and beaming.

Allison's four faces were less deftly drawn, with slits and areas of distortion. She had cut triangles for noses and eyes. The mouths she had made were all just wedges—two turned up and two turned down.

By 1 A.M., they were finished. Clark, who had bent his long torso forward to work, moved over to the glider again and looked out sleepily at nothing. All the neighbors' lights were out across the ravine. For the season and time, the Virginia night was warm. Most of the leaves had fallen and blown away already, and the trees stood unbothered. The moon was round, above them.

Allison cleaned up the mess.

"Your jack-o'-lanterns are much much better than mine," Clark said to her.

"Like hell," Allison said.

"Look at me," Clark said, and Allison did. She was holding a squishy bundle of newspapers. The papers reeked sweetly with the smell of pumpkin innards. "Yours are *far* better," he said.

"You're wrong. You'll see when they're lit," Allison said.

She went inside, came back with yellow vigil candles. It took her a while to get each candle settled into a pool of its own melted wax inside the jack-o'-lanterns, which were lined up in a row on the porch railing. Allison went along and relit each candle and fixed the pumpkin lids over the little flames. "See?" she said. They sat together a moment and looked at the orange faces.

"We're exhausted. It's good-night time," Allison said. "Don't blow out the candles. I'll put in new ones tomorrow."

In her bedroom, a few weeks earlier in her life than had been predicted, she began to die. "Don't look at me if my wig comes off," she told Clark. "Please." Her pulse cords were fluttering under his fingers. She raised her knees and kicked away the comforter. She said something to Clark about the garage being locked.

At the telephone, Clark had a clear view out back and down to the porch. He wanted to get drunk with his wife once more. He wanted to tell her, from the greater perspective he had, that to own only a little talent, like his, was an awful, plaguing thing; that being only a little special meant you expected too much, most of the time, and liked yourself too little. He wanted to assure her that she had missed nothing.

Clark was speaking into the phone now. He watched the jack-o'-lanterns. The jack-o'-lanterns watched him.

MARY ROBISON

5. The following article, "The Endless Autumn," by Nicolaus Mills, was published in the April 16, 1990, issue of *The Nation*. Read this article once quickly. Then reread the article, writing down questions, responses, and ideas for a "strong" reading of it. Your teacher may ask you to write an essay responding to or analyzing this article.

THE ENDLESS AUTUMN

The headline for Adelphi University's full-page *New York Times* ad was apologetic: "Why the Most Interesting University in the Country Stoops So Low as to Advertise Itself." The apology was understandable. Colleges and universities aren't supposed to sell themselves. They are supposed to present themselves—at most in user-friendly fashion—so their future students can make an informed choice.

What Adelphi was doing with its hard sell was, however, similar to what most colleges do now: offer themselves with a Madison Avenue format and treat their students as customers who need to be won over. The change—and with it the rise of firms specializing in institutional promotion and market research—is hardly surprising. Since the baby-boom days of the 1960s the pool of college-age students has shrunk, while in the past ten years the price of a college education has risen by 118 percent at private universities and 82 percent at public ones.

Nonetheless, for most colleges a full-page *New York Times* ad remains too blatant. They prefer a forty- to sixty-page booklet—the viewbook, *a.k.a.* the register or the bulletin. Bigger than a prospectus, smaller than a catalogue, college viewbooks circulate in the millions. For every freshman it accepts, a college often sends out fifty viewbooks. At big schools an annual printing of 100,000 is common.

On these grounds alone, the college viewbook is worth taking seriously. We can no more afford to ignore its mix of rhetoric and social motive than we can that of other mass-circulation publications such as *The Official Boy Scout Handbook* or *The Red Cross First Aid Manual*. But circulation alone is not what makes college viewbooks important. Although the immediate audience is college freshmen and their parents (the paying customers), no other publication so represents college culture as colleges wish it to be seen.

What this idealized picture means in 1990 begins with the college code word of the 1980s—diversity. "Diversity is the hallmark of the Harvard/Radcliffe experience," the first sentence in the Harvard University register declares. "Diversity is the virtual core of University life," the University of Michigan bulletin announces. "Diversity is rooted deeply in the liberal arts tradition and is key to our educational philosophy," Connecticut College insists. "Duke's 5,800 undergraduates come from regions which are truly diverse," the Duke University bulletin declares. "Stanford values a class that is both ethnically and economically diverse," the Stanford University bulletin notes. Brown University says, "When asked to describe the undergraduate life at The College—and particularly their first strongest impression of Brown as freshmen—students consistently bring up the same topic: the diversity of the student body."

What diversity means in this context is that a college is doing its best to abolish the idea that it caters to middle-class whites. By focusing on diversity rather than desegregation or some made-up word like "de-eliting," the college sees itself getting a bargain. It doesn't have to own up to a history of bigotry, and by focusing on the variety that diversity implies, the college avoids the charge of social engineering that it would be subject to if it said it was seeking more minority students.

In an era when racial tensions are on the rise and the Supreme Court has put affirmative action beyond the reach of all but the most determined employer, any institution that insists on diversity is noteworthy. In our colleges and universities, faith in diversity is much more than a political stance, however. It is also an expression of faith in their own transforming power, in their ability to create a special world. Connecticut College puts this specialness most extravagantly when it declares that its students are led into "another universe of discourse." Indeed, in 1990 it's impossible for any leading college to imagine that its students won't, as Oberlin College notes with ten banner headlines in the first five pages of its bulletin, "THRIVE."

What thriving means in this context is exemplified by the boxed cameo portraits of superstudents (for example, the Stanford Rhodes scholar who aids battered women and intends to play basketball on the Oxford team) that every viewbook seems to feature. If ever a student undertook a project that failed, it is never mentioned. Nor is there a hint that a project might have caused a student to see humanity less hopefully.

Above all, there is never an indication that students don't mature on schedule. While even in the Ivy League there is a difference between a Columbia University, which requires its students to take a core curriculum, and a Brown, which emphasizes that it has no core curriculum, the guiding assumption in all cases is that by their junior year at the latest students will find their academic path. As Princeton University, which emphasizes the independent work its juniors and seniors do, notes in its viewbook, "A first-rate education is not something that happens to you, but rather is something you yourself make happen." Never in any viewbook do we get a senior who confesses he coasted through too many courses, nor does any student ever worry that four years of study may make a 9-to-5 job unbearably dull.

What underlies this faith in the college experience is never systematically argued in any viewbook, but it is not hard to find the philosophical source: It is the virtues of a liberal education. "A liberal education must be the thread that weaves a pattern of meaning into the total learning experience," Brown president Vartan Gregorian writes. "By stressing the value of a liberal education we encourage students to seek the infinitely precious affirmation of their most authentic selves," Dartmouth College president James Freedman states. "A liberally educated person is 'liberated' to the extent that education has deepened his or her capacity and inclination for clear thought, analytical reasoning, comprehension and empathy," Wesleyan University's dean of admission declares.

The result is that while viewbooks may read differently (less so if copy as well as graphics have been turned over to a Madison Avenue firm), they remain remarkably similar in structure. Almost all contain the following:

The Melting-Pot Ideal. In addition to their viewbooks, most colleges now have special brochures for minority students. But in the viewbook itself nothing is more important to convey than a picture of students of all races mixing, and doing so in approximately equal numbers of men and women (a problem at single-sex schools that have only marginally turned coed). The result is the ubiquitous posed group photo in which white, black, Asian and Latino students look into the camera and grin like crazy. The photo, if the college can afford it, will be in color, and if not on the cover of its viewbook, within the first few pages. Significantly, candid photos are not used to make the same point.

The Endless Autumn Motif. Falling yellow leaves at Indiana University. Falling red leaves at Smith College. In the college viewbook autumn never seems to stop. At its simplest the point is that college is a beautiful place. But the real function of the endless autumn motif is to convince students that college is a timeless world where they can forget the day-to-day pressures of ordinary life. Even at Columbia, where campus guards have been attacked by New York City muggers, the viewbook makes the school sound like a utopia. "No traffic rumbles across its paths, no skyscrapers skewer its sunshine, no urban tumult disturbs its placid terraces," the Columbia viewbook declares before going on to conclude that the "Columbia landscape is a classic collegiate stage."

The Small-but-Big Paradox. Its aim is to convince students they can have the best of two possible worlds without sacrificing anything. Wesleyan declares that it "brings together the best features of the liberal arts college and the large university." Duke, with 5,800 under-graduate students in contrast with Wesleyan's 2,600, describes its size as "midway between that of small liberal arts colleges and larger research universities." The key here is for the viewbook never to pose the kinds of questions that make the difference between bigness and smallness clear: What percentage of their students do teachers see in office hours? Could an unrecruited athlete expect to play on a varsity team? Do teachers give out written student evaluations or only grades?

The Admissions Fudge. Its intention is to assure prospective students that there is no conflict between selecting a freshman class on merit and opting for a diversity that means, as one admissions dean put it, "We take in more in the groups with weaker credentials and make it harder for those with stronger credentials." There is no attempt to explain why strong board scores will benefit some minorities (blacks) more than other minorities (Asians), or why some minorities (Italian-Americans) are of interest to almost nobody. The result is the kind of admissions statement that, like the following one by Stanford, could mean anything: "The long and labored evaluation process cannot be reduced to a quantifiable formula. . . . While we are focusing on each individual, we also are mindful of putting together a freshman class that cuts across a number of dimensions. Consequently, many factors enter into the process over which individual candidates have no control."

For colleges, even the leading ones, there would of course be a price to pay for turning out a candid viewbook. Harvard, which insists that "good teaching and scholarship go hand in hand," would have to explain why the winners of its 1986 and 1987 Levenson Award for Outstanding Teaching were both rejected for tenure. Yale University, which in its bulletin stresses a folksy concern for student life (you can get Cap'n Crunch for breakfast), would have to explain why it forced clerical employees with an average salary of $13,318 to go through a bitter ten-week strike in 1984 just to get union recognition and improved pay. Stanford, which advertises its social concern with a picture of folk singer Joan Baez at a Stanford antiapartheid rally, would have to explain why so many of its minority students saw its required Western culture courses as racist.

The irony is that in college publications sent to alumni, candor on controversial subjects is usual. In the *Princeton Alumni Weekly* one can read a harrowing account of the rape of a student, and the *Dartmouth Alumni Magazine* carried a series of articles on the racial confrontations that have made Dartmouth national news. Indeed, the assumption our leading colleges make is that the only way to keep the support of students and alumni is to come clean about their troubles. Where they draw the line is with prospective freshmen and their parents.

The closest any viewbook comes to being candid is at Williams

College, where the prospectus in its between-the-pages inserts offers such information about the Williams freshman class as the percentage who admit they cheated on a high school test. But even in the Williams viewbook (yearly cost, $100,000) candor is primarily a tactic, part of an overall antihype strategy. In the final analysis the viewbooks of our leading colleges are a sad performance, made sadder still by the fact that, given what it can cost to visit a far-off school, the viewbook remains the most democratic mechanism a college has for reaching new students.

NICOLAUS MILLS

6. After reading "The Endless Autumn," obtain a copy of your own college's viewbook, the bulletin or register your college sends to prospective students and their parents. Write an essay in which you discuss the degree to which Mills's analysis does or does not apply to or fit your own college's viewbook. Alternatively, you may wish to compare your college's viewbook and that of another college.

CHAPTER 10

UNDERSTANDING ACADEMIC AUDIENCES AND ASSIGNMENTS

As a student in college, you need to understand the textual conventions of academic writing. These conventions are not arbitrary—though they may at first seem confusing to you. Rather, they respond to and reflect the academic rhetorical situation. Like other textual conventions, they represent shared agreements between writers and readers about the construction and interpretation of texts. This chapter describes the values and expectations of an important group of academic readers—your instructors. It also shows you, as a writer, how to analyze academic writing assignments. The next chapter focuses on two important skills required in all academic writing: analysis and argument.

UNDERSTANDING YOUR AUDIENCE: STUDENTS WRITING/INSTRUCTORS READING

Since your instructors are the primary readers of the writing you do in college, you need to understand their values and goals for you and other students. No matter what their disciplines, your instructors are members of an academic community. As such, they share a number of intellectual commitments and values. Perhaps the most central of these is the commitment to the ideal of education as inquiry. All your instructors—in business, liberal arts, agriculture, engineering, and other fields—want to foster students' abilities to think, write, and speak clearly and effectively. When they read your papers and exams, then, your instructors are looking both for your knowledge of a specific subject and for your ability to think and write with sophistication.

Although they might disagree about specifics, those who teach in colleges and universities generally agree about what it means to be a well-educated, thoughtful, knowledgeable person. They believe, for instance, that perhaps the worst intellectual error (after claiming someone else's ideas as your own) is oversimplifying. They want their students to learn how to go beyond obvious and stereotypical analysis and arguments to deeper understandings. Thus a historian might urge his students to recognize that more was at stake in the American Civil War than freeing the slaves, while an engineer might encourage her students to realize that the most obvious way to resolve a design problem is not necessarily the best.

Most college instructors want their students to be able to do more than memorize or summarize information. They want to develop their students' abilities to analyze, apply, question, and evaluate information read and discussed in class. College instructors also want their students to be able to consider issues from multiple perspectives. They tend to believe that nearly every issue or problem has at least two sides—if not more. Because most intellectual issues are so complex, college instructors believe that to explore an idea adequately you must often limit the issue, question, or problem under discussion. They also believe that arguments should be supported by substantial and appropriate evidence, not emotional appeals or logical fallacies. Various disciplines accept different kinds of evidence and follow different methodologies to insure that conclusions are as accurate and meaningful as possible. But all share the conviction that those arguing a point should support their assertions with more than just an "in my opinion."

The habits of thinking your college instructors are committed to helping you acquire are intrinsically rewarding. The knowledge that you can analyze a complex issue or problem, work through various arguments, and develop your own position on a subject brings both intellectual and emotional satisfaction and confidence. These same habits of thinking also bring extrinsic rewards, for they are—as chief executive officers in business and industry emphasize—precisely the habits of mind required to succeed in positions of responsibility in any field.

Exploration

Freewrite for five or ten minutes about your experiences thus far as an academic writer. What has frustrated or confused you? What has excited you? What questions do you have about the academic rhetorical situation and the conventions of academic writing?

What *do* instructors look for when they read students' writing? Most broadly, your instructors want writing that demonstrates learning and a real commitment to and engagement with the subject being discussed. They want writing that reveals that you are making connections between the issues discussed in class and your life and personal values. And they want writing that adheres to the standards of clear thinking and effective communication that they share as members of the academic community. Specifically, most instructors would agree that they hope to find qualities such as those listed here in their students' papers.

CHARACTERISTICS OF EFFECTIVE STUDENT WRITING

Effective college writing:

- addresses a limited but significant topic
- establishes a meaningful context for the discussion of this topic
- presents a sustained and full discussion, given the limitations of the topic, the time to do the assignment, and the page length
- follows a clear pattern of organization
- discusses sources (if included) fairly and effectively
- provides adequate details and evidence for generalizations
- uses appropriate, concise language
- avoids serious errors of grammar, punctuation, and usage

The following essay, written by Tessa McGlasson for a class in European history, fulfills the above criteria. This essay was written in response to this assignment for a take-home midterm exam: "What does Francesco Guicciardini's biography of Lorenzo de Medici reveal about the realities and ideals of fifteenth century Italy?" Tessa's instructor, Dr. Lisa Sarasohn, presented students with excerpts from the biography that Guicciardini, a contemporary Florentine historian, wrote shortly after Medici's death. These excerpts are included here. Read both the excerpts from Guicciardini's biography and Tessa's essay with care. As you read, note how Tessa uses these excerpts to support her conclusions about "the realities and ideals of fifteenth century Italy."

A PORTRAIT OF LORENZO DE MEDICI
By Francesco Guicciardini

The city was in a state of perfect peace, the citizens of the state united and bound together, and the government so powerful that no one dared to oppose it. Every day the populace delighted in spectacles, feasts and novel diversions. The city was sustained both by its abundant supplies and its flourishing and well-established business enterprises; men of talent and ability were rewarded through the recognition and support given to all letters, all arts, all gifts. And finally when the city was in a state of profound tranquility and quiet within, and at the height of glory and reputation without—as a result of having a government and a head of the greatest authority, of having recently extended its dominion, of having been in great part responsible for the salvation of Ferrara and then of King Ferrante, of controlling completely Pope Innocent, of being allied with Naples and Milan, and of being a kind of balance for Italy as a whole—something happened which turned everything upside down, to the confusion not only of the city but of all Italy. And this was the fact that in the said year, Lorenzo de Medici, having had a long illness, finally on the 8th day of April, 1492, passed from this life.

This death was marked out as one of the greatest consequence by many omens: a comet had appeared a short time before; wolves had been heard to howl; a mad woman in Santa Maria Novello had cried out that an ox with fiery horns was burning up the whole city; some lions had fallen into a fight and the most beautiful had been killed by the others; and finally a day or two before his death lightning had struck at night the lantern of the dome of Santa Liparate [Reparata] and knocked down some enormous stones, which fell toward the house of the Medici. . . .

Lorenzo de Medici was forty-three years old when he died, and . . . although he was so young and supposedly under the control of Messer Tommaso Soderini and other elders of the state, nevertheless, in a short time he gained such strength and reputation that he governed the city in his own way. Since his authority multiplied every day and then reached its height through the political crisis of 1478 and later on his return from his successful mission to Naples, he continued until his death to govern the city and to arrange matters entirely according to his own will, as if he were the sole and absolute master. . . .

There were in Lorenzo many and most excellent virtues; there were also in him some vices, due partly to nature, partly to necessity. He possessed such great authority that one could say that in his time the city was not free although it abounded in all the glory and felicity that a city can have; free in name, but in fact and in truth tyrannized over by one of its citizens. His deeds, although they can be censured in part, were very great nonetheless, and so great that they win much more admiration from careful consideration of the facts than from mere hearsay, because they are lacking in those feats of arms and in that military art and discipline for which the ancients are so famous. This was due not to any fault of his but to the age. . . .

No one, even among his adversaries and those who maligned him, denies that there was in him a very great and extraordinary genius. To have governed the city for twenty-three years, and always with increasing power and glory, is such proof of it that anyone who denies it is mad; especially since this is a city most free in speech, full of the most subtle and restless talents. . . . Proof also is the friendship and great reputation he enjoyed with many princes both inside and outside Italy. . . . This reputation sprang from nothing else than knowing how to keep the friendship of these princes with great dexterity and skill. Proof also to those who heard him was his public and private discourse, full of acumen and subtlety, by which in many times and places . . . he gained very great advantage. Proof also are the letters dictated by him, full of such art that one could not ask for more; these seemed the more beautiful inasmuch as they were accompanied by a great eloquence and a most elegant style.

He desired glory and excellence beyond that of anyone else, and in this he can be criticized for having had too much ambition even in regard to minor things; he did not wish to be equalled or imitated by any citizen even in verses or games or exercises, turning angrily against any who did so. He was too ambitious even in great affairs, inasmuch as he wished in everything to equal or emulate all the princes of Italy. . . . In general, however, such ambition was praiseworthy and was responsible for making his renown celebrated everywhere, even outside Italy, because he strove to bring it about that in his time all the arts and talents should be more excellent in Florence than in any other city of Italy. Chiefly for the sake of letters he refounded in Pisa a university of law and the arts. . . . And therefore there always taught in Pisa in his time, with the highest salaries, all the most excellent and famous men of Italy, whom he did not spare expense or trouble to secure. And similarly there flourished in Florence the studies of the humanities. . . . He showed the same favour to vernacular poetry, to music, architecture, painting, sculpture, and all the fine and mechanical arts, so that the city was overflowing with all these graces. These arts developed all the more because he, being most versatile, could pass judgment on them and distinguish among men, with the result that all strove with one another in order to please him more. Of advantage also was the boundless generosity with which he showered pensions on talented men and supplied them with all the tools necessary to their arts. For example, when he wanted to create a Greek library, he sent Lascaris, a most learned man who taught Greek in Florence, as far as Greece to seek out ancient and good books.

The same liberality preserved his renown and his friendship with the princes outside Italy, since he neglected no show of magnificence, even at the greatest expense and loss, by which he might influence great men. And so, through such display and lavishness, his expenditures multiplied in Lyons, Milan, Bruges, and in various centres of his trade and his company, while his profits diminished from being neglected by incompetent agents. . . . His accounts were not well kept because he did not understand commerce or pay enough attention to it, and as a result his affairs more than once fell into such disorder that he was on the point of bankruptcy, and it was necessary for him to help himself out both with money from his friends and with public funds.

TESSA MCGLASSON, HISTORY 331, EXAM TWO

The late fifteenth century, when Lorenzo de Medici ruled Florence, was a prosperous, progressive era for that city, and indeed all of Italy. A more enlightened way of thinking had arrived, and human activity strove to use this new light to illuminate everything that was good and right. But in any rapidly progressing time period there are less desirable elements which come hand in hand with the good. This document reveals much information about the clash of human ideal and human reality in fifteenth century Florence.

The first paragraph of Guicciardini's biography sets forth the overlying cultural and political climate of the period: the city was flourishing and "in a state of perfect peace." What we think of as the Renaissance was underway; "recognition and support" was fully given to the arts and letters, and the citizens enjoyed "spectacles, feasts, and novel diversions" every day. Florence had risen to become one of the most powerful cities on the Italian peninsula under the Medici by the time Lorenzo took power despotically after his father's death in 1469. He ruled

Florence "in his own way" and "according to his own will, as if
he were the sole and absolute master." Medici traveled to Naples
in 1479 and made friends with its king, Ferrante. Since Ferrante
was allied with the pope, this shrewd move earned Florence two
worthy allies at once and ended the city's ongoing wars with the
papal states. This resulted in Medici's "controlling completely
Pope Innocent" and "of being allied with Naples." Another al-
liance existed with Milan. Since we know that city-state al-
liances were constantly shifting during these years, the first
paragraph takes on a fleeting, one-moment-in-time sort of quality;
indeed it should, since it is describing only where Florence was
in early April of 1492, at the time of Lorenzo de Medici's death.

The second paragraph of the biography reveals another interesting characteristic of this period--that is the increasing importance being placed upon the relationship between humans and the
universe. People had begun to believe that the events in the universe affected humans, and vice-versa. Medici's death was apparently "marked out as one of greatest consequence by many omens."
Included in these are astrological and meteorological signs (the
comet and lightning), signs from the animal kingdom (howling wolves
and fighting lions), and strange, inexplicable behaviors of other
humans (the mad woman's ravings). Everything in the universe was
believed to be connected somehow to everything else, and this assumption rests behind much of the advancement made in the era.

The ideals and realities of the late fifteenth century are
illustrated clearly in this manuscript by the personality and actions of Lorenzo de Medici himself. "There were in Lorenzo many
and most excellent virtues," we are told, among them a "very
great and excellent genius." He was a great diplomat: he knew
"how to keep the friendship of these princes with great dexterity

and skill." He spoke and wrote eloquently: his discourse "full
of acumen and subtlety" and his letters in a "most elegant
style." Medici was highly educated and patronized the arts in
every way. He paid well for "all the most excellent and famous
men of Italy" to teach at his university in an effort to make
Florence a center for all types of learning--great evidence of the
"civic pride" and love of liberal education so valued in the Renaissance. Like an ideal noble, Medici patronized talented people
with "boundless generosity." The study of the classics was important to him, as shown by his quest for the best Greek books.
These traits and passions were considered ideal by fifteenth century Florentines as well as other Italians.

With Medici's position of power, however, came opportunities
for corruption and greed. Guicciardini points out that "there
were also in him some vices." The absolute power of his rule in-
vited tyranny, and Guicciardini admits that no matter how "tranquil" and "glorious" Florence was, it "was not free." Medici
was intensely ambitious and egotistical: he "did not wish to be
equalled" and "turned angrily against" anyone who tried. He was
often overly extravagant and his lavishness cost him dearly. Con-
trary to his status as the ideal "Renaissance prince," matters of
commerce escaped his understanding, and so he ignored and neglected them, letting his greed and vanity take over and eventually bring him to "the point of bankruptcy." We further are
told that to "help himself out," he took money from "public
funds." Although in other sources about him we read mostly about
his idealized genius and virtue, this document points out some of
Medici's real-life faults as well.

With any despotism or other form of absolute government comes
the unlimited power of tyranny and all its opportunities for im-

moral human behavior. Likewise, with the ideal must come a dose

of reality. Lorenzo de Medici and his life as detailed in this

document represent the grand, honorable, civilized elements of

fifteenth century Florence. Guicciardini's biography also reminds

us that anything involving humans is always far from perfect.

Italy's fifteenth century, and indeed the entire Renaissance, was

no exception.

Group Activity

Working with a group of classmates, discuss how Tessa McGlasson's essay demonstrates the characteristics of effective student writing listed on page 222. Locate at least one specific example of each characteristic in Tessa's essay. Appoint a recorder to write down the results of your discussion, which your instructor may ask you to present to the class.

LEARNING TO ANALYZE ACADEMIC WRITING ASSIGNMENTS

Understanding your instructors' shared values and goals as members of the academic community can enable you to respond more appropriately to the demands of academic writing. In addition to understanding these values and goals, however, you must know how to analyze the assignments given to you by instructors. Such analysis is crucial, for assignments (whether presented orally or distributed in writing) provide the clearest, most concrete indications of instructors' expectations. You can improve your understanding of your academic assignments by analyzing each assignment, identifying its assumptions, developing strategies to increase your commitment to it, and making action-oriented plans you can use as you work on the assignment.

Analyzing the assignment as presented by your instructor

All assignments are not alike. Sometimes instructors present students with broad, unstructured topics. These assignments are usually relatively brief and open-ended. A political science instructor might ask you to write a twenty-page research paper discussing an important political consequence for America of the Vietnam War. Or a psychology instructor might ask you to write a four- to six-page essay exploring how your family background has influenced your current attitudes about marriage or parenthood. With broad assignments like these, you must often determine not only the specific topic but also the approach to take in analyzing and presenting your material.

In other instances, instructors develop quite limited or specific assignments. Such assignments may substantially restrict your freedom of choice in regard to a topic; they may also include a format or sequence of steps or activities you should follow in completing the assignment. On still other occasions, an assignment may represent a middle ground between these two extremes.

Application

The following assignments are from four different classes. Analyze each assignment, determining if it is broad, limited, or somewhere in the middle.

1. *Take-home final examination question for a political science class.* In a paragraph or two, describe the American public's generally accepted (or "mainstream") view of the role of the United States in the world. Then, in no more than three typewritten, double-spaced pages, do the following:
   - discuss how this view came to be held so widely
   - use logic and evidence to demonstrate significant flaws, distortions, and dangers inherent in the view
   - explain the major factors that must be taken into consideration in devising a new, more accurate, and more viable view
2. *Paper topic for a literature class.* Select from our anthology one of the tales that we didn't read for class. Discuss the tale in the manner in which we discussed the others. Take whatever approach to this tale you choose, but avoid merely summarizing the plot.
3. *Take-home final essay question for a philosophy class.* Explain why Plato considers works of art to be illusions. Why does he see this as a flaw in art? Your answer should address Plato's conceptions of artistry, the art object itself, and the connections between these two topics.
4. *Research paper assignment for a sociology class.* This assignment requires you to complete a content analysis of letters

to the editor from a newspaper for a large urban community (population 500,000 or more) and a newspaper for a small town (population 15,000 or fewer). In completing this assignment, follow the instructions below carefully.

The Content Analysis: Conducting Your Research
- Choose two communities, as described above.
- Read all the letters to the editor in all issues of a newspaper for each community for the same two months.
- Use the letters to the editor as the data for your content analysis.
- In performing your content analysis, follow the attached guidelines [not reprinted here] carefully.

The Content Analysis: Reporting Your Research
- Your research report should be 8 to 10 typed, double-spaced pages long.
- Follow this format in presenting your report: abstract, problem, method, results, discussion, references.
- Use the APA style guidelines for all reference citations.

Whether your instructors give you broad or limited assignments, the words they use to describe these assignments, especially certain key words, can tell you a great deal about their intentions. These key words—words like *define, analyze, evaluate, defend, show, describe, review, prove, summarize,* and *classify*—are usually action verbs. They are crucial in essay examination questions because you must quickly determine how to respond to a topic, but they are important in any writing assignment. An assignment that asks you to *summarize* Freud's oedipal theory, for instance, is quite different from one that asks you to *criticize* or *evaluate* it. To summarize Freud's oedipal theory, you need merely to recount its major features. Criticizing this theory challenges you to identify its major strengths and weaknesses and to provide evidence for your assessment.

Identifying the assumptions behind the assignment

To effectively complete an assignment, you need to know more than whether it is broad or limited. You need to know the criteria your instructor will use to evaluate the assignment and the processes and resources you can best use as you work on it. Some instructors provide information about these and related matters for students. Here, for instance, are suggestions that Dr. David Robinson provides students in his literature classes at Oregon State University.

PROFESSOR DAVID ROBINSON'S SUGGESTIONS FOR WRITING ESSAYS ABOUT LITERATURE

1. Begin from your experience as a reader. Perhaps you found a certain phrase striking or moving, or a character that puzzles or interests you, or a turn in the plot that seems especially apt. There may be a remark or question in class that helps you put things together. Begin there, formulating your paper around that experience.

2. Have a central point, a unifying idea, or a thesis. Either make an argument, or illustrate an observation, or answer a question. Make everything in your paper relate to this thesis. A thesis need not be dogmatic or overly definite. It can be the admission of what you see as irreconcilable contradictions in your response to a text. But that admission can hold your paper together.

3. Use examples and illustrations from the text, direct quotations where appropriate, to illustrate your point. The text of the literary work is the ultimate source for proof of your thesis. But do not simply quote long passages with minimal commentary. The quotes and examples must work to support the line of reasoning you are establishing.

4. The following are some criteria for grading:
   - Originality
   - Accuracy of your analysis of the text (Did you make factual errors? Did you make unsupportable claims about the work?)
   - Thoroughness of your treatment of the topic (Are important elements of the story overlooked? Have elements of the story been given a reasonable relative weight?)
   - Use of examples, illustrations, and quotations from the work to support your arguments
   - Style
   - Grammatical correctness, including spelling and punctuation, but especially sentence construction

If your instructor provides suggestions such as these, you should study them with care. If you don't understand how to act on your instructor's suggestions—how to carry them out as you work on an assignment—make an appointment to speak with your instructor.

Not all instructors provide this kind of information about assignments, however. Sometimes they think that the criteria for evaluation and the processes and resources students might best use to complete an assignment are so obvious that they don't need explicitly to be presented to students. Some instructors believe that students learn more effectively when they take full responsibility for all aspects of an assignment. For this reason, these instructors want students to discover for themselves how they can best work on an assignment and the features that characterize a successful response to an assignment.

Whenever you are presented with an assignment—even one that includes suggestions such as those Dr. David Robinson provides students—you need to "read between the lines." For even detailed suggestions cannot tell you exactly what processes and resources you should use as you work on an assignment. One way to begin this process of reading between the lines is to think about the ways your assignment relates to the objectives, class discussions, and readings for a course. Your instructor may not comment specifically on this connection—yet you can be sure that such a connection does exist. Asking yourself the following questions should help you to recognize such connections and to analyze the assumptions inherent in an assignment.

QUESTIONS FOR DISCOVERING THE ASSUMPTIONS BEHIND AN ASSIGNMENT

1. How does this assignment reflect the objectives of this course? (If you don't understand the course objectives, discuss this problem with your instructor.)
2. What general analytical and argumentative strategies does my instructor emphasize during class discussions? In discussions of readings, what organizational, stylistic, and logical qualities does my instructor praise or criticize? How might this assignment represent my instructor's effort to help me develop the critical abilities he or she emphasizes in class?
3. How much class time has my instructor spent on discussions of readings or on activities related to the content or form of this assignment? What has the instructor emphasized in these discussions or activities? How do these discussions and activities relate to this specific assignment?
4. Does this assignment call for a specific type of writing? How can I use my experience with previous writing assignments to help me successfully complete this assignment?
5. If this is one of several assignments for this course, can I

apply comments my instructor has made in response to earlier essays to my current project?

If you find it difficult to answer these questions, you may want to meet with your instructor to discuss your assignment. This conference will be most useful (for both of you) if you prepare ahead. Before seeing your instructor, ask yourself the questions listed above. Try rewriting the assignment in your own words, and then draw up a plan describing how you intend to complete it. Come to the conference prepared with your plan and with a list of specific questions, if possible. Most instructors are happy to discuss assignments with students, especially students who have prepared carefully for the conference. Don't expect your instructor to give you a step-by-step list of dos and don'ts for an assignment, however. What you want to clarify—and what an instructor will be glad to discuss with you—is your general understanding of and approach to the assignment.

Exploration

Look again at the four assignments included in the Application on page 229. How much information does each assignment provide about the criteria for evaluation and the processes and resources students should use to complete the assignment? If such information is absent, how would you go about "reading between the lines" to discover this information? After rereading each assignment, list the criteria that you believe an instructor would use to evaluate essays turned in by students. Then make a brief list of the processes and resources you believe a student might appropriately use to complete each assignment.

Group Activity

Bring your response to the preceding Exploration to class. Meet with a group of students and, after appointing a recorder, compare your responses to this Exploration. After doing so, formulate at least three statements that indicate what you have learned as a result of this process.

Building commitment to the assignment

Most academic writing is, by definition, *required* writing—writing done to fulfill a requirement. As a student, you are inevitably aware that you are writing not necessarily because you want to but because you have to. These conditions may make it hard for you to feel a strong sense of "ownership" of your writing. Furthermore, even if you're genuinely interested in your topic, you may feel so pressed by deadlines and other demands that all you can think is "I've just got to get this essay out of the way, so I can get ready for biology lab." All writers face these problems, including those who write on the job. Successful writers know, however, that they can't write well unless they are interested in and committed to their subjects. Consequently, they develop strategies to help them build this interest and commitment so that they can transform a required assignment (whether a research paper or a report for the boss) into a question or problem they care about and feel challenged to resolve.

This is not to suggest that you must become passionately absorbed in and excited by every writing assignment. That would not be possible. But if you can't find some way to interest yourself in an assignment, to view it as an intellectual challenge you want to meet, you're going to have trouble getting beyond stale formulas. Some students in this situation simply put off working on their assignments for so long that they must complete them in a desperate, chaotic frenzy. They then blame their poor performance and low grades on their last-minute efforts. There are better ways to respond to the challenge of required writing assignments.

You can, for instance, try to build your interest by using invention strategies—strategies explained in Chapter 5, such as freewriting, looping, brainstorming, and clustering or the more formal journalist's questions, tagmemics, and topical questions. Keeping a writer's journal or notebook may also help you to generate interest in a topic that at first doesn't seem compelling. Suppose, for example, that your economics instructor has asked you to write an essay on some topic connected with the Great Depression of the 1930s. At first you might not find this subject very interesting. After all, the Depression occurred decades ago. You'd rather evaluate one of the current administration's economic policies. But after brainstorming, freewriting, or writing in your journal, you find that you keep coming back to a single image: the much-reproduced photograph of a businessman in a topcoat selling apples on a street corner. Did this actually happen? How often? How representative is this image of the Depression as a whole? Suddenly you've got a series of related questions—questions that you care about and that can help you limit and focus your topic.

When you are building commitment to an assignment, you are looking for reasons to *want* to write, reasons to "own" the assignment your teacher has given you. Talking with your teacher about an assignment is one way you can not only better understand but also care more strongly about an assignment. You can also employ the following guidelines to turn a required assignment into an interesting challenge you want to complete.

Guidelines for generating interest in and commitment to an assignment

1. USE FREEWRITING, BRAINSTORMING, JOURNAL WRITING, OR OTHER INFORMAL KINDS OF WRITING TO EXPLORE WHAT YOU ALREADY KNOW ABOUT YOUR ASSIGNMENT.

As the previous example indicates, freewriting and brainstorming can help you discover images, questions, contradictions, and problems that turn required assignments into questions you want to answer. You may also find it helpful simply to write or list what you already know about a subject; you may be reassured to discover that you have a surprisingly large fund of information on your subject.

2. USE THE SAME STRATEGIES TO EXPLORE HOW YOU FEEL ABOUT AN ASSIGNMENT.

You may find it helpful to freewrite or brainstorm about your feelings about an assignment. While writing in her journal about a required assignment in a journalism class, for instance, Holly Hardin noted that she didn't want to work on a story about whether quarters or semesters are more conducive to learning because it was "just another dead issue." Once she understood the source of her resistance, Holly realized that she should see if her assumption was in fact correct. After interviewing several faculty members on campus, Holly discovered to her surprise that they held widely varying views on this subject. "Once I found a point of conflict," Holly wrote in a later journal entry, "I found a reason to write. From that point on the story was not just easy to work on but interesting."

3. TRICK YOURSELF INTO CARING ABOUT AN ASSIGNMENT BY VARYING YOUR PERSPECTIVE ON IT.

You may find that writing informally about your assignment for different readers may catalyze your ideas and interest. If you're resisting an assignment, write a letter to your parents or a friend describing the reasons why you are finding it difficult. Doing so may help you determine the source of your resistance—and having identified the source you may discover just the right strategy, as Holly Hardin did, to overcome your resistance. At the very least, acknowledging your feelings can be a productive step in the process of moving from resistance to action.

You may find it helpful to conduct a make-believe dialogue with your instructor about an assignment. By forcing yourself to anticipate your instructor's reasons for making the assignment, you may become more engaged with it yourself. (You may wish to follow this dialogue by meeting with your instructor, if you haven't already.)

4. WORK COLLABORATIVELY WITH OTHER STUDENTS IN THE CLASS.

Any assignment can seem overwhelming—something to put off, rather than to begin—when you're sitting alone in your room or the library thinking about it. A much more productive strategy is to meet with other students in the class to discuss your understanding of the assignment and the processes and resources you are employing to respond to it. I'm not talking about a gripe session, or *only* a gripe session. You may want to spend a few moments commiserating with one another about how busy you are, how many assignments you need to do, but you should keep your primary goal in focus. By talking about your assignment and about your current efforts to respond to it, you want to both generate enthusiasm for this project and help one another complete it more effectively.

If you are enrolled in a course in a discipline that you have found difficult in the past, you may wish to form a study group of students who will meet on a regular basis. Simply meeting together can provide discipline and intellectual and emotional reinforcement that you can use to your advantage. Your discussions and responses to works in progress can also help stimulate both your interest in the subject and your ability to respond successfully to assignments.

Exploration

Think back to an academic writing experience that was difficult or frustrating for you. To what extent did this problem result from your inability to build a genuine commitment to the assignment? How might you have responded more effectively to this problem? Freewrite for five or ten minutes about this experience.

Preparing to do the assignment

Analyzing ways to prepare for an assignment may seem like an obvious suggestion, but students surprisingly often don't heed it. Sometimes they may lack commitment to the assignment. Other times they may be simply overwhelmed by all the conflicting demands of academic work. Whatever the motive, the consequence is the same: their writing often suffers.

You need not make elaborate preparations for doing all your assignments, but soon after you receive an assignment, you should be able to answer the following questions about it.

QUESTIONS FOR GETTING STARTED ON AN ASSIGNMENT

- What demands does this assignment make of me?
- How much time should I reserve for research?
- How much time should I reserve for planning, drafting, and revising?
- How will my work for other courses and my personal responsibilities influence my time schedule for completing this assignment?
- What is likely to be most difficult for me about this assignment? How can I anticipate and resolve the potential difficulties?
- What strengths do I have going into this assignment? How can I build on these strengths to make my job easier?
- Do I need to build commitment to the assignment so that I will be better motivated to develop and stick to a plan?
- Am I likely to need help with this assignment? Should I schedule a conference with my instructor or tutor?

These are commonsensical questions, questions that many students ask themselves automatically. They may never write out their answers, but they keep them in mind as they juggle course requirements, schedule their time, and prepare to work on their assignments.

Activities for Thought, Discussion, and Writing

1. Interview either an instructor whose class you are taking this term or an instructor in your major area of study. Ask this person to describe his or her understanding of the goals of undergraduate education and the role your particular class or field of study

plays in achieving these goals. Discuss the special analytic and argumentative skills required to succeed in this course or field. Ask what advice this person would give to someone, like yourself, who is taking a class in this field or planning to major in it. Be prepared to report the results of this interview to your group so that the group can present its collective findings to the class. Your instructor also may ask you to write an essay summarizing and commenting on the results of your interview.

2. Choose a writing assignment that you are currently working on for this or another course. Using the suggestions in this chapter, analyze this writing assignment. Begin by analyzing the assignment as it is presented by your instructor. Then look for the assumptions behind the assignment, developing strategies to help you build commitment to the assignment, and finally prepare to get started using the questions in the chapter.

   After you have completed the assignment, try to determine how this analysis did or did not make your work easier or more productive. Would you follow this process again?

3. Write an essay about the differences between your expectations of what college would be like and your experiences thus far. What have you learned about yourself, and about college, as a result?

CHAPTER 11

UNDERSTANDING ACADEMIC ANALYSIS AND ARGUMENT

As a student, you must respond to a wide range of writing assignments. For your American literature class, you may have to write an essay analyzing the significance of the whiteness of the whale in *Moby Dick*, while your business management class may require a group-written case study. You may need to write a lab report for your chemistry class and critique a reading for sociology.

Although these assignments vary considerably, a close look reveals that they, like most academic writing assignments, draw upon two related skills: analysis and argument. Strengthening these two important academic skills will enable you to respond more effectively to the demands of academic writing.

DEVELOPING EFFECTIVE STRATEGIES FOR ANALYSIS

Analysis is the activity of separating something into parts and determining how these parts function to create the whole. When you analyze something you examine a text, object, or body of data to understand how it is structured or organized and to assess its validity and usefulness. Most academic writing, thinking, and reading involve analysis. Literature students analyze how a play is struc-

239

tured or how a poem achieves its effect; economics students analyze the major causes of inflation; biology students analyze the enzymatic reactions that comprise the Krebs cycle; and art history students analyze how line, color, and texture come together in a painting.

As these examples indicate, analysis is not a single skill but a group of related skills. An art history student might explore how a famous painting by Michelangelo achieves its effect, for instance, by *comparing* it with a similar work by Raphael. A biology student might discuss future acid-rain damage to forests in Canada and the United States by first *defining* acid rain and by then using *cause-effect* reasoning to predict worsening conditions. A student in economics might estimate the likelihood of severe inflation in the 1990s by *categorizing* or *classifying* the major causes of previous inflationary periods and then *evaluating* the likelihood of such factors influencing our current economic situation.

Different disciplines naturally emphasize different analytic skills. But whether you are a history, biology, or business major, you need to understand and practice this crucial academic skill. You will do so more successfully if you establish a purpose and develop an appropriate framework or method for your analysis.

Establishing a purpose for your analysis

Your instructors will often ask you to analyze a fairly limited subject, problem, or process, such as Mrs. Ramsey's role in Virginia Woolf's *To the Lighthouse*, feminists' criticisms of Freud's psychoanalytical theories, or Gregor Mendel's third law of genetics, the law of dominance. Such limited tasks are necessary, your instructors believe, because of the complexity of the material being analyzed. Books have been written on Woolf's masterpiece and Freud's theories, so you can hardly examine these subjects completely in a brief essay or research paper. Even though you are analyzing a limited topic, however, the general purpose of your analysis is much broader; it is to clarify or better understand the material being examined. When you analyze a limited topic, you are like a person holding a flashlight in the dark: the beam of light you project is narrow and highly focused, but it illuminates a much larger area.

Recognizing this larger purpose of analysis can help you make important decisions as you plan, draft, and revise. If your instructor has assigned a limited topic, for instance, you should ask yourself why he or she might have chosen this particular topic. What might make it an especially good means of understanding the larger issues at hand? If you are free to choose your own topic for analysis, your first questions should involve its overall significance. How will analyzing this topic help you better understand the larger subject, process, or problem? As you write, ask yourself regularly if your analysis is leading you to rethink or understand your topic more deeply. If you can answer yes to this question, you are probably doing a good job of analysis.

Even though the general purpose of your analysis is to understand the larger subject, process, or problem, you still need to establish a more specific purpose to provide direction for your writing. Imagine, for instance, that your Shakespeare instructor has asked you to write an essay on the fool in *King Lear*. You might establish one of these specific purposes for your analysis:

- to explain how the fool contributes to the development of a major theme in *King Lear*
- to discuss the effectiveness or plausibility of Shakespeare's characterization of the fool
- to clarify the role the fool plays in the construction of the plot of *King Lear*
- to agree or disagree with a particular critical perspective on the fool's role and significance

Establishing a specific purpose for your analysis helps you define how your analysis should proceed. It enables you to determine the important issues you should address or the questions you should answer. A student analyzing the effectiveness of Shakespeare's characterization of the fool would address different questions, for example, than one who is agreeing with a particular critical perspective on the fool's role and significance.

There are no one-size-fits-all procedures you can follow to establish a purpose for your analysis. Sometimes your purpose will develop naturally as a result of reading, reflection, and discussion with others. In other instances, you may need to draw upon the invention strategies described in Chapter 5. Such informal and formal methods of invention as freewriting, brainstorming, tagmemics, and the topical questions can help you explore your subject and discover one or more fruitful questions that can guide your analysis. You may need to write your way into an understanding of your purpose by composing a rough draft of your essay and seeing, in effect, what you think about your topic. Writing is a dynamic, complex process and thus is variable.

Developing an appropriate method for your analysis

Once you have a purpose, how do you actually analyze something? The answer depends on the subject, process, or problem being analyzed; it also, in academic writing, depends on the discipline within which the analysis is done. The students studying *To the Lighthouse* and Mendel's third law may both use such analytic processes as definition, causal analysis, classification, and comparison to analyze their subjects. But the exact form of the processes each uses— the way each organizes the analysis and the criteria each uses to evaluate it—may well differ. Despite these disciplinary differences, both students must establish some method for analysis if they are to succeed.

In some fields, the appropriate method for analysis is easy to identify. Journalism students, for instance, use the journalistic questions (who, what, where, when, why, and how) to analyze and present news stories. Often, however, as a student you have to discover or establish the method appropriate for a particular task.

There are no hard-and-fast rules for establishing such a method. In general, however, you should look to the methods of inquiry characteristic of the specific discipline for guidance. The following questions can help you develop an appropriate method for your analysis.

QUESTIONS FOR DEVELOPING AN APPROPRIATE METHOD FOR YOUR ANALYSIS

- How have your instructors approached analysis in class? Do they rely upon a systematic procedure, such as case-study or problem-solving methodology, or does their analysis vary depending upon the subject under discussion?
- What kinds of evidence and examples do they draw upon? What criteria seem to influence their choice of evidence and examples?
- What kinds of questions do your instructors typically ask in class discussions? Why might those in the discipline view these as important questions?
- What kind of answers to these questions do your instructors accept or praise as effective? Why might those in this discipline value these kinds of responses to questions?

If after considering these questions and reflecting on your experience in a class, you continue to have difficulty settling on an appropriate method for analysis, meet with your instructor to discuss this problem. You might ask your instructor to recommend student essays or professional articles that you can read. Analyzing these articles and essays can help you understand the analytical methods used by those writing in the field.

RESPONDING TO THE DEMANDS OF ACADEMIC ARGUMENT

What do you think of when you read the word *argument*? Do you imagine two friends disagreeing heatedly about politics? Or do you think of formal debates, like those at forensic competitions or in courts or state legislatures? These are all examples of arguments, but they do not represent its fullest range. *Argument* is not limited to debates or angry confrontations, nor does it necessarily involve the heated exchange of opinions. Argument occurs whenever people make *judgments*, whenever they present *good reasons* for their beliefs and actions. If you and your roommate spend an hour thoughtfully exploring the issues raised by the controversial practice of surrogate motherhood, you are not adversaries but rather partners in inquiry—two friends exploring a complex legal, ethical, and moral question.

As this example indicates, debate is not the only possible model for argument. The debate model of argument can actually pose problems for students writing in the context of the academic rhetorical situation. Think about the words used in debate: opponents "attack" their "adversaries" hoping to "demolish" their arguments in order to "win" the judge's assent and claim "victory" in the "contest." This model of argument may work in forensic and political debates, but it hardly seems appropriate for academic analysis and argument. Your teachers are not interested in whether you can "attack" or "demolish" your opponents; rather, they value the ability to examine an issue or problem dispassionately and from multiple perspectives. Their commitment is not to "winning" but to clear reasoning, substantial evidence, and well-developed arguments. Academic argument is best conceived of as conversation and dialogue—as inquiry—not as debate.

Exploration

Spend five or ten minutes freewriting in response to the following questions.

- In the past, what have you associated with the word *argument*? How have you responded to the word?
- How may these associations or responses have influenced your attitude toward argument?
- If you have adhered in the past to the debate model of argu-

ment, how might you benefit by viewing argument as inquiry and dialogue, rather than debate?

_____

Academic argument complements and builds on analysis. The art history student who analyzes Michelangelo's painting by comparing it with Raphael's might decide that Michelangelo is indeed the superior artist. This comparative analysis would form the foundation of an argument to this effect. The student writing about Shakespeare's portrayal of the fool in *King Lear* is also making an argument. If the instructor finds this student's discussion of the fool effective, it will be because the student has provided *good reasons* in support of his or her major assertions.

As Chapter 10 emphasizes, most college instructors are committed to objective, reasoned argument. In their personal lives, they may have deeply held religious, political, or personal beliefs that influence their thinking and actions—beliefs that they accept "on faith." As members of the academic community, however, they encourage students to adopt a questioning, inquiring approach toward issues and ideas. Consequently, in academic argument you cannot simply assert that something is or is not true, valid, effective, or just; you must provide appropriate evidence for your assertions.

Whether you are interpreting the symbolism of Hester Prynne's scarlet A in *The Scarlet Letter* or evaluating the merits of competing proposals for a business class, you are arguing—presenting good reasons why others should or should not agree with your conclusions. To prepare a successful academic argument, you need to determine what is at stake in an argument, what evidence is appropriate, and what counterarguments are possible.

_____ DETERMINING WHAT'S AT STAKE _____
IN AN ARGUMENT

You can't argue by yourself. If you disagree with a recent legislative decision reported in your morning newspaper, you may mumble angry words to yourself at breakfast—but you'd know that you're not arguing. To argue, you must argue with someone. Furthermore, the person with whom you wish to argue must agree with you that an assertion raises an arguable *issue*. If you like rap music, for example, and your friend, who prefers jazz, refuses even to listen to (much less discuss) your favorite tape, you can hardly argue with your friend's preference. You'll both probably just wonder at the peculiarities of taste.

Similarly, in academic argument you and your reader (most often your instructor) must agree that an issue is worth arguing about if you are to argue successfully. Often this agreement involves sharing a common understanding of a problem, process, or idea. A student who writes an argument on the symbolism of Hester Prynne's scarlet A in *The Scarlet Letter*, for example, begins from a premise, one she believes will be shared by the teacher, that Hester's A has significance for the meaning or theme of the novel.

All argument, in this sense, begins from shared premises. There is, however, an important distinction between the kind of casual arguments you have with family and friends and academic arguments. Academic arguments, unlike casual arguments, must be structured so that they focus on a limited issue or topic. In a late-night discussion with friends, you may easily slip from a heated exchange over the cause of the national budget deficit to a friendly debate about the best way to remedy bureaucratic inefficiency. In an academic argument, however, you must limit your discussion not just to a single issue but to a single *thesis*. It is not enough, in other words, to decide that you want to write about nuclear energy or the need to protect the wilderness. Even limiting these subjects—writing about the Three-Mile Island nuclear reactor or the new Forest Service Land Management Plan for the White Mountain National Forest in New Hampshire—wouldn't help much. That's because your thesis needs to be an assertion—something, in other words, to argue about.

A clear, adequately limited thesis is vital for argument because it indicates (for you and for your reader) what's at stake. For this reason, many instructors and writers suggest that academic arguments should contain an explicit thesis statement, a single declarative sentence that asserts or denies something about the topic. The assertion that "The United States Forest Service's land management plan for the White Mountain National Forest fails adequately to protect New Hampshire's wilderness areas" is an example of a thesis statement.

Thesis statements serve important functions for writers and readers. Developing a clear, limited thesis statement can help insure that a writer stays on track and includes evidence or details relevant to the main point rather than extraneous or only loosely related information. Readers—especially busy readers like your college instructors—also find thesis statements helpful. A limited, clearly worded thesis statement in the introduction of your essay reassures your readers that your essay will be more than a mishmash of loosely connected ideas and examples. Once your readers clearly understand the main point you wish to make in your essay, they also can read your writing both more critically and more efficiently.

Here is the first paragraph of an essay written for a class on Latin American history. The student's thesis statement is underlined. Notice how this statement clearly articulates the student's position on the topic, the role of multinational and transnational corporations in Central America.

Over the past fifty years, Latin American countries have worked hard to gain economic strength and well-being. In order to survive, however, these countries have been forced to rely on multinational and transnational corporations for money, jobs, and technological expertise. In doing so, they have lost needed economic independence and have left themselves vulnerable to exploitation by foreign financiers.

A clear thesis statement can help both writer *and* reader to keep on track as they "compose" an essay.

Application

Look back at the rough and revised drafts of Todd Carpenter's essay, "Why Isn't There a National Bottle Law?" on pages 162–167. Reread both drafts and then answer these questions.

- The rough draft does not contain a clear thesis statement, but the revised draft does. What is the thesis statement in the revised draft? How does this thesis statement improve the effectiveness of Todd's essay? How does this thesis statement help make Todd's essay easier for you as a reader to follow?
- Todd's analysis of his rhetorical situation, presented on page 161, demonstrates his awareness of the academic rhetorical situation and of the demands of academic analysis and argument. Todd notes, for instance, that "even if my instructor agrees that there should be a national bottle law, she won't give me a good grade unless I write an effective argument. In class, my instructor has stressed the importance of looking at both sides of the issue and presenting evidence for my views, so I'll try to do that here." Review Todd's rough and revised drafts, paying particular attention to the ways

Todd's revised draft responds to these concerns. List at least three of these changes and write a brief explanation of why they increase the effectiveness of Todd's essay as an academic argument.

■ Suppose that Todd were writing an essay on this subject not for his instructor but for members of an ecological group whom he hopes to convince to support this effort. How might Todd revise his argument to meet the needs and expectations of these readers, who are likely to support the idea of a national bottle law but may not necessarily view it as a priority for their particular organization?

If you are like many writers, you will at times have to think—and write—your way into a thesis. You may know the subject you want to discuss, and you may have a tentative or *working* thesis in mind from the start. Often, however, you will find that only by actually writing a rough draft, by marshaling your ideas and ordering your evidence, can you finally determine exactly what thesis you can support. In situations like this, you will revise your thesis as you write to reflect your increased understanding of your topic and of your rhetorical situation.

UNDERSTANDING THE ROLE OF VALUES, ASSUMPTIONS, AND BELIEFS IN ARGUMENT

When you argue, you give reasons and provide evidence for your assertions. The student arguing against the Forest Service plan might warn that increased timber harvesting will reduce access to the forest for campers and backpackers or that building more roads will decrease wildlife. This writer also might show that the Forest Service has failed to anticipate some problems with the plan and that cost-benefit calculations are skewed to reflect logging and economic-development interests. These are all potentially good reasons for questioning the proposed plan, but notice that these reasons necessarily imply certain values or beliefs. The argument against increasing the timber harvest and building more roads, for instance, reflects the assumption that preserving wildlife habitats and wilderness lands is more important than the economic development of the resources. It also reflects the more general belief that long-term interests should take precedence over short-term interests.

Is this student's argument flawed because it appeals to values and beliefs? Of course not. When you argue, you can't avoid making some assumptions, nor can—or should—you suppress your own values and beliefs. Your values and beliefs enable you to make sense of the world; they provide links to connect the world you observe and experience with yourself. They thus play an important role in any argument.

Suppose that you and a friend are getting ready to leave your apartment to go out for dinner. You look out the window and notice some threatening clouds. You say, "Looks like rain. We'd better take umbrellas since we're walking. I hate getting soaked." "Oh, I don't know," your friend replies. "I don't think it looks so bad. It usually rains in the mornings in summer. I think we should risk it." Brief and informal as this exchange is, it constitutes an argument. Both you and your friend observed something, analyzed it, and drew conclusions—conclusions backed by reasons. Although you each cite different reasons, your conclusions may most strongly reflect your different personal preferences. You're generally cautious, and you don't like getting caught unprepared in a downpour, so you opt for an umbrella. Your friend is more of a risk-taker.

If your individual preferences, values, and beliefs shape a single situation like this where only getting wet is at stake, imagine how crucial they are in more complicated and contested situations—situations where the central issue is not whether clouds will bring rain but whether a controversial proposal is right or wrong, just or unjust, effective or ineffective. Argument necessarily involves values and beliefs, held by both writer and reader. These values and beliefs cannot be denied or excluded, even in academic argument with its emphasis on evidence and reasoned inquiry. The student arguing against the Forest Service plan cannot avoid using values and beliefs as bridges between reasons and conclusions. And not all of these bridges can be explicitly stated; that would lead to an endless chain of reasons. The standards of academic argument require, however, that the most important values and beliefs undergirding an argument be explicitly stated and defended. In this case, then, the student opposing the Forest Service plan should at some point state and support his or her belief that preserving wildlife habitats and wilderness lands should take priority over economic development.

It's not easy to identify and analyze your own values and beliefs, but doing so is essential in academic argument. Values and beliefs are often held unconsciously, and they function as part of a larger network. Your opinions about the best way for the government to respond to the poor reflect values and beliefs you hold about the family, the proper role of government, the nature of individual responsibility, and the importance of economic security. Thus if your political science instructor asks you to argue for or against workfare programs (programs requiring welfare recipients to work at state-mandated jobs in exchange for economic support), you need to analyze carefully not just these workfare programs but also the role your values and beliefs play in your analysis.

The following guidelines for analyzing your values, assumptions, and beliefs should enable you to respond more effectively to the demands of academic argument.

Guidelines for analyzing your values, assumptions, and beliefs

1. USE THE INFORMAL METHODS OF INVENTION, DESCRIBED IN CHAPTER 5, TO EXPLORE YOUR VALUES, ASSUMPTIONS, AND BELIEFS ABOUT A SUBJECT.

Once you have a general topic, and certainly by the time you have developed a controlling purpose or thesis, you should explore your values, assumptions, and beliefs about your topic. Your goal here is to discover *why* you believe what you believe; to do so you need to consider more than rational, logical arguments: you need to tap into your experiences and emotions. Freewriting, looping, brainstorming, and clustering are excellent ways to gain access to the network or web of assumptions, values, and beliefs that encourage you to adopt a particular stance toward an issue.

2. AFTER EXPLORING YOUR VALUES, ASSUMPTIONS, AND BELIEFS, CONSIDER THE DEGREE TO WHICH THEY ENABLE YOU TO ARGUE EFFECTIVELY ABOUT A SUBJECT.

As noted earlier, college instructors are committed to clear reasoning, substantial evidence, and well-developed arguments. They want their students to be able to consider an issue from multiple perspectives and to respond dispassionately, rather than emotionally, to complex problems and questions. Exploring your own assumptions, values, and beliefs enables you to distance yourself from your habitual ways of thinking and thus encourages the objective habits of mind your instructors want to foster. Your exploration can also help you discover ways to effectively ground your argument in assumptions, values, and beliefs you share with your readers. (You may wish to review Julia Kohashi's and Todd Carpenter's essays, which appear on pages 60–62 and 162–167 to see how they achieve this goal.)

Sometimes your exploration may enable you to realize that you can't write an effective academic argument on a particular subject. Freewriting about your feelings about abortion may help you realize, for instance, that your convictions about this issue are so central to your beliefs, values, and assumptions that you would have difficulty maintaining academic standards of objectivity in an argument about this subject. Understanding this about yourself beforehand can save you a great deal of time and frustration.

3. ENGAGE IN AN INTERNAL DIALOGUE WITH A "DEVIL'S ADVOCATE" TO HELP YOU CRITICALLY EXAMINE YOUR VALUES, ASSUMPTIONS, AND BELIEFS.

Becoming aware of your values, assumptions, and beliefs can help you better understand why you have adopted a particular stance toward an issue or problem. You may nevertheless find it difficult to step outside your habitual ways of thinking to consider whether others might reasonably hold differing views—and yet much academic writing demands just this ability. Many writers find it helpful to engage in an internal dialogue with one or more "devil's advocates," persons whose views differ considerably from their own. If you were writing an essay arguing that the federal government needs to increase funding for college student loans, for instance, you might engage in a mental or written dialogue with a hard-headed pragmatic congressperson or corporate executive whose concerns about the national deficit might cause them to resist such an argument. Their challenges might help you recognize that assumptions you have made about the need for all students to have access to a college education are not universally shared, that other assumptions—such as the need to balance the federal budget—might reasonably take precedence. Your dialogue has helped you learn that you must not only make your own assumptions explicit but provide good reasons why your assumptions are valid and consider competing assumptions as well. Your dialogue might even help you realize that you need to limit or modify your goals for this essay.

4. ENGAGE IN *REAL* DIALOGUES WITH YOUR CLASSMATES ABOUT YOUR SUBJECTS.

You're probably already aware from informal discussions that even friends and family members can disagree about complex or controversial subjects. When you discuss current events with your spouse or roommate, for example, they may naturally formulate questions that require you to reconsider not only your stance toward an issue or problem but also the assumptions, values, and beliefs that undergird this position. You can draw upon this natural activity of mutual inquiry to help you explore—and question—your values, assumptions, and beliefs. This may take the form of informal dinner talk with friends. But additionally, your instructor may ask you to work more formally in groups. If you engage in formal group discussions with classmates, be sure to follow these steps.

- Decide how much time each student will have to discuss his or her work in progress. Appoint a timekeeper to enforce these limits.
- The writer should begin by describing the controlling purpose or thesis of the essay and then briefly list the assumptions, values, and beliefs that have caused him or her to take this position. The writer should then invite group members to ask questions designed to help him or her gain additional perspectives on these assumptions, values, and beliefs and understand how others might reasonably hold different views.
- Group members should let the writer facilitate the resulting discussion. The writer should feel free to ask group members to clarify or elaborate on suggestions. Group members should remember that their goal is not to attack or criticize the writer's assumptions, values, and beliefs but to help the writer gain additional perspectives on them.

When you argue, you must consider not only your own assumptions, values, and beliefs but also those of your readers. The student writing about the Forest Service plan would present a very different argument to the local branch of the Sierra Club than to representatives of the Forest Service. In arguing to the Sierra Club, the student would be almost assured of agreement, so he or she might focus primarily on how the group might best oppose the plan and why members should devote their time and energy to this rather than other projects. The argument to the Forest Service would be quite different. Recognizing that members of the Forest Service would know the plan very well, would have spent a great deal of time working on it, and would obviously be strongly committed to it, the student might decide to focus on a limited number of points, especially those that the Forest Service might be most able and willing to modify. The student might also assume a less aggressive or strident tone since that might needlessly offend the audience.

In academic argument, of course, your reader is generally your instructor. In this rhetorical situation the most useful approach is not to focus on your instructor's individual biases or interests or to try to "psych out" his or her views on your topic. Rather, you should consider the values and beliefs your instructor holds as a member of the academic community. In writing for an economics or political science instructor, the student arguing against the Forest Service plan should provide logical, accurate, and appropriate evidence for assertions. He or she should avoid strong emotional appeals and harsh expressions of outrage or bitterness, focusing instead on developing a succinct, clearly organized, carefully reasoned essay.

Application

Think of an issue that concerns you. Perhaps you are involved with or have been following a campus controversy. You may oppose a decision made recently by your city council or some other elected body. Or you may be committed (or opposed) to broad national movements such as the efforts to provide public child-care facilities, house the homeless, or improve public transportation.

After reflecting on this issue, use the guidelines presented earlier in this section (pages 249–252) to analyze your values, assumptions, and beliefs. Then respond to the following questions.

1. Given your assumptions, values, and beliefs, what challenges would writing an academic essay on this subject pose for you?
2. To what extent did your analysis help you understand that others might reasonably hold different views on this subject? Make a list of the opposing arguments that others might make in response to your subject, then briefly describe the assumptions, values, and beliefs that might lead readers to make these counterarguments. How might you respond to these arguments?
3. Now write the major assertions or arguments you would use to support your controlling idea or thesis. Below each assertion, list the assumptions, values, or beliefs your readers must share with you to accept each assertion.
4. How have the guidelines and this application helped you better understand how to write an effective academic argument? If you were to write an academic argument on this issue, how would you now organize and develop your ideas? What strategies would you now use to respond to the assumptions, values, and beliefs of your readers?

USING EVIDENCE
APPROPRIATE FOR YOUR ARGUMENT

Whenever you argue, you are engaged in the process of giving good reasons why your reader should accept your conclusions or judgment. All arguments are not alike, however. A student reviewing a play or a movie faces different challenges than one advocating laws requiring mandatory use of seat belts in cars. These two tasks require not only different analytic skills but different kinds of evidence.

Arguments can be characterized in a number of ways. All of these systems are somewhat artificial, for the categories describe "pure," unmixed arguments, while in actuality many arguments are hybrids. Still, considering your potential kind or type of argumentative task can help you determine how best to limit your thesis, to select appropriate and persuasive evidence or support, and to organize your ideas. In *Elements of Argument*, Annette T. Rottenberg categorizes arguments according to the nature of the thesis or claim. All arguments, she notes, involve *claims of fact*, *claims of value*, or *claims of policy*. Some essays focus on only one of these claims. More often, however, writers draw upon all these approaches to support and develop their ideas.

Claims of fact

These claims state that something is or will be true; as such, they are—or should be—supportable by verifiable data.

- Eastern European weight lifters consistently outperform their Western counterparts.
- ABC University fails to provide adequate funds for the library.
- Orientation programs for freshmen help them adjust to college life.
- When used properly, organic fertilizers and pesticides can be just as effective, and much less harmful, than their chemical counterparts.

When arguing about a claim of fact, you often support your thesis by using examples, statistics, and statements by authorities on the subject. Even though you use data to support your claim, however, you still must define and interpret this information. You should recognize that reasonable people can disagree about just what the facts are. Even scientists sometimes disagree about the results of rigorously controlled studies. In academic argument, the distinction between a fact and an inference (a conclusion or interpretation of a fact) is often subject to debate. Consequently, you should not assume that the facts are obvious. Many facts are open to multiple interpretations; such interpretation plays a crucial role in academic argument.

Claims of value

Claims of value assert a judgment.

- Euthanasia is a humane alternative to the pain suffered by patients with terminal illnesses.
- None of the *Star Trek* movies has matched the original television series for wit and originality.
- Maslow's psychological theories better describe the nature of human motivation than do those of Freud or Pavlov.
- The news media's obsession with the private lives of politicians is harmful to the practice of democracy.

Claims of value attempt to prove that something is right or wrong, just or unjust, effective or ineffective, well crafted or poorly constructed. If you go to a movie with a friend and then argue about how well the script was written or the actors performed, you are arguing about a claim of value.

Your experience arguing about movies may help you understand an essential requirement for a claim of value: acceptable criteria for judgment. You could hardly defend the merits of a movie because you liked the color of the heroine's dress or because you think that gangster movies set in Chicago are always good. Even if you've never studied films or read movie reviews, you know that if you want your opinion to be taken seriously by others, you need to base your arguments on such commonly accepted criteria as the quality of the acting, the script, and the direction; the significance of the theme; or the movie's ability to draw you into the action, to make you care. When writing an academic essay about a claim of value, you need to be especially concerned with identifying criteria or standards for your analysis. Otherwise, you may be charged with relying on mere opinion rather than informed judgment, or with focusing on trivial issues.

Claims of policy

Claims of policy assert that something should or should not exist or occur.

- Student fees should not be used to support this college's athletic program.
- The federal government should direct more funds to public transportation and less to constructing new highways.
- American executives should adopt some aspects of the Japanese style of management.
- Students should boycott the *Playboy* photographer who will visit campus this term to recruit models.

When you assert a claim of policy, you are implicitly arguing that some current problem must be remedied. There would be no reason to provide better child care, for example, if current facilities were adequate. Essays making claims of policy often begin with necessary background information. Next, the proposed policy must be carefully explained and supported. The support for a claim of policy often comes from statistics and similar forms of evidence. A student advocating increased support of child-care programs, for instance, might cite the number of children needing child care as well as the number of placements available or include the comments of a noted child psychologist on the need for high-quality care.

When you argue about a claim of policy, beliefs and values often play a crucial role in your argument. They do so because they strongly influence how you (and your readers) interpret data. Two individuals reviewing statistics about the number of children needing child care might draw very different conclusions. "This is evidence," the first might think, "of the need for our state to provide public child-care facilities." The second might conclude, "This is evidence of the breakdown of the traditional American family. We need to convince mothers that staying home and caring for children is the most important job possible."

As a student writing academic arguments, you need to recognize how personal values and beliefs may influence your advocacy of a policy. You must also recognize that readers will, in turn, be influenced by their values and beliefs. Ignoring their concerns or attempting to force your own preferences on them weakens your argument and creates a negative image of you as the writer.

Application

Think again about the issue you wrote about in response to the Application on page 252. Formulate a tentative or working thesis statement that reflects your current position on this issue. Identify whether this thesis statement asserts a claim of fact, of value, or of policy, and then list the major evidence you would use to support this thesis. Finally, write a brief statement explaining why this evidence is appropriate, given your thesis statement and the kind of claim it makes.

_____ ACKNOWLEDGING POSSIBLE _____ COUNTERARGUMENTS

Academic argument is modeled upon inquiry—upon dialogue—rather than debate. Your task in an academic argument is not so much to persuade your instructor to agree with you but to demonstrate that you can reason, and write, in a logical, coherent manner. This approach requires that you consider both sides of an issue. Discussing and responding to counterarguments in the body of your essay is one of the most effective ways to demonstrate that you have analyzed an issue from a number of perspectives—that you have seriously looked at all sides of the issue and drawn reasonable conclusions from them.

Earlier sections of this chapter provided a number of ways you can discover counterarguments to your own position. You can, for instance, have an internal dialogue with one or more "devil's advocates," or you can discuss your subject with a group of classmates. You might even decide to interview someone who holds a position different from your own in order to benefit from the dialogue. Being aware of your own values and beliefs can also help you identify possible counterarguments. The student arguing against the Forest Service plan might consider the views of someone with different values, perhaps someone who believed in the importance of economic development, such as a worker for a lumber company. Finally, reading and research can expose you to the ideas and arguments of others.

How you use the counterarguments that you identify will depend upon your subject and your rhetorical situation. In some instances, these counterarguments can play an important structural role in your essay. After introducing your essay and indicating your thesis, for example, you might present the major counterarguments to your position, refuting each in turn. You might also group these counterarguments, responding to them at an appropriate point in your essay.

Group Activity

The following activity will help you recognize possible counterarguments to the thesis you have been writing about in the previous activities on pages 252 and 256. To prepare for this Group Activity, be sure that you have a clear, easy-to-read statement of your tentative or working thesis and of the major evidence you would use to support this thesis in an academic essay. Now spend five or ten minutes brainstorming a list of possible counterarguments to your working thesis.

Bring these written materials to your group's meeting. Determine how much time the group can spend per person if each student is to get help with his or her writing. Appoint a timekeeper to be sure that the group stays on time. Then follow this procedure.

1. Have the writer read his or her working thesis, evidence, and possible counterarguments.
2. Have members of the group suggest additional counterarguments that the writer has not considered. Avoid getting bogged down in specific arguments; instead, focus on generating as many additional counterarguments as possible.

Continue following this procedure until each student's work has been discussed.

When you enter a college or university, you join an academic community, one with unique values, beliefs, and methods of inquiry. Yet few in that community will discuss these directly with you. Instead, your history instructor explores the impact of printing on the Renaissance imagination, while your political science instructor focuses on recent events in the Middle East. Your instructors leave it to you to understand the academic rhetorical situation and to master the skills necessary to succeed in their courses. You don't have to face this challenge alone, however. Your composition instructor and your fellow students, acting both as coaches and supporters, can help you understand and develop the critical thinking, reading, and writing skills necessary for success in college. What's at stake in your composition course, then, is not just earning a passing grade or fulfilling a requirement but becoming a fully participating and successful member of the academic community.

The same skills that enable you to succeed as a student will prepare you to join other communities as well. Whatever career or profession you choose to enter, you can succeed as a writer by drawing upon your ability to analyze your rhetorical situation and to make appropriate choices based on that analysis. Your awareness of the writing process—your recognition that writing is not a magical or mysterious activity but a process that involves planning, drafting, and revising—will enable you to approach new and demanding on-the-job writing tasks with confidence and to experience the satisfaction of a job well done.

Activities for Thought, Discussion, and Writing

1. The following editorial was written in 1986 by Lynne V. Cheney, chairperson of the National Endowment for the Humanities. Analyze the strengths and weaknesses of Cheney's argument. Your instructor may ask you to write an essay responding to it.

STUDENTS OF SUCCESS

Not long ago, my college-age daughter read about a software genius who became a multimillionaire before he was 30. "That does it," she said. "I'm going into computers."

This daughter, who has never met a political-science course she didn't like, was only joking. But a study conducted by the Carnegie Foundation shows that many young people do think seriously along these lines. Instead of choosing college majors—and careers—according to their interests, they are channeling themselves into fields that promise to be profitable: business, engineering, computer science, allied health programs.

Given the high cost of a college education, this trend is not surprising. A bachelor's degree now costs $40,000 at an average independent college. Can we expect students to major in the liberal arts when their starting salaries will be significantly lower than they are for business or professional majors? Shouldn't they get the best possible return on their investment?

They should, but I would suggest that there are better ways to calculate profit and loss than by looking at starting salaries. Consider, first of all, that very few people stay in the same line of work over a lifetime. They switch jobs, even change professions, and what is crucial for advancement is not specialized training but the ability to think critically and judge wisely. Given the difficulty of predicting which skills will be in demand even five years from now, let alone over a lifetime, a student's best career preparation is one that emphasizes general understanding and intellectual curiosity: a knowledge of how to learn and the desire to do it. Literature, history, philosophy and the social sciences—majors that students avoid today—are the ones traditionally believed to develop such habits of mind.

History and classics: I recently conducted an informal survey of successful Americans, and while several dozen phone calls aren't proof of the value of a liberal-arts major, the results are suggestive. The communications world, for example, is dominated by liberal-arts majors. Thomas H. Wyman, chairman of CBS, majored in English, as did Cathleen Black, publisher of *USA Today*. *Washington Post* columnist William Raspberry studied history; NBC News anchorman Tom Brokaw, political science.

In public life, too, leaders more often than not were students of the liberal arts. They form a majority of the president's cabinet. Secretary of State George Schultz and Secretary of Energy John Herrington majored in economics. Interior Secretary Donald Hodel majored in government, and Transportation Secretary Elizabeth Dole, political science. Secretary of the Treasury James Baker read history with a minor in classics; Secretary of Education William Bennett studied philosophy.

The president himself majored in economics and sociology. His communications director, Pat Buchanan, majored in English and philosophy. White House chief of staff (and former treasury secretary) Donald Regan was an English major and before he came to government had a remarkably successful business career as the head of Merrill Lynch. Secretary of Commerce Malcolm Baldrige headed Scovill Manufacturing, and now the former English major is leading a campaign for clear writing in government.

Executives like Regan and Baldrige are not unusual. According to a recent report in *Fortune* magazine, 38 percent of today's CEO's majored in the liberal arts, and a close reading of the *New York Times* shows that 9 of the top 13 executives at IBM are liberal-arts majors. At AT&T, a study showed social-science and humanities graduates moving into middle management faster than engineers and doing at least as well as their business and engineering counterparts in reaching top management levels.

For several years now, corporate executives have extolled the wide range of knowledge and interests that a study of the liberal arts encourages. And now under Tom Wyman's direction, CBS has funded an organization that investigates exactly why liberal-arts training is valuable to the American corporation. "In an increasingly competitive, internationally oriented and technologically innovative society,"

Wyman recently wrote, "successful executives will be those who can understand—and interpret—complex relationships and who are capable of continually reconsidering assumptions underlying old operating practices."

Intellectual enthusiasm: In the past, such top-level views did not always filter down to where entry-level hiring is done. But reports from that front are encouraging. A study by Northwestern University shows that many major companies plan to increase their hiring of liberal-arts graduates by some 20 percent in 1986. Or as one employer recently told *Today* show viewers, "Those that are involved in recruiting people to the company are looking for . . . broader skills . . . Then we will worry about teaching them terminology, specifics of the jobs."

I don't mean to argue that liberal arts is the only road to success. The average starting salary for engineers remains impressively high, almost $30,000 compared to $21,000 for a liberal-arts graduate. In fact, my informal survey also shows that engineers are doing well in a variety of fields. Chrysler chairman Lee Iacocca was an engineering major, as was former Delaware Gov. Pete du Pont. My point is that there are many paths to success and students shouldn't force themselves down any single one if their true interests lie elsewhere. College should be a time for intellectual enthusiasm, for trying to read one's way through the library, for heated debate with those who see the world differently. College should be a time for learning to enjoy the life of the mind rather than for learning to tolerate what one doesn't find interesting.

Students who follow their hearts in choosing majors will most likely end up laboring at what they love. They're the ones who will put in the long hours and intense efforts that achievement requires. And they're the ones who will find the sense of purpose that underlies most human happiness.

LYNNE V. CHENEY

2. Read a daily newspaper for a week. (You may want to read one of the well-respected national newspapers, such as the *Christian Science Monitor* or the *Wall Street Journal*.) Paying particular attention to the editorials, see if you can locate examples of arguments making claims of fact, value, and policy. Analyze the effectiveness of these arguments. Be prepared to bring examples of each kind of argument to class for discussion.

While reading the newspaper for the activity above, try to locate at least two or three examples of mixed arguments—arguments that focus on more than a single claim. How do these arguments differ from those that focus on a single claim?

3. This chapter has presented activities designed to help you better understand academic argument. The Application on page 252, for

instance, asked you to identify the values, assumptions, and beliefs that have led you to hold strong views on an issue. The application on page 256 asked you to formulate a tentative or working thesis and to list the major evidence you would use to support it. Finally, the group activity on page 257 encouraged you to acknowledge possible counterarguments to your thesis.

Drawing on these earlier activities, write an essay directed to an academic reader on the topic you have explored. If you need to revise your tentative or working thesis, feel free to do so.

Acknowledgments (continued from copyright page)

From *The River Why* by David J. Duncan. Copyright © 1983 by David J. Duncan. Reprinted by permission of Sierra Book Clubs.

From *Writing with Power: Techniques for Mastering the Writing Process* by Peter Elbow. Copyright © 1981 by Oxford University Press. Reprinted by permission.

John H. Flavell, Eleanor R. Flavell, Francis L. Green, "Development of the Appearance-Reality Distinction," *Cognitive Psychology* 15 (83), 95–120.

John H. Flavell, "Really and Truly," reprinted with permission from *Psychology Today Magazine*, Copyright © 1988 (P. T. Partners, L. P.).

John H. Flavell, "The Development of Children's Knowledge about the Appearance-Reality Distinction," Copyright © 1986 by the American Psychological Association. Reprinted by permission of the American Psychological Association and John H. Flavell.

Four Seasons advertisement. Reprinted by permission, Four Seasons Hotels and Resorts. The name Four Seasons Hotels and Resorts, any combination thereof, and the Tree Design are registered trademarks of Four Seasons Hotels Limited and Four Seasons Hotels (Barbados) Limited.

Ellen Goodman, "Gambling on a Debtor's Degree," © 1987, *The Boston Globe Newspaper Company/Washington Post Writer's Group*. Reprinted by permission.

From "A Portrait of Lorenzo de'Medici" by Francesco Guicciardini. From *The Portable Renaissance Reader*, ed., intro. by James Bruce Ross and Mary Martin McLaughlin. Copyright © 1953, renewed 1981 by Viking Penguin, Inc. Used by permission of Viking Penguin, a division of Penguin Books USA, Inc.

Handgun advertisement, *Ms.* July/August 1982. Reprinted with permission, Handgun Control, Inc., Washington, D. C.

Harper's Index. Copyright © 1991 by *Harper's Magazine*. All rights reserved. Reprinted from the February 1991 issue by special permission.

Burton Hatlen, "Writing Is a Craft that Can Be Learned, Not an Effortless Outpouring by Geniuses," © 1988, *The Chronicle of Higher Education*. Reprinted with permission.

"How to Choose a Liquid Fertilizer? Learn to Read the Labels," *Sunset Magazine*, November 1986. Reprinted by permission of *Sunset Magazine*.

Ken Kesey, "The Blue-Ribbon American Beauty Rose of a Rodeo." Reprinted by permission of Sterling Lord Literistic, Inc. Copyright © 1986.

Jamaica Kincaid, "Girl" from *At the Bottom of the River* by Jamaica Kincaid. Copyright © 1983 by Jamaica Kincaid. Reprinted by permission of Farrar, Straus and Giroux, Inc.

Robin Lakoff, from *Language and Women's Place*. Copyright © 1975 by Robin Lakoff. Reprinted by permission of HarperCollins Publishers.

Nicolaus Mills, "The Endless Autumn." First published in *The Nation*, April 16, 1990. Reprinted by permission of the author and The Nation Co., Inc. Copyright © 1990.

Cullen Murphy, "Going to the Cats," © 1987, Cullen Murphy, as first published in *The Atlantic Monthly*, August 1987.

"One out of four women over 50 will get osteoperosis." Advertisement reprinted by courtesy of Wyerth-Ayerst Laboratories, Philadelphia, PA.

Jane Bryant Quinn, "How to Read an Annual Report." Reprinted by permission of International Paper Company.

Mary Robison, "Yours" from *An Amateur's Guide to the Night* by Mary Robison. Copyright © 1981, 1982, 1983 by Mary Robison. Reprinted by permission of Alfred A. Knopf, Inc.

Ellen Ruppel Shell, "First, Do No Harm," *The Atlantic Monthly*, May 1988. Reprinted by permission of *The Atlantic Monthly* and the author.

UNICEF Letter. Reprinted by permission of U. S. Committee for UNICEF.

From *The Work/Stress Connection: How to Cope with Job Burnout* by Robert Veninga and James P. Spradley. Copyright © 1981 by Robert L. Veninga and James Spradley. By permission of Little, Brown and Company.

Index